The **Six Vegan Sisters**

Everyday Cookbook

Coleslaw (page 258)

Easy Creamy Mac and
Cheese (page 83)

BBQ Jackfruit Sliders
(page 94)

Baked Tofu Nuggets
(page 224)

The **Six Vegan Sisters**

Everyday Cookbook

200 Delicious Recipes *for* Plant-Based Comfort Food

Molly Davis, Emily Letchford
and Carrie, Mary-Kate, Hannah
and Shannon Lynch

PAGE STREET
PUBLISHING CO.

PAGE STREET
PUBLISHING CO.

First published in 2021 by

Page Street Publishing Co.

27 Congress Street, Suite 105

Salem, MA 01970

www.pagestreetpublishing.com

Distributed by Macmillan, sales in Canada by The Canadian Manda Group.

25   24   23   22   21   1   2   3   4   5

ISBN-13: 978-1-64567-277-7

ISBN-10: 1-64567-277-8

Library of Congress Control Number: 2021931387

Cover and book design by Julia Tyler for Page Street Publishing Co.

Photography by Hayden Stinebaugh

Printed and bound in the United States

To our parents, John and Kate.

WE WOULD NOT BE HERE WITHOUT YOUR UNCONDITIONAL LOVE AND SUPPORT.
THANK YOU FOR EVERYTHING. THIS BOOK IS FOR YOU.

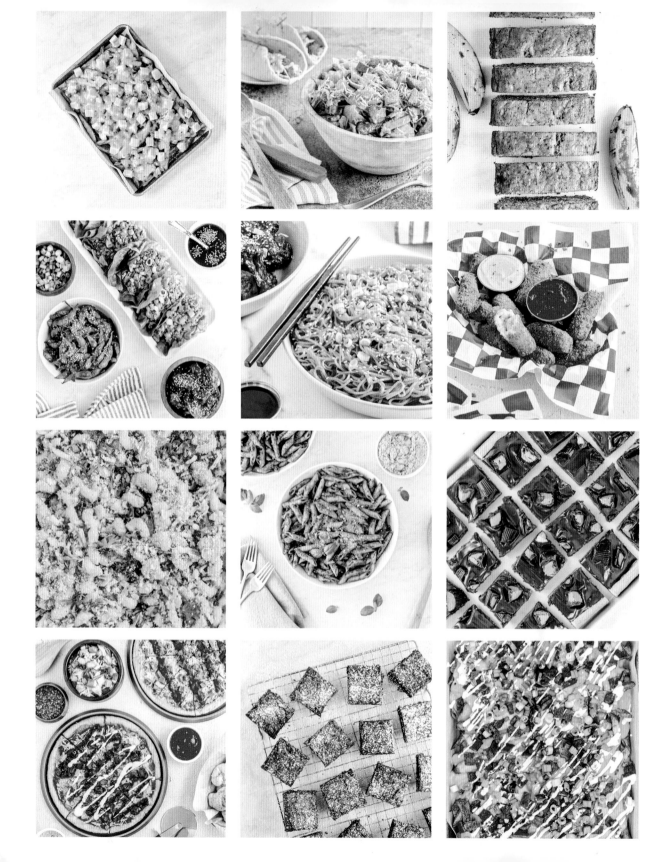

Contents

Butternut Squash Soup with Sautéed Pepitas (page 200)

Roasted Veggie and Quinoa Salad (page 203)

Introduction

Hi there! We are Molly, Emily, Carrie, Mary-Kate, Hannah and Shannon, a.k.a. the Six Vegan Sisters. We are six biological sisters from Michigan with a passion for the vegan lifestyle. Our parents did not raise us vegan, but our mom has been vegetarian our entire lives and was the catalyst for all of us going vegan. She has always been our biggest inspiration and greatest supporter. Even though we all had our own reasons for going vegan, our current mission is the same: to save animals, nourish our bodies and be kinder to the environment.

In 2016, we started our blog, Six Vegan Sisters, and Instagram account, @sixvegansisters, as ways to share our recipes and inspire others through vegan food. We could not have imagined then that we would be here today, reaching millions of people from all around the world. We're so lucky to be able to turn our love for vegan food into a platform that inspires people every day. Our Instagram account and blog have given us opportunities that we would not otherwise have had (including writing this cookbook!) and allowed us to work with some of our all-time favorite brands. The icing on the (vegan!) cake is that we get to do this together—not only as sisters, but as an entire family. Our three brothers (yes, we also have three brothers!), mom and dad are our ultimate taste testers and biggest fans.

Writing a cookbook has always been a dream of ours. When we sat down and talked about what we wanted in a cookbook, we could all agree on one thing: We wanted an approachable, family-friendly book. After all, we come from a family of eleven, so we are no strangers to our mom whipping up four (or more) different meals for dinner in an attempt to please all of us (have we mentioned our mom is basically Superwoman?). Our goal with this cookbook is to be your go-to source for all things vegan cooking and baking. Whether you are just starting out or well into your vegan journey, this cookbook is the one for you. It has recipes to please all palates, including vegans and nonvegans alike.

You'll notice that this book has twelve chapters. From Crowd-Pleasing Pasta and Pizza (page 59) to Sweet Treats (page 279), there is something for everyone. We even have Meat Substitutes (page 331) and Homemade Staples and Basics (page 339), if you're looking to dive a little deeper into the world of vegan home cooking. But don't worry; store-bought options typically work just fine, as noted in each recipe. Most of our recipes include Sister Tips, which we encourage you to read to ensure the recipe is successful and delicious (as it should be!). We've also noted which recipes are (or have the option of being) gluten-free, nut-free and/or soy-free. There are 200 recipes in this cookbook, so get to it—there's a world of delicious vegan food waiting for you. We are honored and excited to share our first cookbook with you and hope these recipes spark joy and bring as much comfort to your family as they do to ours.

xo,

The Six Vegan Sisters

Can't get enough of our recipes? Head to sixvegansisters.com for more vegan deliciousness. Share your creations with us on Instagram by tagging us @sixvegansisters and using #sixvegansisters.

Rice Bowls with Marinated Tofu
and Gochujang Sauce (page 152)

Our Must-Have Vegan Ingredients

Whether you're new to vegan cooking and baking or experienced, oftentimes it can feel a bit overwhelming, especially when you come across ingredients you're not familiar with. Although not exhaustive, the following list details our must-have vegan kitchen ingredients. In this list, you will find our favorite dairy alternatives, vegan protein swaps and much more. We've also noted important tidbits, such as why we use these ingredients, what you can swap them for and where you can purchase them.

DAIRY ALTERNATIVES

Nondairy milk: Throughout this book, there are times when we call for specific nondairy milks that will give the best results for a recipe. Otherwise, you can take your pick of nondairy milks, such as oat, soy, almond or coconut milk. When cooking a savory dish, you will always want to choose a plain, unsweetened nondairy milk. When baking desserts, you have some more leeway, but we recommend that you choose a thick milk, such as soy or oat.

- **Rice milk:** Due to its neutral flavor and similarity in consistency to dairy milk, we call for plain, unsweetened rice milk in many of our savory dishes. We do not recommend substituting other milks for rice milk.

- **Soy milk:** We call for soy milk in both sweet and savory dishes. When using it in savory dishes, be sure to use a plain, unsweetened milk. When using it in sweet dishes, feel free to use plain or vanilla, either sweetened or unsweetened.

- **Canned coconut milk:** Canned coconut milk is much thicker than typical nondairy milks and should not be confused for coconut milk beverage from a carton. We will always note which you should use in a recipe. It should not be replaced when specifically called for.

Nondairy sour cream: You'll want to have this on hand to add richness to both savory and sweet dishes. It can often be replaced with Cashew Cream (page 343) and occasionally with nondairy yogurt, which we have noted when possible.

Nondairy yogurt: Yogurt is used for its richness and unique consistency in both savory and sweet dishes. When using it in savory dishes, be sure it is plain and unsweetened. We recommend coconut- or almond-based yogurt. You can also use nondairy yogurt in the baked goods throughout this book as a substitute for vegan sour cream, which is used to add moisture and acidity.

Vegan cream cheese: You'll use vegan cream cheese in both sweet and savory dishes throughout this book. You can buy it at many grocery stores or make it at home (page 344).

Vegan cheese: You can buy vegan cheese in shredded, block or sliced form. You can also make your own (pages 340–342) that shreds and melts.

VEGETABLE BROTH AND BOUILLON CUBES/PASTE

We use vegetable broth in many recipes throughout this book. You can use broth from a carton, homemade broth or vegan bouillon mixed with water. In this book, you will also come across bouillon cubes or paste used on their own (without water), which have no substitution.

FATS AND OILS

Vegan butter: You can buy vegan butter in stick or tub form. Many recipes in this book will specify whether you must use one or the other, and it's important to use that kind for the best results. If the recipe does not specify which type, feel free to use either.

Olive, canola and avocado oils: We primarily use olive oil in savory dishes, often when sautéing vegetables and tofu, whereas we use canola oil for its neutral flavor and high smoke point in both sweet and savory dishes. We use avocado oil in homemade staples, such as Mayo (page 353) and Creamy Caesar Dressing (page 348), for its mild taste.

Refined coconut oil: Coconut oil is a unique fat that firms up at a temperature below 76°F (24°C) and melts above that temperature, making it perfect for homemade staples, such as Cream Cheese (page 344), Cheddar (page 341) and Mozzarella (page 340). Be sure to use refined coconut oil, as it has no coconut flavor.

Toasted peanut oil and sesame oil (toasted and untoasted): You will come across these oils in a few recipes. Because of their strong flavors, they should be used sparingly, as specified in the recipe, or they could overpower the dish. Toasted peanut oil and toasted sesame oil are finishing oils, meaning you should not use them at a high heat. Pure (untoasted) sesame oil has a milder flavor and can be more widely used.

PROTEINS

A common misconception when it comes to eating vegan is a lack of protein, but that's far from the truth. There are many different plant protein sources, including (but definitely not limited to) the following:

Tofu: When using tofu, we typically prefer the extra-firm variety, but firm and superfirm work on occasion as well. We often press tofu (see page 358 for a tutorial) to remove excess water prior to using.

Tempeh: Tempeh is made from fermented soybeans. It has a chunky texture and a nutty, mushroomy flavor, making it much different from tofu. You'll come across it in our Kale Tahini Salad with Baked Tempeh (page 210).

TVP: Textured vegetable protein, a.k.a. TVP, is a great meat alternative made from defatted soy flour that is rich in protein. It's naturally gluten-free. You'll find this used in our Sloppy Joes (page 109).

Seitan: Made from vital wheat gluten, seitan has a meatlike texture that's great for a variety of different vegan dishes. You can find it at the grocery store, or if you'd prefer to make homemade, we've got you covered—check out Steamed Seitan (page 332), Simmered Seitan (page 333) and even Crispy Seitan (page 336).

ACIDS

Lemon juice, apple cider vinegar and white vinegar: These are often interchangeable in recipes throughout this book. Unless otherwise noted, you can use bottled or freshly squeezed lemon juice.

Rice vinegar: We use unseasoned rice vinegar in many recipes in our Travel-Inspired Eats chapter (page 123). It's perfect for adding a bit of sweetness and acidity.

OTHER INGREDIENTS

Kappa carrageenan: This is an ingredient used to make vegan cheese. It helps the cheese melt when heated and firm up when refrigerated. It may be found at a specialty food store, but we suggest ordering it online.

Tapioca flour: Another important ingredient for vegan cheese, tapioca flour (also known as tapioca starch) is used as a thickener and causes vegan cheese to become thick and stretchy.

Nutritional yeast: You will come across nutritional yeast in many of the recipes throughout this book, including Tofu Scramble (page 27) and Cheddar (page 341). It is a great source of protein, B vitamins and trace minerals. It gives dishes a "cheesy" flavor, making it great for vegan cooking.

Soy sauce or tamari: Made from fermented soybeans, these salty liquids are used widely throughout the cookbook. Tamari is slightly less salty and thicker, and is a gluten-free alternative. If you're looking for a soy-free alternative, you can use coconut aminos.

Mirin: Mirin is a rice wine that adds acidity and sweetness to dishes. You'll come across this ingredient in Spicy Braised Tofu (page 132), Gochujang Brussels Sprouts (page 133) and Rice Bowls with Marinated Tofu and Gochujang Sauce (page 152).

Miso paste: This savory, umami-rich paste made from fermented soybeans is a must-have in every kitchen. We use this in a variety of recipes throughout this book, including Cheddar (page 341), Soy-Miso Edamame (page 219) and Miso Sweet Potato (page 254). It can be found at many grocery stores.

Xanthan gum: Xanthan gum is a fine powder used for thickening and stabilizing. It's imperative for our Cream Cheese (page 344) recipe. It may be found at specialty food stores, but we suggest ordering it online.

BREAKFAST
AND BRUNCH

Sunday brunch has been a tradition in our house for as long as we can remember. Some of our best memories involve gathering around the table as a family and stuffing our faces full of Cinnamon Rolls (page 18), Tofu Scramble (page 27), Sweet Potato Hash (page 26) and Mom's Banana Bread (page 34), or in Shannon's case, a Loaded Açai Bowl (page 50). Because we are a family of eleven (yes, we have three brothers, too!), it's a rarity when we're all together and even rarer when we can all sit around a table and enjoy a meal together. So, this chapter is a tribute to our favorite memories of us all together, enjoying brunch as a family. We hope you can take these recipes and make your own memories with your family, as we have with ours.

Cinnamon Rolls

These ooey-gooey cinnamon rolls are absolute perfection. They're loaded with vegan butter and cinnamon-sugar goodness, then topped with a vanilla glaze for the ultimate cinnamon rolls. We love serving these at brunch for a sweet treat paired with savory dishes, such as Tofu Scramble (page 27) and Tofu "Bacon" (page 335).

PREP TIME:
40 minutes, plus inactive time for rising

COOK TIME:
18 to 22 minutes

YIELD:
12 cinnamon rolls

DOUGH

1 cup (240 ml) warm nondairy milk (heated to 100 to 110°F [37 to 43°C]) (nut-free and/or soy-free if needed)

4 tbsp (48 g) granulated sugar, divided

2¼ tsp (1 [7-g] packet) active dry yeast

2¾ to 3¼ cups (343 to 406 g) all-purpose flour (spooned and leveled or weighed [see page 359 for How to Measure Flour]), plus more for kneading if needed

1 tsp salt

5 tbsp (70 g) vegan butter, cut into 4 pieces, at room temperature (nut-free and/or soy-free if needed)

FOR RISING

1½ tsp (7 ml) canola oil

Make the dough: In a small bowl, whisk together the warm milk with 1 tablespoon (12 g) of the granulated sugar. Sprinkle the yeast on top and whisk until it is mostly dissolved. Set aside for 5 to 10 minutes, until the mixture has foamed.

Meanwhile, in the bowl of a stand mixer fitted with the hook attachment, or in a large bowl, stir together 2¾ cups (343 g) of the flour, the salt and the remaining 3 tablespoons (36 g) of granulated sugar. Add the butter and beat until incorporated. Alternatively, you can mix it with a rubber scraper or large wooden spoon—the butter should break up slightly into the flour, but it's okay if large pieces remain. Once the yeast mixture is foamy, add it to the flour mixture. Beat on low speed or stir with the rubber scraper or wooden spoon, scraping the sides as necessary, until you have a soft but manageable dough. Add more flour, up to ½ cup (62 g), as needed, to ensure the dough is not too sticky to handle.

Either beat the dough in the stand mixer on low speed for 5 to 7 minutes, or transfer the dough to a lightly floured surface and knead by hand for 5 to 7 minutes, incorporating more flour as needed so that the dough does not stick to the sides of the bowl or to your hands. The dough is ready when you gently press into it and it slowly bounces back. Coat a large bowl with the canola oil. Form the dough into a ball and place in the bowl. Turn to lightly coat the ball with the oil. Place a clean towel over the bowl. Let rest in a warm place until the dough has doubled in size, about 1 hour.

(continued)

Cinnamon Rolls (Continued)

FILLING

¾ cup (165 g) packed light brown sugar

2 tbsp (16 g) ground cinnamon

½ cup (113 g) vegan butter, at room temperature, plus more for pan (nut-free and/or soy-free if needed)

GLAZE

3 tbsp (42 g) vegan butter, at room temperature (nut-free and/or soy-free if needed)

1½ cups (187 g) powdered sugar

1 tsp pure vanilla extract

1 tbsp (15 ml) nondairy milk, plus more as needed (nut-free and/or soy-free if needed)

Prepare the filling: In a small bowl, stir together the brown sugar and cinnamon until well combined. Set aside.

Fill and shape the rolls: Butter a 9 x 13-inch (23 x 33-cm) baking dish. Once the dough has doubled, gently punch it down to release any air bubbles and transfer to a lightly floured surface. Roll out the dough into a large rectangle, about 14 x 16 inches (36 x 40 cm) in size. Spread the butter evenly over the dough. Sprinkle the cinnamon sugar mixture evenly over the butter and lightly press it into the butter. Beginning on the longer side, tightly roll the dough into a log. Cut into 12 equal pieces (see Sister Tip). Place the rolls, swirly side up, evenly in the pan. Cover with plastic wrap or a large towel and set in a warm place to rise again until doubled in size, 30 minutes to 1 hour.

Once the rolls are close to doubled in size, preheat the oven to 350°F (180°C). Once doubled in size, bake the rolls for 18 to 22 minutes, until golden brown.

Make the glaze: In a small bowl, mix together the butter, powdered sugar, vanilla and milk until well combined. If necessary, add more milk, 1 teaspoon at a time, until the desired consistency is reached—it should be slightly thick but still pourable.

Once the rolls are out of the oven, allow them to cool slightly, then spread the glaze evenly over the rolls. Serve warm or at room temperature.

Sister Tip

For an easy way to cut the rolls, wrap unflavored dental floss around the spot to be cut, then pull tightly.

Bagels with Veggie Cream Cheese

One of our absolute favorite breakfast foods is a New York–style bagel with tofu veggie cream cheese. Honestly, if you've never had one, you must. Because we're not able to head to NYC every time we're craving a bagel, we set out to create our own homemade bagels with veggie cream cheese to satisfy our cravings. Make the flavorful veggie cream cheese using store-bought or homemade vegan Cream Cheese (page 344) or top these bagels with avocado or vegan butter. We promise, you will not be disappointed.

PREP TIME:
40 minutes, plus inactive time for rising

COOK TIME:
18 to 22 minutes

YIELD:
8 bagels

BAGELS
1⅓ cups (320 ml) warm water (heated to 100 to 110°F [37 to 43°C])

1 tbsp (11 g) diastatic dry malt powder (can substitute for packed light brown sugar or granulated sugar if needed) (see Sister Tips)

2¼ tsp (1 [7-g] packet) active dry yeast

3¾ to 4¼ cups (450 to 510 g) bread flour (spooned and leveled or weighed [see page 359 for How to Measure Flour]), plus more for kneading if needed

1½ tsp (9 g) salt

FOR RISING
1½ tsp (7 ml) canola oil

Make the bagels: In a small bowl, whisk together the warm water and malt powder. Sprinkle the yeast on top and whisk until it is mostly dissolved. Let stand for 5 to 10 minutes, until the mixture has foamed.

Meanwhile, in the bowl of a stand mixer fitted with the hook attachment, or in a large bowl, stir together 3¾ cups (450 g) of the flour and the salt. Once the yeast mixture is foamy, add it to the flour mixture. Beat on low speed or stir with a rubber scraper or wooden spoon, scraping the sides as necessary, until you have a soft but manageable dough. Add more flour, up to ½ cup (60 g), as needed, so that your dough isn't too sticky to handle.

Either beat the dough in the stand mixer on low speed for 5 to 7 minutes, or transfer the dough to a lightly floured surface and knead by hand for 5 to 7 minutes, incorporating more flour as necessary so that the dough does not stick to the sides of the bowl or to your hands. The dough is ready when you gently press into it and it slowly bounces back. Coat a large bowl with the canola oil. Form the dough into a ball and place in the bowl. Turn to lightly coat the ball with the oil. Place a clean towel over the bowl. Let rest in a warm place until the dough has doubled in size, approximately 1 hour.

Line a large baking sheet with parchment paper. Once the dough has doubled, punch it to release any air bubbles and divide it into eight equal pieces. Shape each piece into a ball and press through the center of each ball to make a hole, creating a bagel shape. Place the shaped balls on the prepared baking sheet and cover with a clean towel. Set aside while you prepare your boiling water.

(continued)

Bagels with Veggie Cream Cheese (Continued)

FOR BOILING

2 quarts (2 L) water

2 tbsp (42 g) barley malt syrup (optional; see Sister Tips)

FOR TOPPING

3 to 5 tbsp (28 to 48 g) Everything Seasoning (page 357) or store-bought (optional)

VEGGIE CREAM CHEESE

1 cup (226 g) plain vegan Cream Cheese (page 344) or store-bought (nut-free and/or soy-free if needed)

2 tbsp (15 g) minced carrot

1 tbsp (10 g) seeded and minced red bell pepper

2 tbsp (12 g) minced green onion

1 tsp dried minced onion (see Sister Tips)

1 tsp dried chives

1 tsp fresh dill

¼ tsp garlic powder

Preheat the oven to 450°F (230°C) and fill a large pot with the water. Stir in the barley malt syrup (if using). Place over high heat and bring to a boil. Working in batches, place a few pieces of the dough into the boiling water, boiling on each side for about 1 minute. Once done, place each piece of dough back on the lined baking sheet. If desired, press 1 to 2 teaspoons (3 to 6 g) of Everything Seasoning onto the top of each bagel immediately after it comes out of the water. Once all of the bagels have been boiled, place in the oven for 18 to 22 minutes, until golden brown.

Make the veggie cream cheese: While the bagels are baking, place the cream cheese in a medium-sized bowl. Stir the carrot, bell pepper, green onion (see Sister Tips), dried minced onion, chives, dill and garlic powder into the cream cheese until well incorporated.

Serve the warm bagels sliced with a schmear of veggie cream cheese.

Sister Tips

Diastatic malt powder and barley malt syrup give these bagels a delicious malt flavor and extra-chewy texture and can be found online or at some grocery stores; however, you can follow the substitutions for malt powder and omit the barley malt syrup if you desire.

Dried minced onion adds a delicious flavor to this cream cheese; however, it can be omitted if necessary. You can find it at your local grocery store or order it online. You will also come across this ingredient in Everything Seasoning (page 357) and Sour Cream and Onion Dip (page 225).

For a smoother cream cheese, in a food processor, add the carrot, bell pepper and green onion and process until finely chopped before adding to the cream cheese.

Loaded Breakfast Casserole

This breakfast casserole is great to serve a crowd or to prep in the beginning of the week and enjoy each morning. It's loaded with tofu, veggies, vegan cheese and spices. Serve it with a slice of toast, Tofu "Bacon" (page 335) and Sweet Potato Hash (page 26) for a breakfast that will fuel you for the day.

PREP TIME:
20 minutes, plus inactive time to press tofu

COOK TIME:
1 hour 8 minutes

YIELD:
8 servings

1 tbsp (15 ml) olive oil, plus more for pan

1 medium-sized white onion, chopped small (about 1 cup [160 g])

1 red bell pepper, seeded and chopped small (about 1 cup [149 g])

3 cloves garlic, peeled and minced, or 1 tbsp (9 g) jarred minced garlic

2 (14- to 16-oz [396- to 453-g]) packages firm or extra-firm tofu, drained and pressed (see page 358 for tutorial)

½ tsp ground turmeric

1 tsp onion powder

2 tsp (5 g) garlic powder

2 tsp (4 g) paprika

1 tsp salt

½ tsp freshly ground black pepper

½ cup (120 ml) plain, unsweetened rice milk

⅓ cup (26 g) nutritional yeast

2 tbsp (30 ml) soy sauce (or tamari for gluten-free)

1 lb (453 g) russet potatoes, peeled and diced into ½ to 1" (1- to 2.5-cm) pieces (about 3 cups)

1½ cups (170 g) vegan Cheddar shreds (page 341) or store-bought, divided (nut-free if needed)

Chopped green onion, for topping

Preheat the oven to 375°F (190°C) and oil a 9 x 13-inch (23 x 33-cm) baking dish. Set aside.

In a large skillet, heat the olive oil over medium heat. Add the onion and bell pepper. Cook, stirring often, for 5 to 7 minutes, or until the onion is translucent and the bell pepper is fork-tender. Stir in the garlic and cook for 30 seconds to 1 minute, or until the garlic is fragrant. Remove from the heat and set aside.

Crumble the tofu into a large bowl. Add the turmeric, onion powder, garlic powder, paprika, salt, black pepper, rice milk, nutritional yeast, soy sauce, potatoes and 1 cup (113 g) of the Cheddar shreds. Mix until combined. Mix in the cooked veggies. Pour into the prepared baking dish. Evenly sprinkle the top with the remaining ½ cup (56 g) of Cheddar shreds.

Cover the dish with foil and bake for 45 minutes. Then, remove the foil and bake for another 15 minutes, or until the Cheddar is melted and the potatoes are fork-tender. Remove from the oven and let cool slightly. Serve topped with green onion.

Sweet Potato
Hash (page 26)

Sweet Potato Hash

This breakfast hash is made in less than 30 minutes and is the perfect addition to brunch. We love eating this with a drizzle of ketchup or sriracha. Serve it with our Loaded Breakfast Casserole (page 24) and Tofu "Bacon" (page 335).

PREP TIME:
10 minutes

COOK TIME:
13 to 18 minutes

YIELD:
4 to 6 servings

---

1 tbsp (15 ml) olive or canola oil

½ medium-sized sweet onion, chopped (about ½ cup [80 g])

½ red bell pepper, seeded and chopped (about ½ cup [74 g])

5 cups (710 g) peeled and diced sweet potato (diced into ½" [1.3-cm] pieces)

2 tbsp (30 ml) water

2 tbsp (30 ml) pure maple syrup

1 tsp garlic powder

½ tsp ground cumin

½ tsp paprika

½ tsp onion powder

½ tsp salt, plus more to taste

¼ tsp freshly ground black pepper, plus more to taste

3 cloves garlic, peeled and minced, or 1 tbsp (9 g) jarred minced garlic

In a large sauté pan with a lid, heat the oil over medium heat. Add the onion and bell pepper. Sauté for 3 to 5 minutes, stirring often.

Add the sweet potato and sauté for about 5 minutes, stirring often. Stir in the water, maple syrup, garlic powder, cumin, paprika, onion powder, salt and black pepper. Cover and cook for another 5 to 7 minutes, or until the sweet potato is fork-tender, stirring halfway through.

Remove the lid and add the garlic. Cook, stirring, for another 30 seconds to 1 minute, or until the garlic is fragrant. Serve topped with more salt and black pepper, if desired.

*See in Loaded Breakfast Casserole image on the previous page.

Tofu Scramble

This recipe is always a must-have for our Sunday brunch, especially because it comes together in less than ten minutes. The nutritional yeast adds a cheesy flavor, while the turmeric provides a color reminiscent of scrambled eggs. Serve this classic scramble as is or serve it on a Breakfast Sandwich (page 29).

PREP TIME:
2 minutes

COOK TIME:
6 to 8 minutes

YIELD:
4 servings

1 tbsp (15 ml) olive oil

1 (14- to 16-oz [396- to 453-g]) block firm or extra-firm tofu

1½ tsp (7 ml) soy sauce (or tamari for gluten-free) (low-sodium if desired)

3 tbsp (15 g) nutritional yeast

¼ tsp ground turmeric

1 tsp garlic powder

½ tsp onion powder

½ tsp paprika

¼ tsp salt, plus more to taste

⅛ tsp freshly ground black pepper, plus more to taste

Crushed red pepper flakes (optional)

In a large skillet, heat the oil over medium-low heat. Drain the tofu and crumble it into the pan. Stir for a minute, allowing some water to evaporate. Add all the remaining ingredients, except the red pepper flakes, stirring to combine completely. Increase the heat to medium and cook, stirring occasionally, for 5 to 7 minutes. Add water as needed to keep the tofu from sticking to the pan. Taste and add red pepper flakes and more salt and pepper, if desired.

*See in Breakfast Sandwich image on the next page.

Breakfast Sandwich

As we mentioned in the chapter intro, Sunday brunch has always been a staple in our house, and we always serve the same things: Tofu Scramble (page 27), Tofu "Bacon" (page 335) and Sweet Potato Hash (page 26). But we are always split on how we enjoy our favorite breakfast foods. Half of us are "Team Breakfast Sandwich," whereas the other half of us enjoy our food as is. So, this recipe is for those who are "Team Breakfast Sandwich." Here, we serve Tofu Scramble, Tofu "Bacon," avocado and vegan cheese between slices of buttery, garlicky, crispy bread.

PREP TIME:
10 minutes, plus prep time for Tofu Scramble

COOK TIME:
10 to 20 minutes

YIELD:
4 sandwiches

Vegan butter (nut-free if needed)

8 slices Italian bread or vegan bread of choice (gluten-free if needed)

Garlic Salt (page 356) or store-bought, as needed

4 slices store-bought vegan Cheddar cheese, or 1 cup (113 g) Cheddar shreds (page 341 or store-bought), divided (nut-free if needed)

2 medium-sized ripe avocados, peeled and pitted

1 batch Tofu Scramble (page 27) (gluten-free if needed)

8 slices Tofu "Bacon" (page 335), or prepared store-bought alternative (gluten-free if needed)

Butter each slice of bread on one side and sprinkle with your desired amount of garlic salt.

Heat a large, lidded sauté pan over medium-low heat. For each sandwich, place 2 slices of bread on the skillet, butter side down. To 1 bread slice, add a slice of Cheddar cheese or ¼ cup (28 g) of Cheddar shreds; leave the other bread slice plain. Cover and cook for about 5 minutes, until the bottoms are golden brown and the cheese is melted. Remove from the pan.

Place the peeled avocado in a small bowl. Mash lightly with a fork. To the butter-free side of each cheese-free bread slice, add an equal amount of avocado, an equal amount of Tofu Scramble and 2 slices of Tofu "Bacon." Place a cheese-topped bread slice, melted cheese side down, atop the Tofu "Bacon" to complete each sandwich. Slice each sandwich in half and serve.

Glazed Pumpkin Bread

Not only does this recipe use up a whole can of pumpkin puree (no need to let half of a can go to waste sitting in the fridge), but it makes two loaves of pumpkin bread. It's perfect for giving away a loaf as a gift or wrapping up and freezing to enjoy later. It's moist, flavorful and perfect for fall when you're craving all things pumpkin spice—but it's so good you'll want it year-round!

PREP TIME:
20 minutes

COOK TIME:
48 to 52 minutes

YIELD:
2 loaves, 16 to 20 slices

PUMPKIN BREAD

Nonstick spray, for pans

1 cup (240 ml) soy milk

1 tbsp (15 ml) lemon juice, white vinegar or apple cider vinegar

3½ cups (437 g) all-purpose flour (spooned and leveled or weighed [see page 359 for How to Measure Flour])

2 tsp (9 g) baking soda

2 tsp (9 g) baking powder

1 tsp salt

1½ tsp (4 g) ground cinnamon

1 tsp ground nutmeg

½ tsp ground cloves

¾ cup (180 ml) canola oil

1 cup (200 g) granulated sugar

1 cup (220 g) packed light brown sugar

1 (15-oz [425-g]) can pure pumpkin puree

1 tbsp (15 ml) pure vanilla extract

GLAZE

1½ cups (187 g) powdered sugar

2 tbsp (30 ml) soy milk or nondairy milk of choice, plus more as needed (nut-free if needed)

½ tsp pure vanilla extract

Make the pumpkin bread: Preheat the oven to 350°F (180°C) and spray two 9 x 5-inch (23 x 13-cm) loaf pans with nonstick cooking spray. In a small bowl, whisk together the milk and lemon juice, then set aside for 10 to 15 minutes, until curdled. In a separate, medium-sized bowl, whisk together the flour, baking soda, baking powder, salt, cinnamon, nutmeg and cloves, then set aside.

In a large bowl or the bowl of a stand mixer fitted with the paddle attachment, combine the oil, granulated sugar and brown sugar and beat with a hand mixer or the stand mixer until well mixed. Add the pumpkin, milk mixture and vanilla and beat again until well mixed. Add the flour mixture to the pumpkin mixture and mix until just combined. Distribute the batter equally between the two prepared pans. Bake for 48 to 52 minutes, until a toothpick inserted into the center comes out clean or with only crumbs, no raw batter.

Meanwhile, make the glaze: In a medium-sized bowl, whisk together the powdered sugar, milk and vanilla. Add more milk, ½ teaspoon at a time, until the consistency is thick but pourable. Set aside.

Remove the loaves from the oven and allow them to cool completely in their pans. Flip each pan upside down onto a cutting board, lift up each pan to release the loaves, then carefully turn the loaves upright again. Equally distribute the glaze between the loaves, spreading it to evenly cover the tops of each loaf, allowing some glaze to fall down the sides. For best results, allow the glaze to set for 1 to 2 hours, then slice each loaf into eight to ten equal slices or freeze a loaf for later by wrapping tightly in plastic wrap, then placing in the freezer. Defrost in the fridge overnight before serving.

French Toast Dippers

These dippers are family-friendly and kid-approved. For this recipe, we use a banana mixture in place of eggs, which also adds sweetness and delicious flavor. Serve them topped with powdered sugar and dipped into maple syrup.

PREP TIME:
10 minutes

COOK TIME:
10 minutes

YIELD:
18 dippers

DIPPERS
6 slices thick-cut vegan bread, such as Texas toast (gluten-free if needed)

1 cup (240 ml) nondairy milk (nut-free and/or soy-free if needed)

1 medium-sized ripe banana

2 tbsp (16 g) ground cinnamon

1 tsp pure vanilla extract

Canola oil, for pan

FOR SERVING
Powdered sugar

Pure maple syrup

Cut each piece of bread into three long slices. Set aside.

In a blender or food processer, combine the milk, banana, cinnamon and vanilla, and blend or process until completely blended. Pour into a wide bowl.

Lightly coat the bottom of a large skillet with canola oil and heat over medium heat. Dip each piece of bread into the banana mixture, coating completely, and place in the pan. Lightly fry on each side until golden brown, 2 to 3 minutes per side.

Top with powdered sugar and serve dipped into maple syrup.

Mom's Banana Bread

Let's be honest, there's nothing better than a recipe that reminds you of home, and for us, this is just that. Our mom has been making her banana bread for years, and when we all went vegan, she made a few swaps to her original recipe, cutting out the eggs and dairy. This banana bread is simple, moist and absolute perfection. We love to serve it sliced and topped with plant-based butter or coconut oil.

PREP TIME:
20 minutes

COOK TIME:
48 to 52 minutes

YIELD:
8 to 10 slices

Nonstick spray, for pan

2 tbsp (12 g) flaxseed meal

¼ cup (60 ml) water

1¾ cups (219 g) all-purpose flour (spooned and leveled or weighed [see page 359 for How to Measure Flour])

1 tsp salt

1 tsp baking soda

1 tsp baking powder

2 large or 3 small overripe bananas, mashed (1 heaping cup [250 g])

⅔ cup (133 g) granulated sugar

⅓ cup (80 ml) canola oil

¼ cup (60 g) vegan sour cream, plain nondairy yogurt or Cashew Cream (page 343) (nut-free and/or soy-free if needed)

1 tsp pure vanilla extract

Preheat the oven to 350°F (180°C). Spray a 9 x 5-inch (23 x 13–cm) loaf pan with nonstick spray. Make a flax egg: In a small bowl, stir together the flaxseed meal and water and set aside for 10 to 15 minutes, until gelled.

In a medium-sized bowl, whisk together the flour, salt, baking soda and baking powder. In a large bowl, mash the bananas with a fork or electric mixer—you can either leave some chunks of banana or mash them completely. Mix in the sugar, oil, sour cream, vanilla and flax egg until well incorporated. Add the flour mixture. Mix again until just combined.

Pour into your prepared loaf pan. Bake for 48 to 52 minutes, until a toothpick inserted into the center comes out clean or with just crumbs, no raw batter.

Remove from the oven and let cool for 10 minutes in the pan. Flip the pan upside down onto a cutting board, lift up the pan to release the loaf, then carefully turn the loaf upright again. Let cool for at least 10 more minutes, then slice and serve.

Fluffy Buttermilk Pancakes

Who doesn't love fresh, fluffy pancakes on a lazy Sunday morning? These are delicious plain, but our variations with blueberries and chocolate chips are next level. They're best topped with vegan butter and pure maple syrup.

PREP TIME:
20 minutes

COOK TIME:
15 minutes

YIELD:
8 pancakes

1¼ cups (300 ml) soy milk (see Sister Tips for soy-free option)

1 tbsp (15 ml) lemon juice, white vinegar or apple cider vinegar

1¾ cups (218 g) all-purpose flour (spooned and leveled or weighed [see page 359 for How to Measure Flour])

⅓ cup (66 g) granulated sugar

1 tsp baking powder

½ tsp baking soda

½ tsp salt

2 tbsp (30 ml) canola oil, plus more for pan

1 tsp pure vanilla extract

VARIATIONS

Blueberry Pancakes: 1 cup (148 g) fresh blueberries

Chocolate Chip Pancakes: ¾ cup (126 g) vegan semisweet chocolate chips

In a small bowl, whisk together the milk and lemon juice, then set aside for 10 to 15 minutes, until curdled. In a large bowl, whisk together the flour, sugar, baking powder, baking soda and salt.

Once the milk mixture has curdled, pour it along with the oil and vanilla into the flour mixture. Mix until just barely combined, leaving some chunks. Fold in the blueberries or chocolate chips, if using.

Lightly coat the bottom of a large skillet with oil and heat over medium-low heat. Pour ¼ cup (70 g) of batter into the pan for each pancake (see Sister Tips). Cook for 3 to 5 minutes, until the bottom is golden brown and bubbles form on the surface. Flip and cook on the other side for 1 to 3 minutes, until golden brown. Repeat until all the batter is used and serve immediately.

Sister Tips

Although soy milk is best for this recipe, feel free to use your favorite non-dairy milk with similar results; it may not curdle as well, but your pancakes will still turn out delicious.

This recipe can also make about 32 mini pancakes. For each mini pancake, use 1 tablespoon (17 g) of batter rather than ¼ cup (70 g). Adjust the cook time accordingly.

Double Chocolate Muffins

Double chocolate muffins were one of our favorite store-bought breakfast foods growing up (you know the ones). Making them at home is surprisingly easy, and—bonus—no dairy or eggs are needed. So, what are you waiting for? Double chocolate deliciousness is waiting for you.

PREP TIME:
20 minutes

COOK TIME:
18 to 22 minutes

YIELD:
12 muffins

Nonstick spray, for pan

1 cup (240 ml) soy milk

1 tbsp (15 ml) lemon juice, white vinegar or apple cider vinegar

1¾ cups (218 g) all-purpose flour (spooned and leveled or weighed [see page 359 for How to Measure Flour])

½ cup (50 g) unsweetened natural cocoa powder (spooned and leveled or weighed [see page 359 for tutorial])

¾ cup (150 g) granulated sugar

1 tsp baking powder

1 tsp baking soda

1 tsp salt

½ cup (120 ml) canola oil

⅓ cup (75 g) vegan sour cream, plain nondairy yogurt, Cashew Cream (page 343) or mashed overripe banana (nut-free if needed)

1 tsp pure vanilla extract

1⅓ cups (223 g) vegan semisweet chocolate chips, divided

Preheat the oven to 350°F (180°C). Spray a 12-well muffin pan with nonstick spray and set aside. In a medium-sized bowl, whisk together the milk and lemon juice, then set aside for 10 to 15 minutes, until curdled.

In a large bowl, whisk together the flour, cocoa powder, sugar, baking powder, baking soda and salt. To the milk mixture, add the oil, sour cream and vanilla, and mix to combine. Pour into the flour mixture and mix until just combined, being careful not to overmix. Fold in 1 cup (168 g) of the chocolate chips.

Evenly distribute the batter among the prepared muffin wells, filling all 12 wells. Evenly sprinkle the remaining ⅓ cup (55 g) of chocolate chips over the batter. Bake for 18 to 22 minutes, until a toothpick inserted into the center of a muffin comes out clean or with just crumbs, no raw batter. Remove from the oven and allow to cool slightly, then serve.

These muffins can be stored in an airtight container at room temperature for 2 to 3 days or in the fridge for about a week.

*See in the image to the right (bottom row).

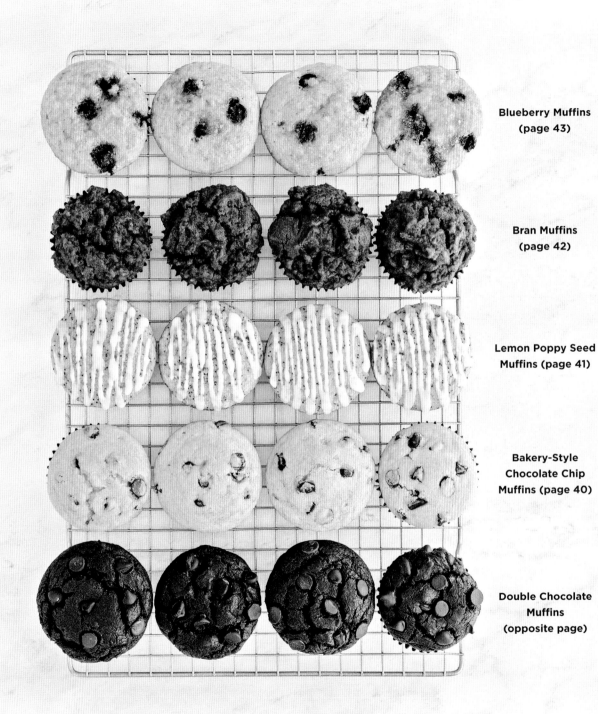

Blueberry Muffins
(page 43)

Bran Muffins
(page 42)

Lemon Poppy Seed
Muffins (page 41)

Bakery-Style
Chocolate Chip
Muffins (page 40)

Double Chocolate
Muffins
(opposite page)

Bakery-Style Chocolate Chip Muffins

These chocolate chip muffins are reminiscent of the ones you would find at your local bakery. They're moist, fluffy and, of course, vegan. They're ready in less than 45 minutes, making them the perfect addition to your morning coffee or brunch.

PREP TIME:
20 minutes

COOK TIME:
18 to 22 minutes

YIELD:
12 muffins

Nonstick spray, for pan

1 cup (240 ml) soy milk

1 tbsp (15 ml) lemon juice, white vinegar or apple cider vinegar

2 cups (250 g) all-purpose flour (spooned and leveled or weighed [see page 359 for How to Measure Flour])

1 tsp salt

1 tsp baking soda

1 tsp baking powder

¾ cup (150 g) granulated sugar

⅓ cup (80 ml) canola oil

2 tsp (10 ml) pure vanilla extract

1 cup (168 g) vegan semisweet chocolate chips

Preheat the oven to 350°F (180°C). Spray a 12-well muffin pan with nonstick spray and set aside. In a medium-sized bowl, whisk together the milk and lemon juice, then set aside for 10 to 15 minutes, until curdled.

In a large bowl, whisk together the flour, salt, baking soda, baking powder and sugar. To the milk mixture, add the canola oil and vanilla and mix to combine. Pour into the flour mixture and mix until just combined, being careful not to overmix. Fold in the chocolate chips.

Evenly distribute the batter among the prepared muffin wells, filling all 12 wells. Bake for 18 to 22 minutes, until a toothpick inserted into the center of a muffin comes out clean or with just crumbs, no raw batter. Remove from the oven and allow to cool slightly, then serve.

These muffins can be stored in an airtight container at room temperature for 2 to 3 days or in the fridge for about a week.

*See in the image on page 39 (fourth row from the top).

Lemon Poppy Seed Muffins

We love everything about these muffins. They are moist, fluffy and the perfect combination of tart and sweet, pairing lemony muffins with a sugary glaze. Make sure to follow the instructions closely, as you'll first bake the muffins at a higher temperature for five minutes, then bring down the temperature for the remainder of the bake time. You should also be sure to zest a lemon prior to squeezing it, as you'll use the zest and juice of approximately one large lemon. These muffins are great to enjoy throughout the week and perfect morning, noon or night.

PREP TIME:
20 minutes

COOK TIME:
14 to 16 minutes

YIELD:
12 muffins

MUFFINS

Nonstick spray, for pan

¾ cup (180 ml) soy milk

¼ cup (60 ml) fresh lemon juice

2 cups (250 g) all-purpose flour (spooned and leveled or weighed [see page 359 for How to Measure Flour])

1 cup (200 g) granulated sugar

1 tsp baking powder

1 tsp baking soda

1 tsp salt

2 tbsp (18 g) poppy seeds

⅓ cup (80 ml) canola oil

¼ cup (60 g) vegan sour cream, plain nondairy yogurt or Cashew Cream (page 343) (nut-free if needed)

1 tbsp (6 g) grated lemon zest

2 tsp (10 ml) pure vanilla extract

GLAZE

½ cup (62 g) powdered sugar

2 tsp (10 ml) soy milk or nondairy milk of choice, plus more as needed (nut-free if needed)

¼ tsp pure vanilla extract

Make the muffins: Preheat the oven to 425°F (220°C) and spray a 12-well muffin pan with nonstick spray. Set aside. In a medium-sized mixing bowl, whisk together the milk and lemon juice. Set aside for 10 to 15 minutes, until curdled.

In a large bowl, whisk together the flour, granulated sugar, baking powder, baking soda, salt and poppy seeds. To the milk mixture, add the oil, sour cream, lemon zest and vanilla, and whisk until combined. Pour the milk mixture into the flour mixture and mix until just combined, being careful not to overmix. Evenly distribute the batter among the prepared muffin wells, filling all 12 wells. Bake for 5 minutes, then lower the oven temperature to 350°F (180°C) and bake for another 9 to 11 minutes, until a toothpick inserted in the center of a muffin comes out clean or with just crumbs, no raw batter.

While the muffins bake, make the glaze: In a small bowl, whisk together the powdered sugar, milk and vanilla. If necessary, add more milk, ½ teaspoon at a time, until your desired consistency is reached. It should be slightly thick yet pourable.

Remove the muffins from the oven, allow to cool slightly, then drizzle evenly with the prepared glaze. Serve slightly warm or at room temperature.

These muffins can be stored in an airtight container at room temperature for 2 to 3 days or in the fridge for about a week.

*See in the image on page 39 (middle row).

Bran Muffins

While we were growing up, our mom and grandma made bran muffins almost weekly; they were a staple in our house. So, when we set out to create recipes for this cookbook, we knew we wanted to include this one. If you've never tried bran muffins before, we encourage you to give these a go. The addition of cinnamon gives them a rich flavor. They're delicious as is or served with a dollop of vegan butter.

PREP TIME:
30 minutes

COOK TIME:
18 to 22 minutes

YIELD:
12 muffins

Nonstick spray, for pan

1 cup (240 ml) soy milk

1 tbsp (15 ml) lemon juice, white vinegar or apple cider vinegar

1¾ cups (218 g) all-purpose flour (spooned and leveled or weighed [see page 359 for How to Measure Flour])

2 tsp (9 g) baking powder

½ tsp baking soda

1 tbsp (8 g) ground cinnamon

¼ tsp salt

2 cups (120 g) vegan bran cereal (preferably stick-shaped, rather than flakes)

1 cup (240 ml) boiling water

½ cup (120 ml) canola oil

¾ cup (150 g) granulated sugar

1 tbsp (15 ml) pure vanilla extract

Preheat the oven to 375°F (190°C). Spray a 12-well muffin pan with nonstick spray and set aside. In a small bowl, whisk together the milk and lemon juice, then set aside for 10 to 15 minutes, until curdled.

In a medium-sized bowl, whisk together the flour, baking powder, baking soda, cinnamon and salt, then set aside.

Place the bran cereal in a large mixing bowl. Pour the boiling water over the cereal and stir. Allow to sit for 3 to 5 minutes, then add the milk mixture. Stir and allow to sit for 3 to 5 more minutes. Add the oil, sugar and vanilla to the bran mixture and mix. Pour the flour mixture into the bran mixture and mix until just combined.

Evenly distribute the batter among the prepared muffin wells, filling all 12 wells. Bake for 18 to 22 minutes, until a toothpick inserted into the center of a muffin comes out clean or with only crumbs, no raw batter. Remove from the oven and allow to cool slightly, then serve.

These muffins can be stored in an airtight container at room temperature for 2 to 3 days or in the fridge for about a week.

*See in the image on page 39 (second row from the top).

Blueberry Muffins

Nothing beats a fresh, warm muffin in the morning, especially when it's loaded with blueberries. These are delicious, moist and much easier to make than you might think. Enjoy them with some of our savory brunch dishes, such as Tofu Scramble (page 27) and Sweet Potato Hash (page 26).

PREP TIME:	COOK TIME:	YIELD:
20 minutes	*18 to 22 minutes*	*12 muffins*

Nonstick spray, for pan

1 cup (240 ml) soy milk

1 tbsp (15 ml) lemon juice, white vinegar or apple cider vinegar

2 cups + 1½ tsp (253 g) all-purpose flour (spooned and leveled or weighed [see page 359 for How to Measure Flour]), divided

¾ cup (150 g) granulated sugar

1 tsp salt

1 tsp baking soda

1 tsp baking powder

⅓ cup (80 ml) canola oil

2 tsp (10 ml) pure vanilla extract

1¼ cups (185 g) fresh blueberries

FOR TOPPING
1 tbsp (13 g) turbinado sugar (see Sister Tip)

Preheat the oven to 350°F (180°C) and spray a 12-well muffin pan with nonstick spray. Set aside. In a medium-sized bowl, whisk together the milk and lemon juice, then set aside for 10 to 15 minutes, until curdled.

In a large bowl, whisk together 2 cups (250 g) of the flour with the granulated sugar, salt, baking soda and baking powder. To the milk mixture, add the canola oil and vanilla, and mix until combined. Pour the milk mixture into the flour mixture and mix until just combined. In a small bowl, combine the blueberries and remaining 1½ teaspoons (3 g) of flour and toss to lightly coat the blueberries. Gently fold them into the batter.

Evenly distribute the batter among the prepared muffin wells, filling all 12 wells. Top each with about ¼ teaspoon of turbinado sugar. Bake for 18 to 22 minutes, until a toothpick inserted into the center of a muffin comes out clean or with just crumbs, no raw batter. Remove from the oven and allow to cool slightly, then serve.

These muffins can be stored in an airtight container at room temperature for 2 to 3 days or in the fridge for about a week.

*See in the image on page 39 (top row).

Sister Tip

You can use any sugar for topping; however, we recommend a sugar with big granules for the best outcome.

Cinnamon Streusel Coffee Cake

This is easily one of the most popular recipes on our blog; it's loved by vegans and nonvegans alike. It's also one of our family favorites and is always served during our weekend brunch and on holidays—it's just that good. This recipe combines a perfectly moist cake with a crumbly cinnamon streusel topping and powdered sugar drizzle—need we say more?

PREP TIME:
30 minutes

COOK TIME:
30 to 35 minutes

YIELD:
20 pieces

CAKE
Nonstick spray, for pan

1 cup (240 ml) soy milk

1 tbsp (15 ml) lemon juice, white vinegar or apple cider vinegar

2 cups (250 g) all-purpose flour (spooned and leveled or weighed [see page 359 for How to Measure Flour])

¾ cup (150 g) granulated sugar

1 tsp baking soda

1 tsp baking powder

1 tsp salt

½ cup (113 g) vegan sour cream, plain nondairy yogurt or Cashew Cream (page 343) (nut-free if needed)

½ cup (120 ml) canola oil

1½ tsp (7 ml) pure vanilla extract

CINNAMON STREUSEL
½ cup (62 g) all-purpose flour (spooned and leveled or weighed [see page 359 for How to Measure Flour])

1 cup (220 g) packed light brown sugar

1 tbsp (8 g) ground cinnamon

¼ cup (½ stick [56 g]) vegan butter, cold, cubed (see Sister Tip) (nut-free if needed)

Make the cake batter: Preheat the oven to 350°F (180°C). Spray a 9 x 13-inch (23 x 33–cm) cake pan with nonstick spray and set aside. In a medium-sized bowl, whisk together the milk and lemon juice, then set aside for 10 to 15 minutes, until curdled.

In a large bowl, whisk together the flour, granulated sugar, baking soda, baking powder and salt. To the milk mixture, add the sour cream, oil and vanilla, and mix to combine. Pour the milk mixture into the flour mixture and mix until just combined. Set aside.

Make the cinnamon streusel: In a separate medium-sized bowl, stir together the flour, brown sugar and cinnamon. Using a fork or pastry cutter, incorporate the butter into the flour mixture by cutting it into smaller and smaller pieces until you have a crumbly, sandlike texture.

(continued)

Cinnamon Streusel Coffee Cake (Continued)

DRIZZLE

¾ cup (94 g) powdered sugar

2 tsp (10 ml) soy milk or nondairy milk of choice, plus more as needed (nut-free if needed)

Layer and bake the cake: Spread about half of the cake batter in the bottom of the prepared pan. Sprinkle with about half of the cinnamon streusel so that it evenly covers the batter. Spread the remaining batter evenly over the topping. Finally, evenly sprinkle with the rest of the topping. Bake for 24 to 28 minutes, until a toothpick inserted into the center comes out clean or with only crumbs, no raw batter. Remove from the oven and allow to cool slightly.

Make the drizzle: In a small bowl, whisk together the powdered sugar and milk. If you think that the icing is too thick, whisk in more milk, ½ teaspoon at a time, until you reach your desired consistency. Drizzle the icing evenly over the cake. Slice into 20 pieces and serve.

Sister Tip

For this recipe, we recommend using vegan buttery sticks, rather than from the tub.

Banana Bread Pancakes

These pancakes use mashed banana to emulate the flavor of banana bread. They require only ten ingredients and are a great way to use up that overripe banana you have sitting on your counter. Have more than one overripe banana? Double this recipe or check out our Mom's Banana Bread (page 34).

PREP TIME:
20 minutes

COOK TIME:
about 15 minutes

YIELD:
9 pancakes

¾ cup (180 ml) soy milk

2 tsp (10 ml) lemon juice, white vinegar or apple cider vinegar

1½ cups (187 g) all-purpose flour (spooned and leveled or weighed [see page 359 for How to Measure Flour])

¼ cup (50 g) granulated sugar

1 tsp baking powder

¼ tsp baking soda

¼ tsp salt

2 tbsp (30 ml) canola oil, plus more for pan

1 overripe medium-sized banana, mashed

½ tsp pure vanilla extract

In a medium-sized bowl, whisk together the milk and lemon juice, then set aside for 10 to 15 minutes, until curdled. In a large bowl, whisk together the flour, sugar, baking powder, baking soda and salt.

To the curdled milk mixture, add the oil, mashed banana and vanilla, and mix to combine. Pour into the flour mixture and mix until just barely combined, leaving some chunks.

Lightly coat the bottom of a large skillet with oil and heat over medium-low heat. Pour ¼ cup (60 g) of batter into the pan for each pancake. Cook for 3 to 5 minutes, until the bottom is golden brown and bubbles form on the surface. Flip and cook on the other side for 1 to 3 minutes, until golden brown. Repeat until all the batter has been used and serve immediately.

French Toast Bake

Nut-free option,
Soy-free option

What's better than plain ol' French toast? This French toast bake, of course. The sweet and sticky bread base is topped with a delicious cinnamon streusel for a next-level breakfast bake. It has the option of being either soft and gooey or a bit crispier, depending on your preference; adjust the cook time accordingly.

PREP TIME:
20 minutes

COOK TIME:
*45 minutes to
1 hour*

YIELD:
12 slices

Nonstick spray, for pan

BASE
¾ cup (78 g) flaxseed meal

1 cup (240 ml) nondairy milk of choice (nut-free and/or soy-free if needed)

1 (20- to 24-oz [566- to 680-g]) loaf Texas toast or French bread

1 (13.5-oz [398-ml]) can full-fat coconut milk

½ cup (110 g) packed light brown sugar

¼ cup (50 g) granulated sugar

1 tbsp (15 ml) pure vanilla extract

TOPPING
½ cup (62 g) all-purpose flour (spooned and leveled or weighed [see page 359 for How to Measure Flour])

½ cup (110 g) packed light brown sugar

1 tbsp (8 g) ground cinnamon

½ cup (1 stick [113 g]) vegan butter, cold, cubed (see Sister Tip) (nut-free and/or soy-free if needed)

FOR SERVING
Pure maple syrup

Preheat the oven to 350°F (180°C). Spray a 9 x 13–inch (23 x 33–cm) baking dish with nonstick spray and set aside.

Make the base: In a large bowl, stir together the flaxseed meal and milk. Let sit for 10 to 15 minutes, until gelled.

Meanwhile, chop the bread into small pieces and set aside. Once the flaxseed mixture has gelled, add the coconut milk, brown sugar, granulated sugar and vanilla, and stir to incorporate. Add the bread pieces and stir to coat the bread completely. Pour into the prepared pan. Set aside.

Make the topping: In a large bowl, mix together the flour, brown sugar and cinnamon. Using a fork or pastry cutter, incorporate the cold butter into the flour mixture by cutting it into smaller and smaller pieces until you have a crumbly, sandlike texture. Sprinkle the topping evenly over the bread mixture.

Bake for 45 minutes to 1 hour; 45 minutes will yield a softer and gooier bake, 1 hour will make it crispier. Allow to cool slightly, then slice into 12 slices and serve with maple syrup.

Sister Tip

For this recipe, we recommend using vegan buttery sticks, rather than from the tub.

Double Chocolate Zucchini Bread

Beyond decadent and chocolaty, this bread is a delicious way to start (or end) the day. The addition of freshly shredded zucchini gives this bread extra moisture and a delicious texture. If you love this recipe, make sure to check out our Double Chocolate Muffins (page 38).

PREP TIME:
25 minutes

COOK TIME:
55 to 65 minutes

YIELD:
8 to 10 slices

Nonstick spray, for pan

⅔ cup (160 ml) soy milk

2 tsp (10 ml) lemon juice, white vinegar or apple cider vinegar

2 cups (250 g) all-purpose flour (spooned and leveled or weighed [see page 359 for How to Measure Flour])

½ cup (50 g) unsweetened natural cocoa powder (spooned and leveled or weighed [see page 359 for tutorial])

1 tsp baking powder

1 tsp baking soda

1 tsp salt

2 cups (270 g) freshly grated zucchini (do not squeeze out excess liquid)

½ cup (120 ml) canola oil

1 cup (200 g) granulated sugar

⅓ cup (80 g) vegan sour cream, plain nondairy yogurt or Cashew Cream (page 343) (nut-free if needed)

1 tsp pure vanilla extract

1¼ cups (210 g) vegan semisweet chocolate chips, divided

Preheat the oven to 350°F (180°C). Spray a 9 x 5-inch (23 x 13-cm) loaf pan with nonstick spray and set aside.

In a small bowl, whisk together the milk and lemon juice, then set aside for 10 to 15 minutes, until curdled. In a medium-sized bowl, whisk together the flour, cocoa powder, baking powder, baking soda and salt, then set aside.

In a separate large bowl, combine the zucchini, oil, sugar, sour cream, vanilla and curdled milk mixture and mix well. Add the flour mixture to the zucchini mixture and mix until just combined, being careful not to overmix. Fold in 1 cup (168 g) of the chocolate chips. Pour into the prepared loaf pan and evenly sprinkle the top with the remaining ¼ cup (42 g) of chocolate chips.

Bake for 55 to 65 minutes, until a toothpick inserted into the center comes out clean or with only crumbs, no raw batter. Remove from the oven and let cool for at least 10 minutes in the pan. Flip the pan upside down onto a cutting board, lift up the pan to release the loaf, then carefully turn the loaf upright again. Let cool for at least 10 more minutes, then slice and serve.

Loaded Açai Bowls

We would be remiss if we didn't include this recipe because Shannon literally eats an açai bowl every single day, so you know this recipe is a winner. Top your bowls with granola, bananas and peanut butter (as we suggest), or any other toppings you please—the possibilities are endless.

PREP TIME:
10 minutes

COOK TIME:
none

YIELD:
2 servings

PEANUT BUTTER TOPPING

¼ cup (65 g) peanut butter, or nut/seed butter of choice (nut-free and/or soy-free if needed)

1 tbsp (14 g) coconut oil

AÇAI BASE

4 (3.52-oz [100-g]) packets frozen açai (see Sister Tips)

½ cup (120 ml) nondairy milk, plus more as needed (nut-free and/or soy-free if needed)

1 medium-sized to large banana

1 to 2 servings plant-based protein powder of choice (optional) (nut-free and/or soy-free if needed)

ADDITIONAL TOPPINGS

1 cup (100 g) Peanut Butter Granola (page 52) or store-bought vegan granola of choice (gluten-free, nut-free and/or soy-free if needed)

1 medium- to large-sized banana, sliced

Prepare the peanut butter topping: In a small, microwave-safe bowl, combine the peanut butter and coconut oil. Microwave in 15-second intervals, stirring in between, until smooth and creamy (see Sister Tips). Set aside.

Prepare the açai base: In a high-speed blender, combine the contents of the açai packets with the milk, banana and protein powder (if using). Blend, occasionally stopping and scraping the sides, until completely blended and creamy. If necessary, add more milk, 1 tablespoon (15 ml) at a time, to get the mixture completely blended.

Assemble the bowls: Distribute the açai mixture equally between two serving bowls. Equally distribute the granola and banana slices between the bowls. Drizzle the peanut butter mixture on top. Serve immediately.

Sister Tips

Smash the frozen açai into small pieces before putting into the blender to achieve a more smoothly blended mixture without the need for excess milk.

Instead of the melted peanut butter mixture, you can create a lower-in-fat drizzle using powdered peanut butter and water.

Peanut
Butter
Granola
(page 52)

Peanut Butter Granola

Up your granola game with this recipe. Making your own granola is not only easy, but it's also much cheaper than buying it at the store. Plus, it fills your kitchen with the delightful smell of peanut butter and maple syrup. Want to take this recipe to the next level? Follow the flavor addition ideas and add ground cinnamon or chocolate chunks (or both!). Use this granola on top of your Loaded Açai Bowls (page 50) or enjoy it with your favorite nondairy yogurt.

PREP TIME:
10 minutes

COOK TIME:
*15 minutes,
plus 1 hour with
oven off*

YIELD:
5 heaping cups (550 g)

2⅓ cups (210 g) gluten-free old-fashioned oats

½ cup (73 g) dry-roasted peanuts, or peanuts of choice

⅓ cup (42 g) powdered peanut butter (see Sister Tip)

1 tsp baking powder

⅛ tsp salt

¼ cup (54 g) refined coconut oil

⅓ cup (86 g) peanut butter (soy-free if needed)

⅓ cup (80 ml) pure maple syrup

2 tsp (10 ml) pure vanilla extract

OPTIONAL FLAVOR ADDITIONS
Cinnamon: 1½ tsp (12 g) ground cinnamon

Chocolate Chunks: ¾ cup (140 g) vegan chocolate chunks

Preheat the oven to 325°F (160°C). Line a 9 x 13-inch (23 x 33–cm) baking dish with parchment paper. In a large bowl, whisk together the oats, peanuts, powdered peanut butter, baking powder, salt and cinnamon (if using). Set aside.

In a large, microwave-safe bowl, combine the coconut oil, peanut butter and maple syrup. Microwave in 15-second intervals, stirring in between, until melted and creamy. Stir in the vanilla.

Add the oat mixture to the peanut butter mixture. Stir until well combined. If adding chocolate chunks, fold them into the mixture. Pour the mixture into the prepared dish. Lightly dampen your hands to prevent sticking and press the mixture firmly into the dish.

Bake for 15 minutes, then turn off the oven and keep the granola in the cooling oven for 1 hour. Remove from the oven and allow to cool completely. Break into chunks.

*See in Loaded Açai Bowls image on the previous page.

Sister Tip

Powdered peanut butter is made from peanuts that have been defatted and powdered. It helps with the texture and flavor of this granola. You can typically find it at the grocery store with the peanut butter or in the natural food section, or order it online. It may also be called peanut butter powder or peanut powder.

Easy Waffles

Here's your new go-to waffle recipe. These waffles are quick to throw together and require just seven ingredients. They are great as is, but feel free to create a variation with your favorite add-ins (hello, chocolate chip waffles).

PREP TIME:
5 minutes

COOK TIME:
varies depending on waffle maker

YIELD:
4 to 6 waffles

1⅓ cups (166 g) all-purpose flour (spooned and leveled or weighed [see page 359 for How to Measure Flour])

2 tsp (8 g) baking powder

2 tbsp (25 g) granulated sugar

¼ tsp salt

1 cup (240 ml) nondairy milk (nut-free and/or soy-free if needed)

¼ cup (60 ml) canola oil

½ tsp pure vanilla extract

FOR SERVING
Vegan butter (nut-free and/or soy-free if needed)

Pure maple syrup

In a medium-sized bowl, stir together the flour, baking powder, sugar and salt. Make a small well in the center of your flour mixture. Pour the milk, oil and vanilla into the well. Mix until just combined, being careful not to overmix.

Cook the batter in your waffle maker according to the manufacturer's instructions. This recipe will make four to six waffles, but the amount will vary based on the size of your waffle maker. Serve immediately, topped with vegan butter and maple syrup.

Monkey Bread

Nut-free option,
Soy-free option

Satisfy your sugar cravings with just one bite of this pull-apart, melt-in-your-mouth monkey bread. The bite-sized pieces are buttery, sweet and reminiscent of cinnamon-sugar donut holes. This recipe requires a 12-cup (2.8-L) Bundt pan, so make sure you have one on hand before you start baking.

PREP TIME:
40 minutes, plus inactive time for rising

COOK TIME:
36 to 42 minutes

YIELD:
40 pull-apart bites

BREAD

1¼ cups (300 ml) warm nondairy milk (heated to 100 to 110°F [38 to 43°C]) (nut-free and/or soy-free if needed)

4 tbsp (50 g) granulated sugar, divided

2¼ tsp (1 [7-g] packet) active dry yeast

3½ to 4 cups (437 to 500 g) all-purpose flour (spooned and leveled or weighed [see page 359 for How to Measure Flour]), plus more for kneading if needed

1½ tsp (9 g) salt

2 tbsp (¼ stick [28 g]) vegan butter, cut into 4 pieces, at room temperature, plus more for Bundt pan (see Sister Tip) (nut-free and/or soy-free if needed)

FOR RISING

1½ tsp (7 ml) canola oil

Make the bread: In a small bowl, whisk together the warm milk with 1 tablespoon (12 g) of the granulated sugar. Sprinkle the yeast on top and whisk until it is mostly dissolved. Set aside for 5 to 10 minutes, until the mixture has foamed.

In the bowl of a stand mixer fitted with the hook attachment, or in a large bowl, stir together 3½ cups (437 g) of the flour, the salt and the remaining 3 tablespoons (36 g) of granulated sugar. Add the butter and beat to incorporate. Alternatively, you can mix it with a rubber scraper or large wooden spoon—the butter should break up slightly into the flour, but it's okay if large pieces remain. Once the yeast mixture has foamed, add it to the flour mixture. Beat on low speed or stir with the rubber scraper or wooden spoon, scraping the sides as necessary, until you have a soft but manageable dough. Add more flour as needed, up to ½ cup (62 g), to ensure the dough is not too sticky to handle.

Either beat the dough in the stand mixer on low speed for 5 to 7 minutes, or transfer the dough to a lightly floured surface and knead by hand for 5 to 7 minutes, incorporating more flour as needed so that the dough does not stick to the sides of the bowl or to your hands. The dough is ready when you gently press into it and it slowly bounces back. Coat a large bowl with the canola oil. Form the dough into a ball and place into the bowl. Turn to lightly coat the ball with oil. Place a clean towel over the bowl. Let rest in a warm place until the dough has doubled in size, about 1 hour.

Meanwhile, butter a 12-cup (2.8-L) Bundt pan and set aside.

(continued)

Monkey Bread (Continued)

BUTTER COATING

½ cup (1 stick [113 g]) vegan butter (see Sister Tip) (nut-free and/or soy-free if needed)

CINNAMON SUGAR COATING

1 cup (200 g) granulated sugar

1 tbsp (8 g) ground cinnamon

CARAMEL

½ cup (1 stick [113 g]) vegan butter (see Sister Tip) (nut-free and/or soy-free if needed)

1 cup (220 g) packed light brown sugar

Prepare the coatings: In a small, microwave-safe bowl, microwave the butter until melted. Alternatively, you can melt the butter in a small saucepan and pour it into a bowl.

In a separate small bowl, stir together the granulated sugar and cinnamon. Once the dough has doubled in size, gently punch into it to release any air bubbles. Take little balls of the dough (creating about 40 total) and coat them with the butter coating, then with the cinnamon sugar coating. Place each in the pan so that they are evenly spread within the pan. You should have two or three layers of pieces. Top with a clean towel or plastic wrap and let rise again until doubled, 30 minutes to an hour.

Once the dough has almost doubled, preheat the oven to 350°F (180°C).

While the oven heats, make the caramel: In a saucepan over medium-low heat, melt the butter, then whisk in the brown sugar. Heat, whisking constantly, for 1 to 2 minutes, or until the brown sugar is mostly dissolved and has incorporated into the butter. Remove from the heat.

Once the dough has doubled in size, pour the caramel evenly over the pieces of dough in the pan. Bake for 35 to 40 minutes, until golden brown. Remove from the oven and allow to cool for 5 to 10 minutes in the pan, then flip onto a large serving plate and lift up the pan to release the monkey bread. Enjoy warm or at room temperature.

Sister Tip

For this recipe, we recommend using vegan buttery sticks, rather than from the tub.

Date Bars

Gluten-free, Soy-free

One of our family's favorite go-to quick snacks on busy days is a breakfast bar. These are made of simple ingredients and take only five minutes to whip up. They are great to have on hand and are a perfect snack for the whole family.

PREP TIME: ——— **COOK TIME:** ——— **CHILL TIME:** ——— **YIELD:**

5 minutes — *none* — *1 to 2 hours* — *8 bars*

1½ cups (219 g) unsalted raw whole cashews

1½ cups (240 g) pitted dates (about 15 Medjool or about 33 Deglet Noor), soaked if necessary (see Sister Tip)

¼ cup + 2 tbsp (30 g) unsweetened natural cocoa powder (spooned and leveled or weighed [see page 359 for tutorial])

1 tsp pure vanilla extract

Add-ins of choice, such as vegan mini chocolate chips or nuts

Line a 9 x 5–inch (23 x 13–cm) loaf pan with parchment paper.

In a high-speed blender or food processor, combine the cashews, dates, cocoa powder and vanilla, and process until a dough forms, scraping the sides as necessary. If the dough isn't forming easily, you can add water, 1 teaspoon at a time, to get the mixture to mix. If desired, stir in mini chocolate chips, nuts or other add-ins to customize to your liking.

Press into the prepared loaf pan. Chill for 1 to 2 hours, then remove from the pan and slice into eight bars.

Sister Tip

If your dates are not very fresh and have hardened, soak them before using. Place the dates in a small bowl and cover with warm water. Soak for 5 to 10 minutes, then drain, rinse and pat dry.

CROWD-PLEASING
PASTA AND PIZZA

Growing up, our family dinners and get-togethers often included 20+ people (after all, we do come from a family of eleven). When we began writing this cookbook, we knew we needed to include all of our favorite crowd-pleasing pasta and pizza recipes that have passed the taste tests of both vegan and nonvegan family members. In this chapter, you'll find recipes that are perfect for parties, barbecues and holidays. From Easy Creamy Mac and Cheese (page 83) and Fettuccine Alfredo (page 71) to Molly's favorite, Detroit-Style Cheese Pizza (page 77), you're sure to find a recipe for any occasion. We hope these dishes bring your family as much comfort and happiness as they do ours.

Classic Garlic Bread
(page 269)

Cashew Tofu Sweet Potato Lasagna

This recipe is our spin on the traditional lasagna we grew up eating. We swapped out the dairy ricotta for a flavorful cashew tofu mixture that pleases vegans and nonvegans alike. The addition of sweet potato adds a slight sweetness that we love, but feel free to omit it if you prefer a more traditional lasagna. Our favorite way to serve this is with our Caesar Salad (page 206) and Classic Garlic Bread (page 269).

PREP TIME:
20 minutes, plus inactive time to press tofu and prep time for Cashew Cream

COOK TIME:
50 to 54 minutes, plus time to boil noodles

YIELD:
15 to 18 slices

LASAGNA
9 wavy lasagna noodles (gluten-free if needed)

1 tbsp (15 ml) olive oil

1 large sweet potato, or 2 small to medium-sized sweet potatoes

2 (24-oz [680-g]) jars vegan marinara sauce, divided

1 cup (113 g) vegan Mozzarella shreds (page 340) or store-bought, for topping

RICOTTA
2 (14-oz [397-g]) blocks extra-firm tofu, pressed (see page 358 for tutorial)

1 tsp salt

½ tsp freshly ground black pepper

2 tsp (5 g) garlic powder

2 tsp (5 g) onion powder

2 tsp (3 g) dried basil

1 heaping tbsp (2 g) dried parsley

1 cup (33 g) chopped spinach

2 heaping cups (540 g) Cashew Cream (2 batches [page 343])

Begin the lasagna: Preheat the oven to 375°F (190°C).

Cook the noodles until al dente, according to the package instructions. Drain and rinse the noodles in cold water. Brush the noodles with the olive oil and lay them flat on a sheet of parchment paper until you need to use them.

Peel the sweet potato and slice lengthwise into ¼- to ½-inch (6-mm to 1.3-cm) slices. Bring a small pot of water to a boil. Boil the sweet potato slices until fork-tender, 5 to 7 minutes. Drain and rinse in cold water. Set aside.

Prepare the ricotta: Crumble the pressed tofu into a large bowl and add the salt, pepper, garlic powder, onion powder, basil, parsley, spinach and Cashew Cream. Mix well.

Assemble the lasagna: Pour about half a jar of marinara sauce into a 9 x 13–inch (22 x 33–cm) baking dish. Top with 3 lasagna noodles, placing them side by side to cover the entire bottom of the dish. Top with about half of the ricotta mixture, spreading it evenly over the noodles. Evenly spread another half a jar of marinara across the ricotta. Layer 3 more lasagna noodles on top of the marinara. Spread the remainder of the ricotta mixture over the noodles. Arrange the sweet potato slices evenly across the top. Evenly spread another half a jar of marinara over the sweet potato. Layer with 3 more noodles, then spread the remaining half a jar of marinara on top of the noodles. Evenly sprinkle the mozzarella shreds on top.

Cover the dish with foil. Bake for 40 minutes, then remove the foil and bake for 5 to 10 more minutes, or until the mozzarella is melted and bubbly. Remove from the oven, allow to cool slightly, then slice into 15 to 18 equal pieces.

Pesto Pasta

Transform our homemade Pesto (page 352) into a simple and easy entrée by combining it with pasta and nutritional yeast. This dish comes together quickly and is perfect for weekend barbecues or busy weeknights. We love it served with Easy Steamed Broccoli (page 258) and Parmesan-Crusted Tofu (page 337).

PREP TIME:
none

COOK TIME:
2 minutes, plus time to boil pasta

YIELD:
6 to 8 servings

1 (16-oz [453-g]) package penne or pasta of choice (gluten-free if needed)

1 tbsp (15 ml) olive oil

1½ cups (390 g) vegan Pesto (1 batch [page 352]) or store-bought (nut-free if needed)

¼ cup (20 g) nutritional yeast

½ tsp salt, plus more to taste

⅛ tsp freshly ground black pepper, plus more to taste

Vegan Parmesan Cheese (page 342) or store-bought, for topping (nut-free and/or soy-free if needed)

Cook the pasta according to the package instructions. Once cooked, drain and rinse in cold water, then rinse with hot water to reheat.

Add the oil to the empty pasta pot over low heat. Stir in the pasta to lightly coat with oil. Add the pesto, nutritional yeast, salt and pepper. Stir until well coated, then remove from the heat. Season with more salt and pepper to taste, if desired.

Serve immediately, topped with Parmesan.

Parmesan Cheese
(page 342)

Cashew Mac

This is one of the easier pasta dishes in this section. The creamy sauce is simply made of cashews, rice milk, vegetable bouillon, nutritional yeast and spices—it's great stirred into any type of pasta, so take your pick! Serve this mac with our Roasted Veggie and Quinoa Salad (page 203) and our Breadsticks (page 266).

PREP TIME:
5 minutes, plus inactive time to soak cashews

COOK TIME:
5 minutes, plus time to boil pasta

YIELD:
6 to 8 servings

1 (16-oz [453-g]) package pasta of choice (gluten-free if needed)

1 tbsp (15 ml) olive oil

1 cup (146 g) raw unsalted whole cashews, soaked (see Sister Tip)

1½ cups (360 ml) plain, unsweetened rice milk

1½ tsp (9 g) vegetable bouillon paste or 1½ vegan bouillon cubes (15 g)

¼ cup (20 g) nutritional yeast

1½ tsp (3 g) paprika, plus more for topping

1 tsp garlic powder

1 tsp onion powder

1 tsp salt, plus more to taste

Freshly ground black pepper

Vegan sriracha, for topping (optional)

Cook the pasta according to the package instructions. Once cooked, drain and rinse in cold water, place back in the pot and toss with the olive oil to keep from sticking.

While the pasta cooks, drain and rinse the cashews. In a high-speed blender, combine the cashews, rice milk, vegetable bouillon, nutritional yeast, paprika, garlic powder, onion powder and salt. Blend until the sauce is creamy and fully blended, scraping the sides as needed.

Pour the sauce into a large skillet and cook over medium-low heat, whisking often, until the mixture thickens, about 5 minutes. Add the pasta and stir until well combined. Season with more salt and pepper to taste, if desired. Serve topped with paprika and a little sriracha, if desired.

Sister Tip

To soak cashews, place in a bowl and cover completely with water. Let sit for at least 2 hours, then drain, rinse and pat dry (see page 358 for more options and tips).

Creamy Spicy Pasta

This recipe puts a spicy twist on a simple creamy sauce. Even though there is no vegan cheese in this dish, it's not missed—the sauce is rich and flavorful enough without it. If you like a kick of spice and lots of flavor, you will love this dish. Serve it with Parmesan-Crusted Tofu (page 337) and homemade Dinner Rolls (page 271).

PREP TIME:
2 minutes

COOK TIME:
10 minutes, plus time to boil pasta

YIELD:
6 to 8 servings

1 (16-oz [453-g]) package pasta of choice

4 tbsp (60 ml) olive oil, divided

3 cloves garlic, peeled and minced, or 1 tbsp (9 g) jarred minced garlic

⅓ cup (41 g) all-purpose flour

3 cups (720 ml) plain, unsweetened rice milk

¾ cup (60 g) nutritional yeast

½ tsp onion powder

1 tsp garlic powder

1½ tsp (3 g) paprika

½ tsp dried oregano

½ tsp cayenne pepper, plus more to taste

1 tsp salt, plus more to taste

¼ tsp freshly ground black pepper, plus more to taste

Cook the pasta according to the package instructions. Once cooked, drain and rinse in cold water, place back in the pot and toss with 1 tablespoon (15 ml) of the olive oil to keep from sticking.

In a large skillet, heat the remaining 3 tablespoons (45 ml) of olive oil over medium-low heat. Add the garlic and cook for 30 seconds to 1 minute, or until fragrant. Whisk in the flour until it is fully incorporated into the oil.

Slowly pour in the rice milk, whisking constantly. Increase the heat to medium-high and bring the mixture to a gentle boil, whisking constantly. Lower the heat to medium-low, bringing the mixture to a simmer. Whisk in the nutritional yeast, onion powder, garlic powder, paprika, oregano, cayenne, salt and black pepper. Simmer, whisking often, for 3 more minutes, or until the sauce thickens.

Stir in the cooked pasta and serve with more cayenne, salt and pepper to taste.

Creamy Tomato Pasta

This recipe is extra rich and creamy, thanks to the addition of cashews. Blending them with sautéed onion and garlic, vegetable broth, crushed tomatoes and spices creates a next-level tomato sauce. Top this dish with Crispy Seitan (page 336) and serve with Dinner Rolls (page 271).

PREP TIME:
10 minutes, plus inactive time to soak cashews

COOK TIME:
15 minutes, plus time to boil pasta

YIELD:
6 to 8 servings

1 (16-oz [453-g]) package pasta of choice (gluten-free if needed)

3 tbsp (45 ml) olive oil, divided

½ medium-sized onion, chopped (about ½ cup [80 g])

3 cloves garlic, peeled and minced, or 1 tbsp (9 g) jarred minced garlic

½ cup (120 ml) vegetable broth

1 cup (146 g) raw unsalted whole cashews, soaked and drained (see Sister Tip)

1 (28-oz [793-g]) can crushed tomatoes

1 tsp garlic powder

1 tsp onion powder

1 tbsp (5 g) dried basil

¼ tsp dried oregano

¼ tsp crushed red pepper flakes

1½ tsp (9 g) salt, plus more to taste

⅛ tsp freshly ground black pepper, plus more to taste

FOR SERVING (OPTIONAL)
Crispy Seitan, sliced (page 336; omit for gluten-free) (soy-fee if needed)

Vegan Parmesan Cheese (page 342) or store-bought (soy-free if needed)

Dried or chopped fresh parsley

Cook the pasta according to the package instructions. Once cooked, reserve ½ cup (120 ml) of pasta water for later, then drain and rinse in cold water. Place the pasta back in the pot and toss with 1 tablespoon (15 ml) of the olive oil to keep from sticking.

In a large skillet, heat the remaining 2 tablespoons (30 ml) of olive oil over medium-low heat. Add the onion. Cook, stirring occasionally, for 5 to 7 minutes, or until translucent. Stir in the garlic and cook for another 30 seconds to 1 minute, until fragrant.

Transfer the onion mixture to a high-speed blender and add the vegetable broth, cashews, tomatoes, garlic powder, onion powder, basil, oregano and red pepper flakes. Blend until smooth and creamy, scraping the sides as necessary.

Pour the blended tomato mixture into the original skillet and cook over medium-low heat, whisking often, until the mixture thickens, about 5 minutes. Add the cooked pasta and stir. If the pasta sauce is too thick, add the reserved pasta water, 2 tablespoons (30 ml) at a time, until your desired consistency is reached. Stir in the salt and pepper and add more to taste, if desired. Serve topped with Crispy Seitan, Parmesan and parsley, if desired.

Sister Tip

To soak cashews, place them in a bowl and cover completely with water. Let sit for at least 2 hours, then drain, rinse and pat dry (see page 358 for more options and tips).

Mushroom Stroganoff

Calling all mushroom lovers—this one's for you. Our vegan spin on Stroganoff pairs pasta with a creamy, flavorful mushroom sauce. It's quick, easy and perfect for any day of the week. Serve it with Breadsticks (page 266) and Kale Tahini Salad with Baked Tempeh (page 210).

PREP TIME:
10 minutes

COOK TIME:
*15 minutes, plus
time to boil pasta*

YIELD:
6 to 8 servings

1 (16-oz [453-g]) package pasta of choice

1 tbsp (15 ml) olive oil

2 tbsp (28 g) vegan butter (nut-free and/or soy-free if needed)

1 medium-sized sweet onion, sliced (about 1 cup [160 g])

3½ cups (245 g) sliced cremini mushrooms

3 cloves garlic, peeled and minced, or 1 tbsp (9 g) jarred minced garlic

⅓ cup (41 g) all-purpose flour

1½ cups (360 ml) vegetable broth

1 cup (240 ml) plain, unsweetened rice milk

3 tbsp (15 g) nutritional yeast

1 tsp Dijon mustard

2 tsp (10 ml) vegan Worcestershire sauce (soy-free if needed)

1 tsp salt, plus more to taste

¼ tsp freshly ground black pepper, plus more to taste

Cook the pasta according to the package instructions. Once cooked, drain and rinse in cold water, place back in the pot and toss with the olive oil to keep from sticking.

In a large sauté pan, melt the butter over medium-low heat. Stir in the onion and mushrooms. Sauté, stirring occasionally, for 5 to 7 minutes, or until the onion becomes translucent.

Stir in the garlic and cook for another 30 seconds to 1 minute, or until fragrant. Stir in the flour until it is completely incorporated. Slowly pour in the vegetable broth and rice milk, stirring constantly. Increase the heat to medium-high, bringing the mixture to a gentle boil, stirring constantly. Lower the heat to low, bringing the mixture to a simmer. Stir in the nutritional yeast, Dijon mustard, Worcestershire sauce, salt and pepper. Let simmer, stirring occasionally, for 3 to 5 minutes, or until the sauce thickens.

Stir in the cooked pasta. Season with more salt and pepper to taste, if desired.

Fettuccine Alfredo

Growing up, dairy-based fettuccine Alfredo was one of our simple go-to dinners—after all, we haven't always been vegan. Our 15-minute version pairs fettuccine pasta with a creamy plant-based sauce that won't have you missing the dairy. We love serving it with Easy Steamed Broccoli (page 258) and Parmesan-Crusted Tofu (page 337).

PREP TIME:
2 minutes

COOK TIME:
10 minutes, plus time to boil pasta

YIELD:
6 to 8 servings

1 (16-oz [453-g]) package vegan fettuccine pasta

1 tbsp (15 ml) olive oil

¼ cup (56 g) vegan butter (nut-free and/or soy-free if needed)

6 cloves garlic, peeled and minced, or 2 tbsp (18 g) jarred minced garlic

⅓ cup (41 g) all-purpose flour

3 cups (720 ml) plain, unsweetened rice milk

½ cup (40 g) nutritional yeast

½ tsp dried oregano

1 tsp dried basil

1 tsp dried parsley

1 tsp salt, plus more to taste

½ tsp freshly ground black pepper, plus more to taste

1 cup (113 g) vegan Mozzarella shreds (page 340) or store-bought (nut-free and/or soy-free if needed)

FOR SERVING
Vegan Parmesan Cheese (page 342) or store-bought (nut-free and/or soy-free if needed)

Dried or fresh chopped parsley

Cook the pasta according to the package instructions. Once cooked, drain and rinse in cold water, place back in the pot and toss with the olive oil to keep from sticking.

In a large skillet, melt the butter over medium-low heat. Stir in the garlic and cook for 30 seconds to 1 minute, or until fragrant. Whisk in the flour until it is completely incorporated. Slowly pour in the rice milk, whisking constantly.

Increase the heat to medium-high and bring mixture to a gentle boil, whisking constantly. Lower the heat to low, bringing the mixture to a simmer.

Whisk in the nutritional yeast, oregano, basil, parsley, salt and pepper. Let simmer, whisking occasionally, for 3 to 5 minutes, or until thickened. Stir in the mozzarella shreds until melted. Stir in the cooked pasta. Add more salt and pepper to taste, if desired.

Remove from the heat and serve topped with Parmesan cheese and parsley.

...combines a rich tomato sauce with vegan "beef," veggies and pasta. ...n this dish are enhanced by the low and slow simmer, so don't be put off ...ng cook time; it's well worth the wait. Serve this dish with Garlic and Herb ...ccia (page 272) and Caesar Salad (page 206).

PREP TIME:
15 minutes

COOK TIME:
1¼ to 1¾ hours

YIELD:
6 to 8 servings

¼ cup (56 g) vegan butter (nut-free and/or soy-free if needed)

1 medium-sized white onion, chopped (about 1 cup [160 g])

⅔ cup (84 g) chopped carrot (chopped small)

⅔ cup (67 g) chopped celery (chopped small)

16 oz (453 g) vegan ground "beef" (we like Impossible and Beyond Beef), defrosted if frozen (gluten-free, nut-free and/or soy-free if needed)

1 (14.5-oz [411-g]) can fire-roasted diced tomatoes

3 cloves garlic, peeled and minced, or 1 tbsp (9 g) jarred minced garlic

½ tsp salt, plus more to taste

⅛ tsp freshly ground black pepper, plus more to taste

¾ cup (180 ml) vegan dry white wine

1 cup (240 ml) plain, unsweetened rice milk

16 oz (453 g) stracci toscani or lasagna noodles (gluten-free if needed)

1 tbsp (15 ml) olive oil

FOR SERVING
Dried or chopped fresh parsley

Vegan Parmesan Cheese (page 342) or store-bought (nut-free and/or soy-free if needed)

In a large, lidded nonstick skillet, melt the butter over medium heat. Stir in the onion and let cook, uncovered, for about 3 minutes. Add the carrot and celery and let cook, stirring occasionally, until tender, 5 to 7 minutes. Stir in the ground "beef" and cook, stirring often, for 6 to 8 minutes, or until lightly browned. Add the fire-roasted tomatoes, stir and allow to cook for a couple of minutes. Next, stir in the garlic, salt and pepper. Cook, stirring, for 30 seconds to 1 minute, or until the garlic is fragrant. Continue by stirring in the white wine, increasing the heat to high and bringing to a boil. Lower the heat to low and bring to a gentle simmer. Let simmer, still uncovered, stirring occasionally, for 30 to 45 minutes, until the excess liquid has evaporated.

Once the liquid has evaporated, stir in the rice milk and increase the heat to high, bringing the mixture to a boil. Lower the heat to low and bring to a gentle simmer. Let simmer, partially covered, stirring occasionally, for another 30 to 45 minutes, or until the sauce has thickened and most of the liquid has evaporated.

When there are about 20 minutes left for the sauce to cook, cook the pasta according to the package instructions. Once cooked, drain and rinse in cold water, place back in the pot and toss with the olive oil to keep from sticking. If using lasagna noodles, chop into 2- to 3-inch (5- to 7.5-cm) pieces before adding to the sauce.

When the sauce is done, stir in the cooked pasta and add more salt and pepper to taste, if desired. Serve topped with parsley and Parmesan.

Broccoli Alfredo Stuffed Shells

You'll be surprised by how much you love this recipe. This dish pairs a creamy Alfredo sauce with broccoli and ricotta–stuffed shells, and is topped with melty Mozzarella (page 340). Serve it with Dinner Rolls (page 271) or Garlic and Herb Focaccia (page 272) for the perfect comfort meal.

PREP TIME:
30 minutes, plus prep time for Cashew Cream

COOK TIME:
50 to 60 minutes, plus time to boil pasta

YIELD:
24 to 26 shells

PASTA

24 to 26 jumbo pasta shells (see Sister Tips)

1 tbsp (15 ml) olive oil

FILLING

1 tbsp (15 ml) olive oil

2 cups (182 g) diced broccoli (diced small)

1 medium-sized sweet onion, chopped (about 1 cup [160 g])

3 cloves garlic, peeled and minced, or 1 tbsp (9 g) jarred minced garlic

1 (14- to 16-oz [396- to 453-g]) block firm or extra-firm tofu, pressed (see page 358 for tutorial)

1½ heaping cups (405 g) Cashew Cream (1½ batches [page 343])

1 tsp dried oregano

1 tsp dried parsley

1 tsp dried basil

1 tsp dried chives

½ tsp garlic powder

½ tsp onion powder

Make the shells: Cook the pasta shells according to the package instructions, until al dente. Once cooked, drain and rinse in cold water, place back in the pot and toss with the olive oil to keep from sticking.

Make the filling: In a large sauté pan with a lid, heat the olive oil over medium heat. Add the broccoli and onion and stir. Cover and cook, stirring occasionally, for 7 to 10 minutes, or until the onion becomes translucent and the broccoli is tender. Stir in the garlic and cook for another 30 seconds to 1 minute. Remove from the heat and set aside.

Crumble the pressed tofu into a large bowl. Add the Cashew Cream, oregano, parsley, basil, chives, garlic powder, onion powder and prepared vegetables. Stir until well combined. Set aside.

(continued)

Broccoli Alfredo Stuffed Shells (Continued)

ALFREDO SAUCE

½ cup (113 g) vegan butter

½ cup (62 g) all-purpose flour

3 cups (720 ml) plain, unsweetened rice milk

⅓ cup (27 g) nutritional yeast

1 tsp garlic powder

1 tsp dried oregano

1 tsp dried basil

1 tsp dried parsley

1 tsp salt

½ tsp freshly ground black pepper

TOPPING

2 cups (226 g) vegan Mozzarella shreds (page 340) or store-bought

Make the sauce: In a medium-sized saucepan, melt the butter over medium-low heat. Whisk in the flour until it is completely incorporated. Slowly pour in the rice milk, whisking constantly. Increase the heat to medium-high and bring the mixture to a gentle boil, whisking constantly. Lower the heat to low, bringing the mixture to a simmer. Whisk in the nutritional yeast, garlic powder, oregano, basil, parsley, salt and pepper. Let simmer, whisking occasionally, for 3 to 5 minutes, or until thickened. Remove from the heat and set aside.

Assemble and bake the shells: Preheat the oven to 400°F (200°C). Spread about half of the Alfredo sauce on the bottom of a 9 x 13–inch (23 x 33–cm) baking dish. Fill each shell with the filling, 2 to 3 tablespoons (30 to 45 g) per shell, arranging them evenly in the baking dish as you go (see Sister Tips). Top evenly with the rest of the sauce. Evenly sprinkle the mozzarella cheese on top. Cover the dish with foil and bake on the middle rack for 30 minutes, remove the foil and bake for another 5 to 10 minutes, or until the cheese is melted and bubbly. Serve warm.

Sister Tips

We recommend cooking a few extra shells, as some break in the cooking process. You will end up using a little more than half of a 16-ounce (453-g) package.

To fit the maximum amount of shells in the baking dish, place them in the dish at a slight angle. You should be able to fit three rows of eight shells each, and may be able to stuff another two in the dish. If not, you can use another small baking dish to cook any remaining shells.

Detroit-Style Cheese Pizza

Pizza Fridays were a tradition in our household growing up. Of course, living in the Detroit area, we would always get Detroit-style pizza. It's traditionally rectangular and fluffy with crispy edges, and our version is no different. We recommend using our homemade Mozzarella (page 340) for this recipe, but of course, you can use store-bought. Serve this with our Garlic Cheese Bread (page 270) and Simple Ranch Salad (page 205).

PREP TIME:
15 minutes, plus prep time for Pizza Dough

COOK TIME:
20 to 25 minutes

YIELD:
8 to 10 slices

1 tbsp (15 ml) olive oil

1 batch Pizza Dough (page 355) (see Sister Tip)

1 cup (240 g) vegan marinara sauce

2 cups (226 g) vegan Mozzarella shreds (page 340) or store-bought (nut-free and/or soy-free if needed)

1 tbsp (14 g) vegan butter, melted (nut-free and/or soy-free if needed)

1 tsp Garlic Salt (page 356) or store-bought

TOPPINGS
Dried oregano

Dried or chopped fresh basil

Preheat the oven to 425°F (220°C). Brush a 9 x 13–inch (23 x 33–cm) baking dish with the olive oil.

Press the dough into the prepared dish, pressing it in at the corners and up the sides for a thinner crust and thicker base. Spread the marinara evenly over the pizza dough and top evenly with the mozzarella shreds. Bake for 20 to 25 minutes, until the crust is crispy and the cheese is melted.

Meanwhile, in a small bowl, stir together the melted butter and garlic salt. Once the pizza is out of the oven, brush the butter mixture on the crust. Top the pizza with oregano and basil, let cool for 3 to 5 minutes, then carefully remove from the dish. Place on a cutting board and slice into eight to ten pieces. Serve immediately.

Sister Tip

If you're in a time crunch, you can use 16 ounces (453 g) of store-bought vegan pizza dough; note that the cook time may vary.

"Bacon" and Caramelized Onion Detroit-Style Pizza

One of Molly's absolute favorite dishes, this recipe levels up our Detroit-Style Cheese Pizza (page 77) by adding Tofu "Bacon" (page 335), caramelized onion and a Garlic Aioli (page 354) drizzle. We can't choose one over the other, so we recommend you make one of each—along with Garlic Cheese Bread (page 270), of course.

PREP TIME:	COOK TIME:	YIELD:
15 minutes, plus prep time for Pizza Dough and Garlic Aioli	50 to 55 minutes	8 to 10 slices

CARMELIZED ONIONS

2 tbsp (28 g) vegan butter (nut-free and/or soy-free if needed)

1 medium-sized white onion, sliced (about 1 cup [160 g])

PIZZA

1 tbsp (15 ml) olive oil

1 batch Pizza Dough (page 355) (see Sister Tip)

1 cup (240 g) vegan marinara sauce

2 cups (226 g) vegan Mozzarella shreds (page 340) or store-bought (nut-free and/or soy-free if needed)

6 slices Tofu "Bacon" (page 335) or prepared store-bought alternative, chopped (soy-free if needed)

1 tbsp (14 g) vegan butter, melted (nut-free and/or soy-free if needed)

1 tsp Garlic Salt (page 356) or store-bought

¼ cup (60 g) Garlic Aioli (page 354) (soy-free if needed)

Make the carmelized onion: In a small skillet, melt the butter over medium-low heat. Stir in the onion slices. Cook, uncovered, stirring occasionally, over low heat for 45 minutes. Increase the heat to medium-high and cook, stirring often, for 5 to 10 minutes.

Make the pizza: Meanwhile, preheat the oven to 425°F (220°C). Brush a 9 x 13-inch (23 x 33–cm) baking dish with the olive oil.

Press the dough into the pan, pressing it in at the corners and up the sides for a thinner crust and thicker base. Spread the marinara evenly over the pizza dough and top with mozzarella shreds. Evenly sprinkle the chopped "bacon" on top. Bake for 20 to 25 minutes, until the crust is crispy and the mozzarella is melty.

In a small bowl, stir together the melted butter and garlic salt. Once the pizza is out of the oven, brush the butter mixture on the crust of cooked pizza. Evenly sprinkle the caramelized onion on top of the pizza. Drizzle the Garlic Aioli on top, let cool for about 3 minutes and carefully remove from the dish. Place on a cutting board, slice into eight to ten pieces and serve immediately.

Sister Tip

If you're in a time crunch, you can use 16 ounces (453 g) of store-bought vegan pizza dough; note that the cook time may vary.

Simple Ranch
Salad (page 205)

Pesto Seitan Pizza
(page 82)

Garlic Knots
(page 267)

BBQ Seitan Pizza

Inspired by the classic nonvegan BBQ chicken pizza, this version uses seitan in place of chicken. The combination of barbecue sauce, marinara, red onion and mozzarella (and topped with a drizzle of ranch, of course) will have you wondering why you don't make this pizza more often. This recipe only calls for a half batch of Pizza Dough (page 355), so use up the rest by making our Pesto Seitan Pizza (page 82).

PREP TIME:
10 minutes, plus prep time for Pizza Dough and Steamed Seitan

COOK TIME:
15 minutes

YIELD:
8 slices

Olive oil, for pan

½ cup (120 ml) vegan barbecue sauce, divided

4 oz (113 g) Steamed Seitan (page 332), chopped into ½" (1.3-cm) pieces (about ¾ cup) (soy-free if needed)

½ batch Pizza Dough (page 355) (see Sister Tip)

½ cup (120 g) vegan marinara sauce

1 cup (112 g) vegan Mozzarella shreds (page 340) or store-bought (nut-free and/or soy-free if needed)

½ medium-sized red onion, chopped (about ½ cup [80 g])

1 tbsp (14 g) vegan butter, melted (nut-free and/or soy-free if needed)

1 tsp Garlic Salt (page 356) or store-bought

Vegan Ranch Dressing (page 345) or store-bought, for serving (nut-free and/or soy-free if needed)

Preheat the oven to 425°F (220°C) and grease a 12-inch (30-cm) round pan with the oil.

In a medium-sized bowl, mix ¼ cup (60 ml) of the barbecue sauce with the seitan pieces to thoroughly coat the seitan and set aside. Using your hands, stretch out the dough into a 12-inch (30-cm) circle with a slightly thicker outer crust and carefully place on the prepared pan. Spread the marinara sauce evenly over the dough, leaving the thicker edge of the crust bare. Sprinkle the mozzarella shreds on top. Evenly sprinkle the seitan pieces and red onion on top. Drizzle the remaining ¼ cup (60 ml) of barbecue sauce on top. Bake for about 15 minutes, until the crust is crispy and the mozzarella is melted.

Meanwhile, in a small bowl, stir together the melted butter and garlic salt. Once the pizza is out of the oven, brush the butter mixture on the outer crust of the pizza. Drizzle with your desired amount of vegan ranch. Let cool for about 3 minutes. Place on a cutting board, slice into eight slices and serve.

Sister Tip

If you're in a time crunch, you can use 8 ounces (227 g) of store-bought vegan pizza dough; note that the cook time may vary.

Pesto Seitan Pizza

This pizza has a pesto base and is topped with our vegan Mozzarella shreds (page 340), Steamed Seitan (page 332)—a great substitute for chicken—and a drizzle of marinara. It has a vegan butter garlic crust (as do all our pizzas!), which puts it over the top. Serve it with our Garlic Knots (page 267) and Simple Ranch Salad (page 205). This recipe only needs a half batch of Pizza Dough (page 355); if you'd like to use up a whole batch, make two of these pizzas or pair this with BBQ Seitan Pizza (page 81).

PREP TIME:	COOK TIME:	YIELD:
15 minutes, plus prep time for Pizza Dough and Steamed Seitan	*15 minutes*	*8 slices*

Olive oil, for pan

½ batch Pizza Dough (page 355) (see Sister Tip)

¼ cup (60 g) vegan Pesto (page 352) or store-bought (nut-free if needed)

1 cup (113 g) vegan Mozzarella shreds (page 340) or store-bought (nut-free and/or soy-free if needed)

4 oz (113 g) Steamed Seitan (page 332), chopped into ½" (1.3-cm) pieces (soy-free if needed)

¼ cup (60 g) vegan marinara sauce

1 tbsp (14 g) vegan butter, melted (nut-free and/or soy-free if needed)

1 tsp Garlic Salt (page 356) or store-bought

Preheat the oven to 425°F (220°C) and grease a 12-inch (30-cm) round pan with the oil.

Using your hands, stretch out the dough into a 12-inch (30-cm) circle with a slightly thicker outer crust and carefully place on the prepared pan. Spread the pesto evenly over the dough, leaving the thicker edge of the crust bare. Sprinkle the cheese evenly over the pesto. Evenly sprinkle the seitan pieces on top. Drizzle the marinara sauce on top. Bake for about 15 minutes, until the crust is crispy and the cheese is melted.

Meanwhile, in a small bowl, stir together the melted butter and garlic salt. Once the pizza is out of the oven, brush the butter mixture on the outer crust of the pizza. Let cool for about 3 minutes. Place on a cutting board, slice into eight slices and serve.

*See in BBQ Seitan Pizza image on page 80.

Sister Tip

If you're in a time crunch, you can use 8 ounces (227 g) of store-bought vegan pizza dough; note that the cook time may vary.

Easy Creamy Mac and Cheese

This dish is simple, delicious and kid-approved. It has everything you love about mac and cheese, without the dairy. You can almost always find this served at our family barbecues and get-togethers—it's just that good. Serve it with our BBQ Jackfruit Sliders (page 94), Baked Tofu Nuggets (page 224) or Sloppy Joes (page 109).

PREP TIME:
none

COOK TIME:
15 minutes, plus time to boil pasta

YIELD:
6 to 8 servings

1 (16-oz [453-g]) package pasta of choice; we prefer elbow macaroni or cellentani

1 tbsp (15 ml) olive oil

⅓ cup (75 g) vegan butter (nut-free and/or soy-free if needed)

⅓ cup (41 g) all-purpose flour

3 cups (720 ml) plain, unsweetened rice milk

1½ tsp (4 g) garlic powder

1 tsp onion powder

1½ tsp (3 g) paprika, plus more for topping

2 tsp (30 g) Dijon mustard

1½ tsp (9 g) salt, plus more to taste

2 cups (226 g) vegan Cheddar shreds (page 341) or store-bought (nut-free and/or soy-free if needed)

Dried or chopped fresh parsley, for topping

Cook the pasta according to the package instructions. Once cooked, drain and rinse in cold water, place back in the pot and toss with the olive oil to keep from sticking.

In a large skillet over medium-low heat, melt the butter. Whisk in the flour until fully incorporated. Slowly pour in the rice milk, whisking constantly. Increase the heat to medium-high and bring the mixture to a gentle boil, whisking constantly. Lower the heat to low, bringing the mixture to a simmer. Whisk in the garlic powder, onion powder, paprika, Dijon mustard and salt. Let simmer, whisking occasionally, for 3 to 5 minutes, or until thickened.

Stir in the Cheddar shreds until melted. Stir in the cooked pasta. Add more salt to taste, if desired.

Serve topped with extra paprika and parsley.

*See in BBQ Jackfruit Sliders image on page 2.

Macaroni Salad

This easy recipe is absolute perfection. We love this salad because the creamy Mayo (page 353) dressing is lighter than the typical nonvegan version. It's also great because you can substitute any veggies you like or have on hand. Serve as a side dish paired with our BBQ Seitan Sandwich (page 166) or Crispy Buffalo Tofu Sliders (page 173).

PREP TIME:
20 minutes

COOK TIME:
time to boil pasta

YIELD:
6 to 8 servings

1 (16-oz [453-g]) package elbow macaroni pasta (gluten-free if needed)

1 tbsp (15 ml) olive oil

¾ cup (113 g) chopped sweet gherkins or your favorite pickle

1 red bell pepper, seeded and chopped (about 1 cup [149 g])

2 large celery ribs, chopped (about 1 cup [101 g])

½ medium-sized red onion, chopped (about ½ cup [80 g])

DRESSING
1¼ cups (282 g) vegan Mayo (page 353) or store-bought (soy-free if needed)

1½ tbsp (22 ml) white vinegar

1 tbsp (15 ml) lemon juice

1 tbsp (15 g) Dijon mustard

1 tbsp (15 g) granulated sugar

1 tsp celery salt (can substitute with regular salt if needed)

1 tsp freshly ground black pepper

TOPPING
Fresh parsley, roughly chopped

Cook the pasta according to the package instructions. Once cooked, drain and rinse in cold water, place back in the pot and toss with the olive oil to keep from sticking.

In a large bowl, combine the chopped vegetables with the cooked pasta and mix well.

In a small bowl, whisk together all the dressing ingredients. Add the dressing to the macaroni mixture and mix well so that everything is evenly coated.

Serve immediately, topped with fresh parsley, or chill for at least an hour in the refrigerator before serving if you prefer a chilled macaroni salad.

*See in BBQ Seitan Sandwich image on page 167.

Creamy Roasted Garlic Pasta

Growing up, our parents always made us simple creamy pasta with white sauce. So, we decided to make our own vegan version with loads of flavor. This simple and delicious creamy pasta is loaded with three heads of roasted garlic. Serve it with Easy Steamed Broccoli (page 258) and Crispy Seitan (page 336).

PREP TIME:
10 minutes

COOK TIME:
50 minutes, plus time to boil pasta

YIELD:
6 to 8 servings

3 heads garlic

2 tbsp (30 ml) olive oil, divided

1 (16-oz [453-g]) package pasta of choice

3 cups (720 ml) plain, unsweetened rice milk

⅓ cup (75 g) vegan butter (nut-free and/or soy-free if needed)

⅓ cup (41 g) all-purpose flour

¼ cup (20 g) nutritional yeast

1 tsp onion powder

1 tsp garlic powder

½ tsp crushed red pepper flakes (optional)

1½ tsp (9 g) salt, plus more to taste

¼ tsp freshly ground black pepper, plus more to taste

2 cups (226 g) vegan Mozzarella shreds (page 340) or store-bought (nut-free and/or soy-free if needed)

Preheat the oven to 400°F (200°C).

Slice off the top of each garlic head, exposing some of the insides of the cloves. Place each head on a piece of foil (cut large enough to be wrapped around the whole head), cut side up. Drizzle each with 1 teaspoon of olive oil, then wrap completely in foil. Place on an ungreased baking sheet and roast in the oven for 40 minutes.

While the garlic is roasting, cook the pasta according to the package instructions. Once cooked, drain and rinse in cold water, place back in the pot and toss with the remaining tablespoon (15 ml) of the olive oil to keep from sticking.

Once the garlic is finished roasting, remove it from the oven and allow to cool slightly. Into a blender, squeeze as much the roasted garlic out of the skins as you can. Add the rice milk and blend until completely blended. Set aside.

In a large skillet, melt the butter over medium-low heat. Whisk in the flour until it is completely incorporated. Immediately add the garlic mixture in a slow, steady stream while whisking constantly. Increase the heat to medium-high, bringing the mixture to a gentle boil, whisking constantly.

Once the mixture is boiling, lower the heat to low, bringing the mixture to a simmer. Whisk in the nutritional yeast, onion powder, garlic powder, crushed red pepper flakes (if using), salt and pepper. Let simmer, whisking occasionally, for 3 to 5 minutes, or until thickened. Stir in the mozzarella shreds until melted. Stir in the cooked pasta. Taste and add more salt and pepper, if desired. Serve immediately.

Baked Mac and Cheese

If you're going to make one (vegan) cheesy dish from this cookbook to impress a nonvegan, please make it this one. This is, hands down, our most requested dish by family and friends. The creamy mac and cheese base is topped with a crispy bread crumb mixture, then baked to perfection. Serve this with our BBQ Seitan Sandwich (page 166) or Crispy Buffalo Tofu Sliders (page 173).

PREP TIME:
5 minutes, plus prep time for Cashew Cream

COOK TIME:
30 minutes, plus time to boil pasta

YIELD:
6 to 8 servings

1 (16-oz [453-g]) package cellentani pasta

1 tbsp (15 ml) olive oil

TOPPING

1 cup (56 g) French-fried onions

½ cup (54 g) vegan Italian bread crumbs

1 tsp Garlic Salt (page 356) or store-bought

1 tsp dried parsley

CHEESE SAUCE

¼ cup (57 g) vegan butter (soy-free if needed)

¼ cup (31 g) all-purpose flour

3 cups (720 ml) plain, unsweetened rice milk

½ cup (40 g) nutritional yeast

2 tsp (5 g) garlic powder

½ tsp onion powder

1 tsp paprika

1¼ tsp (7 g) salt, plus more to taste

2 cups (226 g) vegan Cheddar shreds (page 341) or store-bought (soy-free if needed)

1 heaping cup (270 g) Cashew Cream (1 batch [page 343])

Chopped fresh parsley, for topping (optional)

Preheat the oven to 350°F (180°C) and set aside a 9 x 13–inch (23 x 33–cm) baking dish.

Cook the pasta according to the package instructions, until al dente. Once cooked, drain and rinse in cold water, place back in the pot and toss with the olive oil to keep from sticking.

Prepare the topping: In a small bowl, stir together the French-fried onions, bread crumbs, garlic salt and parsley (alternatively, you can process in a food processor or blender for finer crumbs). Set aside.

Make the cheese sauce: In a large skillet, melt the butter over medium-low heat. Whisk in the flour until it is completely incorporated. Slowly add the rice milk while whisking constantly. Increase the heat to medium-high and bring the mixture to a gentle boil, whisking constantly. Lower the heat to low, bringing the mixture to a simmer. Whisk in the nutritional yeast, garlic powder, onion powder, paprika and salt. Let simmer, whisking occasionally, for 3 to 5 minutes, or until thickened. Stir in the Cheddar shreds and Cashew Cream and cook, stirring, until the shreds have melted.

Stir in the cooked pasta. Season with more salt, if desired. Transfer the pasta mixture to the baking dish. Sprinkle the topping evenly over the top. Cover the pan tightly with foil.

Bake for 15 minutes, then remove the foil. Bake, uncovered, for another 5 minutes, until the topping is golden brown. Serve warm, topped with parsley, if desired.

Classic Stuffed Shells

Growing up, stuffed shells were a dinner staple in our house. Our mom would always serve them with a side of garlic bread and a simple salad. So, this vegan recipe is an ode to one of our favorite recipes that reminds us of our childhood. It pairs jumbo pasta shells with a flavorful tofu and cashew cream "ricotta" mixture, topped with marinara and mozzarella. Serve these with Classic Garlic Bread (page 269) and Caesar Salad (page 206).

PREP TIME:
25 minutes, plus prep time for Cashew Cream and inactive time to press tofu

COOK TIME:
35 to 40 minutes, plus time to boil pasta

YIELD:
24 to 26 shells

Olive oil, for baking dish

SHELLS
24 to 26 jumbo shells (see Sister Tips) (gluten-free if needed)

1 tbsp (15 ml) olive oil

TOFU CASHEW RICOTTA
1 (14- to 16-oz [396- to 453-g]) block firm or extra-firm tofu, pressed (see page 358 for tutorial)

3 cloves garlic, peeled and minced, or 1 tbsp (9 g) jarred minced garlic

1 tbsp (5 g) dried oregano

1 tbsp (2 g) dried parsley

1 tbsp (5 g) dried basil

1 tbsp (0.2 g) dried chives

1 tsp garlic powder

1 tsp onion powder

1 tsp salt

¼ tsp freshly ground black pepper

2 heaping cups (540 g) Cashew Cream (2 batches [page 343])

FOR ASSEMBLING AND SERVING
1 (24-oz [680-g]) jar vegan marinara sauce

2 cups (226 g) vegan Mozzarella shreds (page 340) or store-bought

Chopped fresh parsley, optional

Preheat the oven to 400°F (200°C). Oil a 9 x 13-inch (23 x 33–cm) baking dish with olive oil and set aside.

Make the shells: Cook the shells according to package instructions, until al dente. Once cooked, drain and rinse in cold water, place back in the pot and toss with the olive oil to keep from sticking.

Make the ricotta: In a large bowl, crumble the pressed tofu. Add the garlic, oregano, parsley, basil, chives, garlic powder, onion powder, salt, pepper and Cashew Cream. Mix until well combined.

Spread half of the marinara sauce on the bottom of the prepared dish. Fill each shell with 2 to 3 tablespoons (30 to 45 g) of the ricotta and arrange the shells evenly in the dish (see Sister Tips). Spread the rest of the marinara sauce over the shells. Evenly sprinkle the mozzarella shreds on top. Cover the dish with foil and bake for 30 minutes. Remove the foil and bake for another 5 to 10 minutes, or until the mozzarella is melted and bubbly. Serve warm, topped with parsley, if desired.

Sister Tips

We recommend cooking a few extra shells, as some break in the cooking process. You will end up using a little more than half of a 16-ounce (453-g) package.

To fit the maximum amount of shells in the baking dish, place them at a slight angle. You should be able to fit three rows of eight shells each, and may be able to stuff another two in the dish. If not, you can use another small dish to cook any remaining shells.

FAMILY WEEKNIGHT FAVORITES

Growing up, we were lucky enough to have dinner together as a family most nights. As you can probably imagine, pleasing eleven people was no small feat, but somehow our mom always made it look easy. The dishes found in this chapter have been known to please everyone, especially when served with a couple of Go-To Sides (pages 247 to 261), a batch of soup or a large salad (pages 189 to 211). From Loaded Cheese Fries (page 118) to BBQ Jackfruit Sliders (page 94) and One-Pot Cheeseburger Macaroni (page 111), there's something for everyone. We hope that you can enjoy these recipes as a family, as we have.

Spinach Artichoke Flatbreads

This is a re-creation of one of our childhood favorites—veganized. We would often smother pita bread with spinach and artichoke dip and top it with mozzarella, cooking it to melty perfection. This recipe is an ode to that creation. It works as an appetizer, a side or an entrée. Pair it with Creamy Tomato Soup (page 194) or Butternut Squash Soup with Sautéed Pepitas (page 200).

PREP TIME:
5 minutes

COOK TIME:
15 to 17 minutes

YIELD:
4 flatbreads

3 tbsp (42 g) vegan butter, divided (nut-free and/or soy-free if needed)

3 cloves garlic, peeled and minced, or 1 tbsp (9 g) jarred minced garlic

2 tbsp (15 g) all-purpose flour

¾ cup (180 ml) plain, unsweetened rice milk

½ cup (113 g) vegan Cream Cheese (page 344) or store-bought (nut-free and/or soy-free if needed)

1 packed cup (30 g) spinach, chopped

1½ tsp (6 g) Garlic Salt (page 356) or store-bought, divided

½ tsp dried parsley

1 tsp lemon juice

1 (14-oz [396-g]) can quartered artichoke hearts

4 vegan pitas, vegan naan bread or vegan flatbread of choice

1 cup (113 g) vegan Mozzarella shreds (page 340) or store-bought (nut-free and/or soy-free if needed)

Chopped fresh parsley, for topping

Preheat the oven to 400°F (200°C).

In a skillet, melt 2 tablespoons (28 g) of the butter over medium-low heat. Add the garlic and sauté, stirring often, until fragrant, 30 seconds to 1 minute. Whisk in the flour until well incorporated. While whisking constantly, slowly pour in the rice milk. Whisk until fully incorporated. Increase the heat to medium-high, bringing the mixture to a gentle boil. Lower the heat to low, bringing the mixture to a simmer. Let simmer, whisking often, for 1 to 2 minutes, or until slightly thickened. Whisk in the cream cheese and spinach until fully incorporated. Whisk in 1 teaspoon of the garlic salt, the parsley and the lemon juice. Remove from the heat and set aside.

Drain and rinse the artichokes, then pat them dry with a clean towel. Chop them into small pieces and set aside. Place the pitas on a large ungreased baking sheet. In the microwave or in a saucepan over medium-low heat, melt the remaining 1 tablespoon (14 g) of butter and place in a small bowl. Stir in the remaining ½ teaspoon of garlic salt. Brush evenly over the tops of the pitas. Top each pita evenly with the spinach mixture. Distribute the mozzarella shreds evenly among the pitas. Sprinkle the chopped artichoke evenly on the top of the pitas.

Bake the pitas for 8 to 10 minutes, until the bottoms are crispy and the mozzarella is melty. Slice the flatbreads into your desired amount of slices and serve topped with parsley, if desired.

BBQ Jackfruit Sliders

Gluten-free option, Nut-free, Soy-free option

No get-together is complete without these simple sliders. The BBQ jackfruit is easily made by cooking jackfruit with a bit of diced onion and BBQ sauce. Toss it on a slider bun with some homemade Coleslaw (page 258) and voilà, you've got a delicious slider that will please vegans and nonvegans alike. Serve these sliders at any gathering and pair them with our Easy Creamy Mac and Cheese (page 83) or Baked Tofu Nuggets (page 224).

PREP TIME:
10 minutes, plus prep time for Coleslaw

COOK TIME:
20 to 22 minutes

YIELD:
12 to 16 sliders

2 (20-oz [567-g]) cans young jackfruit in brine

1 tbsp (15 ml) olive oil

½ medium-sized white onion, chopped (about ½ cup [80 g])

1¾ cups (420 ml) vegan BBQ sauce

1 batch Coleslaw (page 258) (soy-free if needed)

12 to 16 vegan slider buns (gluten-free if needed)

Drain and rinse the jackfruit and squeeze out as much water as possible, using a cheesecloth or clean towel. Chop it into small pieces and set aside.

In a large skillet, heat the olive oil over medium-low heat. Stir in the onion and cook, stirring occasionally, for 5 to 7 minutes, or until translucent. Stir in the jackfruit and cook, stirring often, for about 5 minutes. Add the BBQ sauce and cook, stirring often, for another 10 minutes.

Assemble the sliders by placing equal amounts of the jackfruit mixture and coleslaw in each bun.

Coleslaw (page 258)

Easy Creamy Mac and
Cheese (page 83)

Baked Tofu Nuggets
(page 224)

Jackfruit Quesadillas

Gluten-free option, Nut-free option, Soy-free option

If you're not familiar with jackfruit, it's a versatile fruit grown in tropical regions of the world. Not only is it full of fiber and other nutrients, it has a "meaty" texture that's great for vegan dishes. For this recipe, we sauté it with onion, pepper, garlic and Taco Seasoning (page 357), making it a perfect filling for these quesadillas. Serve them with our Roasted Tomato Salsa (page 217), Cashew Cream (page 343) and our Fresh and Easy Guacamole (page 242).

PREP TIME:
10 minutes

COOK TIME:
25 minutes

YIELD:
6 quesadillas

JACKFRUIT FILLING

2 (20-oz [567-g]) cans young jackfruit in brine

1 tbsp (15 ml) canola oil

¾ medium-sized white onion, chopped (about ¾ cup [120 g])

¾ red bell pepper, chopped (about ¾ cup [112 g])

1 tbsp (9 g) Taco Seasoning (page 357) or store-bought

¼ cup (60 ml) water

3 cloves garlic, peeled and minced, or 1 tbsp (9 g) jarred minced garlic

1 cup (112 g) vegan Mozzarella shreds (page 340) or store-bought (nut-free and/or soy-free if needed)

1 cup (113 g) vegan Cheddar shreds (page 341) or store-bought (nut-free and/or soy-free if needed)

FOR SERVING

Vegan butter, as needed (nut-free and/or soy-free if needed)

6 large flour tortillas (gluten-free if needed)

Garlic Salt (page 356) or store-bought, as needed (optional)

Make the jackfruit filling: Drain and rinse the jackfruit and squeeze out as much water as possible, using a cheesecloth or clean towel. Chop it into small pieces and set aside.

In a large skillet with a lid, heat the oil over medium-low heat. Stir in the onion and bell pepper and cook, stirring occasionally, for 5 to 7 minutes, or until the onion is translucent and the pepper is fork-tender. Stir in the jackfruit, taco seasoning and water. Let the mixture cook, covered, for about 5 minutes. Remove the lid and cook, stirring often, for another 3 to 5 minutes, or until most of the water has evaporated. Stir in the garlic and cook for 30 seconds to 1 minute, until fragrant. Stir in the mozzarella and Cheddar shreds until they melt. Remove from the heat and set aside.

To assemble: Spread a thin coat of butter on one side of a tortilla and, if desired, sprinkle with a bit of garlic salt, then place, butter side down, on a skillet over medium heat. Spread about one-sixth of the filling over just half of the tortilla. Fold in half and cook each side for 2 to 3 minutes, until lightly browned and crispy. Repeat with the remaining quesadillas, cooking two at a time, if desired. Serve with your preferred dip.

Loaded Nachos

This is the perfect dish to feed a crowd because not only is it absolutely amazing, but it also makes a (seriously) huge platter of nachos. Topped with Nacho Cheese (page 218), Easy Taco "Meat" (page 332), beans, salsa, shredded lettuce, Fresh and Easy Guacamole (page 242), Cashew Cream (page 343), green onions, jalapeño and cilantro, these are called Loaded Nachos for a reason.

PREP TIME:
15 minutes plus prep time for Easy Taco "Meat" and Nacho Cheese

COOK TIME:
3 to 5 minutes

YIELD:
8 servings

1 batch Easy Taco "Meat" (page 332) (gluten-free and/or soy-free if needed)

1 cup (264 g) Roasted Tomato Salsa (page 217) or store-bought salsa of choice

1 (15-oz [425-g]) can pinto or black beans, drained and rinsed

1 (13-oz [368-g]) bag vegan tortilla chips

1 batch Nacho Cheese (page 218), warm

1 cup (72 g) shredded lettuce

½ cup (120 g) Fresh and Easy Guacamole (page 242) or store-bought

¼ cup (60 g) Cashew Cream (page 343) or store-bought vegan sour cream

2 green onions, chopped

1 jalapeño pepper, sliced

2 tbsp (3 g) minced fresh cilantro leaves

In a skillet over medium-low heat, mix the taco "meat" with the salsa and beans. Cook, stirring often, for 3 to 5 minutes, or until warmed.

Spread the tortilla chips on a large serving tray. Top with the warm Nacho Cheese. Sprinkle the bean mixture on top. Evenly sprinkle the lettuce on top, then dollop the guacamole and Cashew Cream on top.

Top with the green onions, jalapeño and cilantro. Serve immediately.

Twice Baked Potatoes

When you hear "twice baked potatoes," you may think of traditional cream, butter and bacon. Our version uses vegan alternatives (whether homemade or store-bought), so it has all the flavor without any of the meat or dairy. Pair these with our Caesar Salad (page 206) or our Kale Tahini Salad with Baked Tempeh (page 210).

PREP TIME:
35 minutes

COOK TIME:
1 hour 20 minutes

YIELD:
6 baked potatoes

6 baking or russet potatoes (2 lb [907 g])

1 tbsp plus ½ cup (130 g) vegan butter, divided, plus more for topping (nut-free and/or soy-free if needed)

½ cup (113 g) vegan sour cream or Cashew Cream (page 343), plus more for topping (nut-free and/or soy-free if needed)

½ tsp garlic powder

1 tbsp (0.2 g) dried chives

1 tsp dried parsley

½ tsp salt, plus more to taste

⅛ tsp freshly ground black pepper, plus more to taste

1 tbsp (15 ml) plain, unsweetened rice milk, plus more as needed

6 slices Tofu "Bacon" (page 335) or prepared store-bought alternative, chopped (gluten-free and/or soy-free if needed)

1 cup (113 g) vegan Cheddar shreds (page 341) or store-bought, divided (nut-free and/or soy-free if needed)

Chopped green onion, for topping

Preheat the oven to 400°F (200°C).

Scrub the potatoes clean and pat dry with a clean towel. Place ½ teaspoon of the butter on top of each potato and place in a piece of foil big enough to cover the entire potato. Seal the foil tightly to ensure no butter can melt out. Place the wrapped potatoes directly on the middle baking rack. Bake for 1 hour. Remove the potatoes from the oven (leaving the oven on) and carefully unwrap the foil, then allow to cool for at least 10 minutes, or until they can be handled.

Cut off about one-third of the top of each potato horizontally. Carefully remove the insides with a spoon and place them in a large bowl, leaving ⅛ inch (3 mm) of potato around the inside of the skins.

In the microwave or on the stovetop, melt the remaining ½ cup (113 g) of butter. To the bowl of potato chunks, add the melted butter, sour cream, garlic powder, chives, parsley, salt, pepper and rice milk. Mash with a potato masher, stirring and scraping the bowl's sides with a rubber scraper as needed. Add more rice milk, as necessary, until your desired consistency is reached. Stir in the "bacon" and ½ cup (56 g) of the cheese. Season with more salt and pepper to taste, if desired.

Spoon the mashed potatoes back into the potato skins, overfilling them slightly, and place them on an ungreased baking sheet. Evenly sprinkle the remaining ½ cup (56 g) of cheese shreds over the potatoes. Bake for another 20 minutes. Serve topped with extra butter and sour cream and sprinkled with green onion.

Creamy Vegetable Risotto

If you've ever made risotto, you know it takes time and a little patience, but is well worth it. This creamy risotto is packed with veggies and is the perfect complement to many dishes. Serve it as a side or make it a meal by topping it with our Parmesan-Crusted Tofu (page 337).

PREP TIME:
5 minutes

COOK TIME:
1 hour

YIELD:
6 servings

---

1 tbsp (15 ml) olive oil

½ medium-sized white onion, chopped small (about ½ cup [80 g])

3 cloves garlic, peeled and minced, or 1 tbsp (9 g) jarred minced garlic

4 cups (960 ml) vegetable broth, divided

2 cups (140 g) chopped white mushrooms

1 cup (180 g) uncooked Arborio rice

1 cup (134 g) frozen peas

½ packed cup (18 g) baby spinach

¼ cup (20 g) nutritional yeast

1 tsp garlic powder

1 tsp onion powder

1 tsp salt, plus more to taste

1 tbsp (15 g) vegan butter (nut-free and/or soy-free if needed)

1 tsp lemon juice

Vegan Parmesan Cheese (page 342) or store-bought, for topping (optional) (nut-free and/or soy-free if needed)

In a large sauté pan, heat the olive oil over medium-low heat, add the onion and stir. Cook, stirring often, for 5 to 7 minutes, until translucent. Stir in the garlic and cook for 30 seconds to 1 minute, until fragrant. Stir in ½ cup (120 ml) of the vegetable broth and the mushrooms. Cook, stirring occasionally, for another 5 minutes. Lower the heat to low and add the rice, evenly covering the bottom of the pan. Let cook, without stirring, for 2 to 3 minutes, until you hear faint snapping noises.

Stir in another ½ cup (120 ml) of the vegetable broth. Let cook, stirring every minute or so, for 6 to 8 minutes, or until all the broth has absorbed. Repeat six more times, until the remaining 3 cups (720 ml) of vegetable broth are absorbed.

Mix in the frozen peas and spinach. Cook, stirring often, for 1 to 3 minutes, or until the peas are warm and the spinach has wilted. Stir in the nutritional yeast, garlic powder, onion powder and salt. Add the butter and lemon juice. Stir well. Season with more salt to taste. Serve topped with Parmesan, if desired.

Balsamic Roasted Veggies and Tofu

This recipe combines veggies and tofu with a sweet and flavorful balsamic sauce. Don't be intimidated by the long cook time; this recipe is quite easy and absolutely worth the wait. Serve it on its own or over a bed of Perfect White Rice (page 350).

PREP TIME:
15 minutes, plus inactive time to press tofu

COOK TIME:
1 hour

YIELD:
6 servings

TOFU
1 (14- to 16-oz [396- to 453-g]) block firm or extra-firm tofu

Canola or olive oil (or spray version), for baking dish

SAUCE
3 tbsp (45 ml) balsamic vinegar

⅓ cup (80 ml) olive oil

1 tbsp (3 g) Italian seasoning

1 tsp onion powder

1 tsp garlic powder

3 tbsp (45 ml) pure maple syrup or agave

1 tsp salt

¼ tsp freshly ground black pepper

VEGETABLES
3 cups (426 g) diced sweet potato

1 red bell pepper, seeded and chopped (about 1 cup [149 g])

1 medium-sized white onion, chopped (about 1 cup [160 g])

1½ cups (192 g) peeled and chopped carrots

FOR SERVING (OPTIONAL)
Chopped fresh parsley

Prepare the tofu: Drain the tofu and slice lengthwise into four long, equal slices. Press the slices (see page 358 for tutorial). Cut each slice into ½- to 1-inch (1.3- to 2.5-cm) cubes (40 to 50 total).

Preheat the oven to 425°F (220°C) and oil a 9 x 13-inch (23 x 33-cm) baking dish with canola or olive oil.

Make the sauce: In a large bowl, combine all the sauce ingredients. Stir well.

Incorporate the vegetables and tofu: Add all the vegetables and cubed tofu to the sauce. Gently stir, evenly coating everything with the sauce. Transfer the mixture to the prepared baking dish.

Cover with foil and bake for 45 minutes. Remove the foil, stir and bake for 15 more minutes, or until the sweet potato and carrots are fork-tender. If desired, broil on high for 1 to 2 minutes to crisp slightly. Serve topped with parsley, if desired.

Veggie Pot Pie Casserole

This pot pie is reminiscent of the classic dish, but is (of course!) vegan. It pairs a creamy vegetable base with homemade vegan biscuits that will please the entire family. Don't be intimidated by the long ingredient list; this recipe is well worth it.

PREP TIME:	COOK TIME:	YIELD:
30 minutes	*about 50 minutes*	*6 servings*

Canola or olive oil (or spray version), for baking dish

BISCUITS
¾ cup (180 ml) plain, unsweetened soy milk

2 tsp (10 ml) apple cider vinegar, white vinegar or lemon juice

6 tbsp (¾ stick [84 g]) vegan butter (see Sister Tips) (nut-free if needed)

2 cups (250 g) all-purpose flour (spooned and leveled or weighed [see page 359 for How to Measure Flour]), plus more as needed

1 tbsp (12 g) granulated sugar

2 tsp (9 g) baking powder

¼ tsp baking soda

½ tsp salt

POT PIE FILLING
¼ cup (56 g) vegan butter (nut-free if needed)

1 medium-sized white onion, chopped (about 1 cup [160 g])

1 cup (110 g) shredded carrot

1 cup (101 g) diced celery

2 cups (300 g) peeled and diced russet potatoes

2 tbsp (30 ml) water

Preheat the oven to 425°F (220°C) and oil a 9 x 13–inch (23 x 33–cm) baking dish with canola or olive oil.

Begin preparing the biscuits: In a small bowl, whisk together the soy milk and vinegar. Place in the fridge to curdle, for later use. Place the butter in the freezer for later use.

Make the pot pie filling: In a large, lidded skillet, melt the butter over medium heat. Stir in the onion and cook, uncovered, for 5 to 7 minutes, or until translucent. Stir in the carrot, celery and potatoes. Pour in the water, cover and cook, stirring occasionally, for 10 minutes. Add more water, as necessary, to ensure the vegetables don't stick to the pan.

(continued)

POT PIE FILLING (CONTINUED)

1 cup (134 g) frozen green peas

1 cup (136 g) frozen corn

3 cloves garlic, peeled and minced, or 1 tbsp (9 g) jarred minced garlic

½ tsp salt

¼ tsp freshly ground black pepper

¼ tsp ground celery seed

1 tbsp (2 g) dried parsley

1 tsp garlic powder

⅓ cup (41 g) all-purpose flour

1 cup (240 ml) plain, unsweetened rice milk

1½ cups (360 ml) vegetable broth

TOPPING

2 tbsp (28 g) vegan butter, melted (nut-free if needed)

1 tsp dried parsley

When the 10 minutes have passed, stir in the peas, corn and garlic and cook for 30 seconds to 1 minute, or until the garlic is fragrant. Stir in the salt, pepper, ground celery seed, parsley, garlic powder and flour until the veggies are completely coated. Slowly add the rice milk and broth, stirring constantly. Increase the heat to medium-high and bring to a gentle boil, stirring constantly. Lower the heat to low and let simmer, stirring occasionally, for 3 to 5 minutes. The pot pie filling will thicken. Remove from the heat and set aside.

Meanwhile, finish the biscuit dough: In a large bowl, whisk together the flour, sugar, baking powder, baking soda and salt. Use cheese grater to shred the cold butter into the flour mixture and stir until well mixed (see Sister Tips). Add the cold milk mixture and stir to incorporate. Transfer to a floured surface. Add in a bit of flour until the dough is workable.

Using your hands, gently press the dough into a rectangle that is about 1 inch (2.5 cm) thick. Fold the dough in half widthwise and press into a rectangle. Repeat this four times, creating layers of dough. Then, press into a rectangle that is ¾ to 1 inch (2 to 2.5 cm) thick. Using a biscuit cutter that is 2¾ to 3 inches (7 to 7.5 cm) in diameter, cut out six circles (cut straight down without wiggling the cutter).

Assemble and bake the casserole: Pour the veggie mixture into the baking dish and evenly top with the biscuit dough. Bake for 16 to 20 minutes, until the biscuits are golden brown. Meanwhile, make the topping by placing the melted butter in a small bowl and stirring in the parsley.

Remove the dish from the oven and brush the topping evenly over the biscuits. Serve warm.

Sister Tips

For this recipe, we recommend using vegan buttery sticks, rather than from the tub.

Using a cheese grater is a simple way to cut the cold butter into the flour mixture without the need for much handling of the dough. However, you can also use a pastry cutter or fork to cut the butter into the flour mixture (see page 359 for tutorial).

Sloppy Joes

This vegan Sloppy Joes recipe does not disappoint—it's easy, flavorful and takes just 30 minutes to whip up. For this recipe, we use textured vegetable protein (see Sister Tip for more information). Serve these with our Coleslaw (page 258) or Baked Seasoned Fries (page 251).

PREP TIME:
10 minutes

COOK TIME:
20 minutes

YIELD:
6 to 8 sloppy joes

2 cups (184 g) textured vegetable protein (TVP) (see Sister Tip)

2 cups (480 ml) boiling water

1 tbsp (15 ml) olive oil

⅓ red bell pepper, seeded and chopped (about ⅓ cup [49 g])

⅓ medium-sized white onion, chopped (about ⅓ cup [53 g])

3 cloves garlic, peeled and minced, or 1 tbsp (9 g) jarred minced garlic

3 tbsp (50 g) tomato paste

⅓ cup (80 ml) vegetable broth

¾ cup (180 g) ketchup

1 tbsp (15 ml) hot sauce

¼ cup (60 ml) vegan Worcestershire sauce (gluten-free if needed)

½ tsp chili powder

½ tsp garlic powder

½ tsp onion powder

2 tbsp (27 g) packed light brown sugar

1 tbsp (15 ml) apple cider vinegar

¼ tsp salt, plus more to taste

⅛ tsp freshly ground black pepper, plus more to taste

FOR SERVING
6 to 8 vegan burger buns (gluten-free if needed)

Place the textured vegetable protein into a large, heat-resistant bowl. Pour the boiling water over it and stir until combined. Set aside.

In a large sauté pan, heat the olive oil over medium-low heat. Add the bell pepper and onion and cook, stirring often, for 5 to 7 minutes, or until the onion is translucent and the bell pepper is fork-tender. Stir in the garlic and cook for another 30 seconds to 1 minute, or until fragrant. Stir in the tomato paste until the veggies are coated. Stir in the prepared textured vegetable protein. Cook, stirring, for 1 to 2 minutes, or until lightly sautéed.

Stir in the rest of the ingredients and cook, stirring occasionally, for about 10 minutes, or until thickened. Add more salt and black pepper, if desired.

Assemble the Sloppy Joes by scooping your desired amount of the TVP mixture onto each burger bun.

Sister Tip

Textured vegetable protein, or TVP, is a complete protein made from soy. It's a great alternative to meat. You can find it at specialty stores or order it online.

One-Pot Cheeseburger Macaroni

This recipe is family-friendly and kid-approved. It's made simply in one pot—hello, easy cleanup! In less than 30 minutes, you can prepare this flavorful pasta dish packed with vegan "beef," a creamy tomato sauce, vegan cheese and spices. Serve this with our Dinner Rolls (page 271) and Simple Ranch Salad (page 205).

PREP TIME:	COOK TIME:	YIELD:
prep time for Cashew Cream	*25 to 30 minutes*	*4 to 6 servings*

1 tbsp (15 ml) olive oil

12 oz (340 g) vegan ground "beef" (we like Impossible and Beyond Beef), defrosted if frozen (soy-free if needed)

3 tbsp (48 g) tomato paste

2 tsp (5 g) garlic powder

1 tsp onion powder

1 tsp paprika

½ tsp salt, plus more to taste

1½ cups (360 ml) plain, unsweetened rice milk

2 cups (480 ml) water

2 cups (6 oz [170 g]) uncooked cellentani pasta

1 cup (113 g) vegan Cheddar shreds (page 341) or store-bought (soy-free if needed)

¼ cup (60 g) Cashew Cream (page 343)

Dried or chopped fresh parsley, for topping (optional)

In a large skillet, heat the oil over medium heat. Add the ground "beef" and stir often until cooked, 7 to 10 minutes. Stir in the tomato paste, garlic powder, onion powder, paprika and salt, stirring to coat the "beef." Add the rice milk, water and cellentani. Stir to fully mix, then increase the heat to high and bring to a boil. Lower the heat to low, bringing the mixture to a simmer. Simmer, stirring occasionally, for 15 to 17 minutes, or until the pasta is cooked and most of the liquid is absorbed. Remove from the heat.

Mix in the Cheddar shreds until melted. Finally, mix in the Cashew Cream. Season with more salt and serve warm, topped with parsley, if desired.

Taco Pasta

This unique recipe marries two of our favorite dishes: tacos and pasta. It's creamy, cheesy and loaded with the flavors you'd typically find in a taco. Obsessed with tacos? Check out our Taco Salad (page 209) and Fried Avocado Tacos (page 187).

PREP TIME:
none

COOK TIME:
10 to 15 minutes, plus time to boil pasta

YIELD:
6 to 8 servings

12 oz (340 g) medium pasta shells or pasta of choice (gluten-free if needed)

2 tbsp (30 ml) olive oil, divided

16 oz (453 g) vegan ground "beef" (we like Impossible and Beyond Beef), defrosted if frozen (gluten-free, nut-free and/or soy-free if needed)

2 tbsp (5 g) Taco Seasoning (page 357) or store-bought

½ cup (120 ml) plain, unsweetened rice milk

1 cup (240 g) Roasted Tomato Salsa (page 217) or store-bought salsa of choice

1 (14.5-oz [411-g]) can petite diced tomatoes

2 tbsp (14 g) canned chopped green chiles

1 cup (113 g) vegan Cheddar shreds (page 341) or store-bought (nut-free and/or soy-free if needed)

1 cup (113 g) vegan Mozzarella shreds (page 340) or store-bought (nut-free and/or soy-free if needed)

½ tsp salt, plus more to taste

¼ tsp freshly ground black pepper, plus more to taste

Chopped fresh cilantro, for topping (optional)

Cook the pasta according to the package instructions. Once cooked, drain and rinse in cold water, place back in the pot and toss with 1 tablespoon (15 ml) of the olive oil to keep from sticking.

In a large skillet, heat the remaining 1 tablespoon (15 ml) of olive oil over medium-low heat. Stir in the ground "beef." Cook, stirring occasionally, for 3 to 5 minutes, or until lightly browned. Sprinkle the taco seasoning on top and stir until the "beef" is coated. Add the rice milk and stir to completely combine. Cook for 3 to 5 minutes, or until the "beef" is completely cooked.

Stir in the salsa, tomatoes, green chiles, Cheddar shreds and mozzarella shreds. Cook, stirring occasionally, for about 3 minutes, or until the shreds have melted. Stir in the cooked pasta, salt and pepper. Add more salt and pepper to taste, if desired. Serve topped with cilantro, if desired.

Creamy Garlic Orzo

This dish is made in one pot and is ready in just 30 minutes. It's creamy, garlicky and buttery. We love topping it with our Parmesan-Crusted Tofu (page 337) and pairing it with Easy Steamed Broccoli (page 258), making it a full meal.

PREP TIME:
5 minutes

COOK TIME:
25 minutes

YIELD:
6 to 8 servings

4 tbsp (56 g) vegan butter, divided (nut-free and/or soy-free if needed)

½ medium-sized onion, diced (about ½ cup [80 g])

1 (16-oz [453-g]) package orzo

3 cloves garlic, peeled and minced, or 1 tbsp (9 g) jarred minced garlic

3½ cups (840 ml) vegetable broth

1 cup (240 ml) plain, unsweetened rice milk

½ cup (40 g) nutritional yeast

1 tsp salt

¼ tsp freshly ground black pepper

½ tsp dried parsley

½ tsp garlic powder

1 tsp fresh lime juice

FOR SERVING (OPTIONAL)
Parmesan-Crusted Tofu (page 337), sliced (omit for nut-free and/or soy-free)

Dried or chopped fresh parsley

In a large skillet, melt 2 tablespoons (28 g) of the butter over medium-low heat. Stir in the onion and orzo and sauté, stirring often, until the orzo is lightly browned, about 7 minutes.

Add the garlic and let cook for 30 seconds to 1 minute, or until fragrant. Stir in the vegetable broth and rice milk and increase the heat to high, bringing the mixture to a boil. Lower the heat to low and bring to a simmer. Cook, stirring occasionally, for 13 to 15 minutes, or until the orzo is fully cooked and most of the liquid is absorbed. Remove from the heat.

Stir in the remaining 2 tablespoons (28 g) of butter and the nutritional yeast until they are fully incorporated and the butter has melted. Stir in the salt, pepper, parsley, garlic powder and lime juice. Serve warm topped with Parmesan-Crusted Tofu and parsley, if desired.

BBQ Tofu Bowls

These bowls top white rice with crispy BBQ tofu, sautéed broccoli and sweet potato, beans, corn and a drizzle of vegan ranch dressing. They're quick, easy and absolutely delicious. Feel free to get creative and customize these bowls with any veggies or toppings you please!

PREP TIME:
10 minutes, plus inactive time to press tofu and prep time for rice

COOK TIME:
about 20 minutes

YIELD:
4 bowls

CRISPY TOFU

1 (14- to 16-oz [396- to 453-g]) block firm or extra-firm tofu

⅓ cup (40 g) cornstarch

¼ cup (60 ml) canola oil

⅓ cup (96 g) vegan BBQ sauce, plus more as desired

SAUTÉED VEGETABLES

1 tbsp (15 ml) canola or olive oil

1 medium- to large-sized head broccoli, stemmed and chopped into bite-sized pieces (about 4 cups [200 g])

1 medium- to large-sized sweet potato, peeled and diced (2 heaping cups [320 g])

¼ cup (60 ml) water

FOR THE BOWLS

4½ cups (750 g) Perfect White Rice (1½ batches [page 350])

1 (15.5-oz [439-g]) can red kidney beans, drained and rinsed

1 cup (136 g) corn (fresh [cooked], frozen [defrosted] or canned [drained and rinsed])

Vegan Ranch Dressing (page 345) or store-bought (nut-free if needed)

Begin the crispy tofu: Drain the tofu and slice lengthwise into four long, equal slices. Press the slices (see page 358 for tutorial). Cut each slice into ½- to 1-inch (1.3- to 2.5-cm) cubes (40 to 50 total).

Prepare the sautéed vegetables: Heat the canola oil in a large sauté pan with a lid over medium heat. Add the broccoli and sweet potato. Cook, stirring occasionally, for 5 minutes. Stir in the water, cover and cook, stirring occasionally, for another 5 to 7 minutes, or until fork-tender.

Meanwhile, finish the crispy tofu: In a large bowl, add the tofu pieces and cornstarch. Gently shake the bowl to coat all the pieces with the cornstarch (alternatively, you can coat each piece separately). In a large skillet, heat the canola oil over medium heat. Carefully transfer the cornstarch-coated tofu to the pan, leaving excess cornstarch in the bowl. Cook, stirring occasionally, for 7 to 10 minutes, until the tofu pieces are crispy on all sides. Stir the BBQ sauce into the crispy tofu until well coated.

Prepare the bowls: Distribute the prepared white rice among four serving bowls. Place an equal amount of crispy BBQ tofu, sautéed vegetables, kidney beans and corn in each serving bowl. Drizzle ranch dressing and extra BBQ sauce over the bowls, as desired. Serve warm.

Sautéed Veggie Flatbreads

These quick and simple flatbreads are perfect for busy weeknights when you want something delicious but also easy. They are loaded with sautéed veggies and topped with (vegan) cheese and ranch dressing. Want to add hummus or pesto? See our Sister Tip for these variations and feel free to customize these flatbreads with any veggies you have on hand.

PREP TIME:
10 minutes

COOK TIME:
about 25 minutes

YIELD:
4 flatbreads

1 tbsp (15 ml) olive oil

1 small head or ½ large head cauliflower, stemmed and chopped small (about 4½ cups [425 g])

1 cup (128 g) chopped carrot, chopped small

½ red bell pepper, seeded and chopped (about ½ cup [74 g])

½ medium-sized white onion (about ½ cup [80 g])

¼ cup (60 ml) water

3 cloves fresh garlic, minced, or 1 tbsp (9 g) jarred minced garlic

2 packed cups (74 g) baby spinach

Vegan butter (nut-free and/or soy-free if needed)

4 flatbreads or pitas (gluten-free if needed)

Garlic Salt (page 356) or store-bought

1 cup (113 g) vegan Mozzarella shreds (page 340) or store-bought (nut-free and/or soy-free if needed)

Vegan Ranch Dressing (page 345) or store-bought, for serving (nut-free and/or soy-free if needed)

In a large sauté pan with a lid, heat the olive oil over medium heat. Add the cauliflower, carrot, bell pepper and onion. Cook, stirring occasionally, for 5 minutes. Stir in the water, cover and cook for another 5 minutes, or until the cauliflower and carrot are fork-tender. Remove the lid, stir in the garlic and cook for 30 seconds to 1 minute, or until fragrant. Lower the heat to low and add the spinach. Cook, covered, for another minute, or until the spinach has wilted. Remove from the heat.

Butter one side of each flatbread. Evenly sprinkle your desired amount of garlic salt on top of the butter. Place each flatbread, buttered side down, in a large skillet over medium-low heat. You may need to do this one or two at a time. Place an equal amount of cooked veggies on each flatbread (see Sister Tip). Sprinkle each flatbread with ¼ cup (28 g) of the cheese. Cover and cook for 5 to 7 minutes, or until the bottom is lightly browned and crispy and the cheese has melted. Slice each flatbread into 4 to 6 slices and serve with a drizzle or dip into a side of ranch dressing.

Sister Tip

For extra flavor, spread Hummus (page 243) or Pesto (page 352) on the pitas before topping with veggies.

Loaded Cheese Fries

French fries topped with perfect cheese sauce, Tofu "Bacon" (page 335), green onion and Ranch Dressing (page 345)—what more could you ask for? We could argue that this is one of our favorite weeknight meals (Mary-Kate would eat it every day if she could). We love to serve it with BBQ Jackfruit Sliders (page 94).

PREP TIME:
5 minutes

COOK TIME:
about 10 minutes

YIELD:
4 to 6 servings

CHEESE SAUCE

2 tbsp (28 g) vegan butter (nut-free and/or soy-free if needed)

2 tbsp (16 g) all-purpose flour

1½ cups (360 ml) plain, unsweetened rice milk

1 cup (113 g) vegan Cheddar shreds (page 341) or store-bought (nut-free and/or soy-free if needed)

1 cup (113 g) vegan Mozzarella shreds (page 340) or store-bought (nut-free and/or soy-free if needed)

LOADED FRIES

8 slices Tofu "Bacon" (page 335) or prepared store-bought variation, chopped (soy-free if needed)

4 green onions

¼ cup (60 g) vegan Ranch Dressing (page 345) or store-bought (nut-free and/or soy-free if needed), plus water to thin

1 batch Fries (Baked or Fried) (page 259), or 2½ lb (1 kg) store-bought fries, prepared according to package instructions

Make the cheese sauce: In a small saucepan, melt the butter over medium-low heat. Whisk in the flour until it is completely incorporated. Slowly pour in the rice milk while whisking constantly. Increase the heat to medium-high and bring the mixture to a gentle boil, whisking constantly. Lower the heat to low, bringing the mixture to a simmer. Let simmer, whisking occasionally, for 3 to 5 minutes, or until thickened. Stir in the Cheddar and mozzarella shreds until melted.

Assemble the fries: Chop the "bacon" into small pieces and chop the green onions. Mix the ranch dressing with a bit of water to thin it out. Place the freshly prepared, hot fries on a serving tray. Pour the warm cheese sauce on top. Sprinkle the chopped bacon on top. Drizzle the ranch dressing and sprinkle the chopped green onions all over. Serve immediately.

Broccoli Cheddar Rice

Inspired by one of our favorite dishes, Broccoli Cheddar Soup (page 191), this rice is cheesy, flavorful and loaded with broccoli. It's kid-approved and a great way to sneak in those extra veggies. Our favorite way to serve this dish is topped with Parmesan-Crusted Tofu (page 337).

PREP TIME:	COOK TIME:	YIELD:
5 minutes, plus inactive time to soak cashews and prep time for rice	*10 minutes*	*4 servings*

½ cup (120 ml) vegetable broth

½ cup (120 ml) plain, unsweetened rice milk

1 cup (146 g) raw unsalted whole cashews, soaked (see Sister Tip)

1 tsp garlic powder

½ tsp onion powder

½ tsp ground celery seed

½ tsp salt

¼ cup (20 g) nutritional yeast

1 tbsp (15 ml) olive oil

1½ cups (150 g) finely chopped broccoli

½ medium-sized white onion, chopped (about ½ cup [80 g])

½ cup (60 g) vegan Cheddar shreds (page 341) or store-bought (soy-free if needed)

3 cups (500 g) Perfect White Rice (1 batch [page 350])

FOR SERVING
Dried or chopped fresh parsley

Vegan Parmesan Cheese (page 342) or store-bought (soy-free if needed)

In a high-speed blender, combine the vegetable broth, rice milk, soaked cashews, garlic powder, onion powder, ground celery seed, salt and nutritional yeast. Blend until smooth, then set aside.

In a large, nonstick skillet, heat the olive oil over medium heat. Add the broccoli and onion and let cook, stirring often, for 7 to 10 minutes, or until the broccoli is fork-tender and the onion becomes translucent.

Add the blended cashew sauce and vegan cheese to the pan and cook, stirring, until the Cheddar is melted.

Stir in the white rice. Serve topped with parsley and Parmesan.

Sister Tip

To soak cashews, place in a bowl and cover completely with water. Let sit for at least 2 hours, then drain, rinse and pat dry (see page 358 for more options and tips).

TRAVEL-INSPIRED
EATS

We absolutely love traveling and immersing ourselves in the cultures of new places. Trying authentic dishes and discovering new flavors is one of our favorite things to do while exploring different parts of the world. Many of the recipes in this chapter are inspired by our travels, especially to Asia, Emily's absolute favorite place to visit. The floral and aromatic flavors of ingredients, such as makrut lime leaves, remind her of time spent in Thailand and Cambodia, while the salty and umami flavors of miso and soy sauce bring her back to her time in Japan.

Of course, nothing beats enjoying these flavors in the places where we discovered them, but we hope our take on many traditional dishes pays tribute to our love and appreciation for the cultures from which they originated. In this chapter, you'll find everything from Sweet and Sour Tofu (page 128) and Gochujang Brussels Sprouts (page 133) to Butter Tofu (page 140).

**Spicy Braised Tofu
(page 132)**

Sesame Noodles

This dish pairs rice noodles with a sweet and savory sesame sauce. The addition of the cornstarch slurry makes the sauce thick and sticky. Serve these Sesame Noodles with Spicy Gochujang Broccoli Wings (page 126) or Orange Tofu (page 131).

PREP TIME:
5 minutes

COOK TIME:
10 minutes, plus time to cook noodles

YIELD:
6 to 8 servings

1 tbsp (8 g) cornstarch

2 tbsp (30 ml) water

3 tbsp (45 ml) pure (untoasted) sesame oil

4 cloves garlic, peeled and minced, or 4 tsp (12 g) jarred minced garlic

⅓ cup (80 ml) soy sauce (or tamari for gluten-free or coconut aminos for soy-free)

⅓ cup (73 g) packed light brown sugar

1 tbsp (15 ml) chili garlic sauce

1 tbsp (15 ml) unseasoned rice vinegar

½ tsp garlic powder

1 (14-oz [396-g]) package rice noodles (use the thickness of your choice; any type will work)

FOR SERVING
2 green onions, thinly sliced

Sesame seeds

In a small bowl, combine the cornstarch with the water. Set aside.

In a large sauté pan, heat the sesame oil over medium-low heat. Stir in the garlic and cook for 30 seconds to 1 minute, or until fragrant. Stir in the soy sauce, brown sugar, chili garlic sauce, rice vinegar and garlic powder. Increase the heat to medium-high and bring the mixture to a gentle boil, whisking constantly. Whisk in the cornstarch slurry. Lower the heat to low, bringing the mixture to a simmer. Let the sauce cook, whisking often, until it becomes thick and sticky, 3 to 5 minutes.

Meanwhile, cook the rice noodles according to the package instructions. Drain and rinse in cold water.

Stir the cooked noodles into the sauce. Serve topped with green onion and sesame seeds.

Spicy Gochujang Broccoli Wings

These spicy broccoli wings are baked, not fried. The sauce on these wings combines spicy gochujang with maple syrup and liquid smoke for a combination of spicy, sweet and smoky. If you aren't familiar with gochujang, it's a red chili paste made from red pepper flakes, glutinous rice and fermented soybeans, and is popular in Korean cooking. If you're a fan of gochujang and this recipe, make sure to try our Rice Bowls with Marinated Tofu and Gochujang Sauce (page 152).

PREP TIME:
15 minutes

COOK TIME:
35 to 40 minutes

YIELD:
4 servings

BATTERED BROCCOLI
1 large head broccoli

1 cup (125 g) all-purpose flour

1 cup (240 ml) water

SAUCE
3 tbsp (60 g) gochujang

1 tsp sesame oil

1 tbsp (15 ml) soy sauce

1 tbsp (15 ml) pure maple syrup or agave

¼ tsp liquid smoke (optional; see Sister Tip)

1 (1" [2.5-cm]) piece fresh ginger, peeled and minced

FOR SERVING
1 green onion, chopped

Sesame seeds

Make the broccoli: Preheat the oven to 400°F (200°C) and line a baking sheet with parchment paper. Chop the broccoli into bite-sized pieces and set aside.

In a large bowl, whisk together the flour and water. Dunk each piece of broccoli into the mixture—this can be done by putting all the broccoli into the bowl and mixing or individually dunking each piece. Arrange the battered broccoli in a single layer on the prepared baking sheet, letting any excess batter drip off into the bowl before placing down. Bake the broccoli for 35 to 40 minutes, or until crispy, flipping halfway through.

Meanwhile, make the sauce: In a large bowl, whisk together the gochujang, sesame oil, soy sauce, maple syrup, liquid smoke (if using) and ginger.

Once the broccoli is done cooking, place all the pieces in the bowl with the sauce and toss until they are all covered. Serve topped with green onion and sesame seeds.

Sister Tip

Liquid smoke adds a strong smoky flavor to this dish. If you are not typically a fan of smoky dishes, we recommend omitting the ingredient altogether.

Cold Peanut Noodles

If we could eat these noodles every day, we would. They really are that good. The creamy peanut sauce is made with just six ingredients and takes less than ten minutes to whip up. Because these noodles are served cold, they can easily be prepped ahead of time and set in the fridge until they are ready to be served. They are great as a side dish served with our Gochujang Brussels Sprouts (page 133) and Spicy Braised Tofu (page 132).

PREP TIME:
10 minutes

COOK TIME:
time to cook noodles

YIELD:
6 to 8 servings

¼ cup (65 g) creamy peanut butter (soy-free if needed)

⅓ cup (80 ml) low-sodium soy sauce (or tamari for gluten-free, or coconut aminos for soy-free)

2 tbsp (30 ml) unseasoned rice vinegar

1 tbsp (15 g) vegan sriracha

1 tbsp (15 ml) pure maple syrup or agave

1 tbsp (15 ml) pure (untoasted) sesame oil

1 (14-oz [396-g]) package medium-width rice noodles

FOR SERVING
2 to 3 green onions, chopped

Sesame seeds

In a large bowl, whisk together the peanut butter, soy sauce, rice vinegar, sriracha, maple syrup and sesame oil. Place in the fridge while you prepare the noodles.

Cook the rice noodles according to the package instructions. Drain and rinse with cold water.

Add the cooked noodles to the sauce and stir to evenly coat with the sauce. Serve immediately, topped with the green onions and sesame seeds, or chill for at least an hour in the refrigerator before serving.

Sweet and Sour Tofu

This dish has been one of the most popular recipes on our blog for a while now, so of course it deserves a spot in this cookbook. The crispy tofu pairs perfectly with the sticky sweet and sour sauce. Serve this saucy dish over our Perfect White Rice (page 350).

PREP TIME:
10 minutes, plus inactive time to press tofu

COOK TIME:
about 20 minutes

YIELD:
4 servings

CRISPY TOFU

1 (14- to 16-oz [396- to 453-g]) block firm or extra-firm tofu

⅓ cup (40 g) cornstarch

¼ cup (60 ml) canola oil

SWEET AND SOUR SAUCE

2 tsp (5 g) cornstarch

2 tbsp (30 ml) water

⅓ cup (80 ml) low-sodium soy sauce (or tamari for gluten-free)

⅓ cup (80 ml) pure maple syrup or agave

2 tbsp (30 ml) unseasoned rice vinegar

1 tbsp (15 ml) pure (untoasted) sesame oil

1 clove garlic, peeled and minced, or 1 tsp jarred minced garlic

1 (½" [1.3-cm]) piece fresh ginger, peeled and minced (can substitute for ¼ tsp ground ginger if needed)

1 tsp chili garlic sauce (see Sister Tip)

FOR SERVING

Sesame seeds

Chopped green onion

Make the crispy tofu: Drain the tofu and slice lengthwise into four long, equal slices. Press the slices (see page 358 for tutorial). Cut each slice into ½- to 1-inch (1.3- to 2.5-cm) cubes (40 to 50 total). In a large bowl, add the tofu pieces and cornstarch. Gently shake the bowl to coat all the pieces with the cornstarch (alternatively, you can coat each piece separately).

In a large skillet, heat the canola oil over medium heat. Carefully transfer the cornstarch-coated tofu to the pan, leaving excess cornstarch in the bowl. Cook, stirring occasionally, for 7 to 10 minutes, or until the tofu pieces are crispy on all sides.

Make the sauce: In a small bowl, combine the cornstarch with the water. Set aside. In a large skillet over medium heat, whisk together the soy sauce, maple syrup, rice vinegar and sesame oil. Add the garlic, ginger and chili garlic sauce and whisk again. Increase the heat to medium-high, bringing the mixture to a gentle boil, whisking constantly. Add the cornstarch slurry to the skillet and whisk. Lower the heat to low, bringing the sauce to a simmer. Let the sauce cook until it becomes thick and sticky, 3 to 5 minutes.

Once the sauce has thickened, add the crispy tofu to the pan. Mix to completely coat the tofu. Serve topped with sesame seeds and green onion.

Sister Tip

If you like spice, add more chili garlic sauce for an extra kick.

Perfect White Rice
(page 350)

**Easy Steamed
Broccoli (page 258)**

Orange Tofu

Another tofu recipe for the win! Here, we pair crispy panfried tofu with a sticky, sweet and tangy orange sauce that is sure to change the mind of any tofu-hater. Enjoy this tofu on its own or serve it with Easy Steamed Broccoli (page 258) and Perfect White Rice (page 350).

PREP TIME:	COOK TIME:	YIELD:
10 minutes, plus inactive time to press tofu	about 20 minutes	4 servings

CRISPY TOFU

1 (14- to 16-oz [396- to 453-g]) block firm or extra-firm tofu

⅓ cup (40 g) cornstarch

¼ cup (60 ml) canola oil

ORANGE SAUCE

1 tbsp (8 g) cornstarch

2 tbsp + ¼ cup water (90 ml), divided

1½ tsp (3 g) orange zest

2 tbsp (30 ml) fresh orange juice

2 tbsp (30 ml) unseasoned rice vinegar

2 tbsp (30 ml) low-sodium soy sauce (or tamari for gluten-free)

2 tbsp (30 ml) pure maple syrup or agave

¼ cup (50 g) granulated sugar

1 (½" [1.3-cm]) piece fresh ginger, peeled and minced (can substitute for ¼ tsp ground ginger if needed)

1 clove garlic, peeled and minced, or 1 tsp jarred minced garlic

FOR SERVING

Chopped green onion

Sesame seeds

Crushed red pepper flakes (optional)

Make the crispy tofu: Drain the tofu and slice lengthwise into four long, equal slices. Press the slices (see page 358 for tutorial). Cut each slice into ½- to 1-inch (1.3- to 2.5-cm) cubes (40 to 50 total). In a large bowl, add the tofu pieces and cornstarch. Gently shake the bowl to coat all the pieces with cornstarch (alternatively, you can coat each piece separately).

In a large skillet, heat the canola oil over medium heat. Carefully transfer the cornstarch-coated tofu to the pan, leaving excess cornstarch in the bowl. Cook, stirring occasionally, for 7 to 10 minutes, or until the tofu pieces are crispy on all sides.

Make the sauce: In a small bowl, combine the cornstarch with 2 tablespoons (30 ml) of the water. Set aside. In a large skillet over medium-low heat, whisk together ¼ cup (60 ml) of the water with the orange zest and juice, rice vinegar, soy sauce, maple syrup, sugar, ginger and garlic. Increase the heat to medium-high, bringing the mixture to a gentle boil. Add the cornstarch slurry to the skillet and whisk. Lower the heat to low, bringing the sauce to a simmer. Let the sauce cook, whisking often, until it becomes thick and sticky, about 5 minutes.

Once the sauce has thickened, add the crispy tofu to the pan. Mix to completely coat the tofu. Served topped with green onion, sesame seeds and crushed red pepper flakes (if using).

Spicy Braised Tofu

If you ask Emily, few things are better than fried, spicy tofu. This recipe combines many of her favorite ingredients, including soy sauce, sesame oil and gochugaru. If you're not familiar with gochugaru, it's a Korean chili powder that adds a robust flavor with a nice balance of smoky, spicy and sweet. Enjoy this tofu served over Perfect White Rice (page 350) with a side of Sesame Noodles (page 125).

PREP TIME:
10 minutes, plus inactive time to press tofu

COOK TIME:
10 minutes

YIELD:
2 to 4 servings

1 (14- to 16-oz [396- to 453-g]) block extra-firm tofu

¼ cup (60 ml) low-sodium soy sauce (or tamari for gluten-free)

1 tbsp (15 ml) mirin

1 tsp pure (untoasted) sesame oil

1 (1" [2.5-cm]) piece fresh ginger, peeled and minced (can substitute ½ tsp ground ginger if needed)

3 cloves garlic, peeled and minced, or 1 tbsp (9 g) jarred minced garlic

1 tbsp (5 g) gochugaru

3 tbsp (45 ml) canola oil

Chopped green onion, for serving

Drain the tofu and slice lengthwise into four long, equal slices. Press the slices (see page 358 for tutorial).

In a small bowl, whisk together the soy sauce, mirin, sesame oil, ginger, garlic and gochugaru. Set aside.

Slice each piece of pressed tofu diagonally, creating eight triangles. In a large skillet (see Sister Tip), heat the canola oil over medium-high heat. Once the oil begins to shimmer, add the tofu slices. Let the tofu fry until golden brown, 2 to 4 minutes, then flip and let fry for an additional 2 to 4 minutes, until golden brown.

Pour the prepared sauce into the pan and allow the sauce to cook with the tofu for a minute or two, flipping the tofu around to ensure they are coated with the sauce. Serve the tofu drizzled with any remaining sauce from the pan and topped with green onion.

Sister Tip

We recommend using a nonstick or seasoned cast-iron skillet for this recipe. Otherwise, the tofu may stick when you are attempting to flip.

Gochujang Brussels Sprouts

These Brussels sprouts are easy to make and super simple, requiring just four main ingredients. Roasted Brussels sprouts are tossed in a gochujang sauce for a delicious spicy and slightly sweet dish. Pair this side with our Cold Peanut Noodles (page 127) or Spicy Braised Tofu (page 132).

PREP TIME:
5 minutes

COOK TIME:
30 to 35 minutes

YIELD:
2 to 4 servings

Canola or olive oil (or spray version), for pan

1 lb (453 g) Brussels sprouts

3 tbsp (54 g) gochujang (gluten-free if needed)

1 tsp sesame oil

2 tsp (10 ml) mirin

Sesame seeds, for serving

Preheat the oven to 400°F (200°F) and oil a baking sheet with canola or olive oil.

Chop the Brussels sprouts in half. Place them, cut side down, on the prepared baking sheet. Roast in the oven for 30 to 35 minutes, or until fork-tender, flipping halfway through.

Meanwhile, in a medium-sized bowl, combine the gochujang, sesame oil and mirin and whisk well.

Once roasted, stir the Brussels sprouts into the sauce. Serve topped with sesame seeds.

Sweet Fire Tofu

This is our spin on a nonvegan takeout dish that we grew up eating. For this recipe, we pair crispy tofu, veggies and pineapple with a thick, sweet and spicy sauce. Serve it over a bed of Perfect White Rice (page 350), topped with green onion and sesame seeds.

PREP TIME:
20 minutes, plus inactive time to press tofu

COOK TIME:
about 25 minutes

YIELD:
4 servings

CRISPY TOFU
1 (14- to 16-oz [396- to 453-g]) block firm or extra-firm tofu

⅓ cup (40 g) cornstarch

¼ cup (60 ml) canola oil

VEGETABLES
1 tbsp (15 ml) canola oil

1 red bell pepper, sliced (about 1 cup [149 g])

½ medium-sized white onion, sliced (about ½ cup [80 g])

2 cups (370 g) diced fresh ripe pineapple (1" [2.5-cm] cubes), or frozen (defrosted), or canned (drained and rinsed)

3 cloves garlic, peeled and minced, or 1 tbsp (9 g) jarred minced garlic

SWEET FIRE SAUCE
2 tsp (5 g) cornstarch

7 tbsp (105 ml) water, divided

¼ cup (60 ml) unseasoned rice vinegar

¼ cup (50 g) granulated sugar

1 tbsp (15 ml) soy sauce (or tamari for gluten-free)

1 tbsp (15 ml) chili garlic sauce

FOR SERVING
Chopped green onion

Sesame seeds

Make the crispy tofu: Drain the tofu and slice lengthwise into four long, equal slices. Press the slices (see page 358 for tutorial). Cut each slice into ½- to 1-inch (1.3- to 2.5-cm) cubes (40 to 50 total). In a large bowl, combine the tofu pieces and cornstarch. Gently shake the bowl to coat all the pieces with cornstarch (alternatively, you can coat each piece separately).

In a large skillet, heat the canola oil over medium heat. Carefully transfer the cornstarch-coated tofu to the pan, leaving excess cornstarch in the bowl. Cook, stirring occasionally, for 7 to 10 minutes, or until the tofu pieces are crispy on all sides.

Prepare the vegetables: In a large sauté pan, heat the canola oil over medium heat. Add the bell pepper, onion and pineapple. Cook for about 7 minutes, or until the bell pepper is fork-tender and the onion becomes translucent. Add the garlic and cook for 30 seconds to 1 minute, or until fragrant. Remove from the heat and set aside.

Prepare the sauce: In a small bowl, combine the cornstarch with 1 tablespoon (15 ml) of the water. Set aside. In a large sauté pan over medium-low heat, whisk together the remaining 6 tablespoons (90 ml) of water, the rice vinegar, sugar, soy sauce and chili garlic sauce. Increase the heat to medium-high and bring the mixture to a gentle boil, whisking constantly. Whisk in the cornstarch slurry. Lower the heat to low, bringing the sauce to a simmer. Let the sauce cook, whisking often, until it becomes thick and sticky, 3 to 5 minutes. Stir in the tofu and cooked vegetables.

Serve topped with green onion and sesame seeds.

Coconut Panko Tofu
with Peanut Sauce
(page 138)

Red Coconut Curry Noodles

This recipe is inspired by a dish from one of our favorite restaurants. These noodles are saucy, flavorful and a little bit spicy. Top them with our Baked Tofu (page 334) or serve them as a side to our Coconut Panko Tofu with Peanut Sauce (page 138).

PREP TIME:
10 minutes

COOK TIME:
about 10 minutes, plus time to cook noodles

YIELD:
6 to 8 servings

1½ tsp (7 ml) pure (untoasted) sesame oil

4 cloves garlic, peeled and minced, or 4 tsp (13 g) jarred minced garlic

1 (15.5-oz [439-ml]) can full-fat coconut milk

3 tbsp (45 g) red curry paste

¼ cup (60 ml) soy sauce (or tamari for gluten-free, or coconut aminos for soy-free)

2 tbsp (30 ml) pure maple syrup or agave

1 tbsp (15 ml) chili garlic sauce

1 (14-oz [396-g]) package medium-width rice noodles

FOR SERVING (OPTIONAL)
½ cup (52 g) fresh bean sprouts

¼ cup (22 g) diced green onion

2 tbsp (2 g) minced fresh cilantro leaves

¼ cup (37 g) crushed peanuts (omit for nut-free)

Sesame seeds

In a large skillet, heat the sesame oil over medium-low heat. Stir in the garlic and cook for 30 seconds to 1 minute, or until fragrant. Stir in the coconut milk, curry paste, soy sauce, maple syrup and chili garlic sauce and increase the heat to medium-high, bringing the sauce to a boil. Lower the heat to low, bringing the sauce to a simmer. Simmer, stirring occasionally, for 7 to 10 minutes, or until thickened.

Meanwhile, prepare the rice noodles according to the package instructions. Drain and rinse in cold water.

Stir the cooked noodles into the sauce. Serve topped with bean sprouts, green onion, cilantro, peanuts and sesame seeds, if desired.

Coconut Panko Tofu with Peanut Sauce

This is one of our favorite ways to enjoy tofu because it's so flavorful. The coconut milk and panko coating give the tofu a perfectly crisp outer texture that will impress even the pickiest of eaters. Enjoy it as is or serve it on top of our Coconut Rice (page 351) or Perfect White Rice (page 350) with a side of Red Coconut Curry Noodles (page 137).

PREP TIME:	COOK TIME:	YIELD:
30 minutes, plus inactive time to press tofu	*40 minutes*	*4 servings*

COCONUT PANKO TOFU

1 (14-oz [396-g]) block firm or extra-firm tofu

Canola or olive oil (or spray version), for pan

¼ cup (31 g) all-purpose flour

½ cup (120 ml) canned full-fat coconut milk, stirred well before measuring

1 cup (60 g) vegan panko bread crumbs

COCONUT PEANUT SAUCE

½ cup (120 ml) canned full-fat coconut milk, stirred well before measuring

¼ cup (65 g) creamy peanut butter

1 tbsp (15 ml) pure maple syrup

1 tbsp (15 ml) low-sodium soy sauce or tamari

Juice of ¼ lime (about 1½ tsp [7 ml])

Salt to taste

Make the coconut panko tofu: Drain the tofu and slice lengthwise into four long, equal slices. Press the slices (see page 358 for tutorial). Cut each slice into ½- to 1-inch (1.3- to 2.5-cm) cubes (40 to 50 total).

Preheat the oven to 400°F (200°C) and oil a baking sheet with canola or olive oil. Set aside.

Line up three bowls. Add the flour to the first, the coconut milk to the second and the panko to the third. Dip each piece of tofu into the flour, then the coconut milk, then coat with the panko. Place on the prepared baking sheet. Bake for 40 minutes, flipping halfway through.

Meanwhile, make the coconut peanut sauce: In a small bowl, whisk together the coconut milk, peanut butter, maple syrup, soy sauce and lime juice until smooth. If desired, heat the coconut peanut sauce in the microwave or on the stovetop over low heat until warmed. Taste and add salt as desired. Serve the tofu drizzled with the peanut sauce.

*See in Red Coconut Curry Noodles image on page 136.

Veggie Fried Rice

Looking for a quick and easy restaurant-style fried rice recipe? Well, look no further. This recipe uses simple ingredients, comes together in less than 30 minutes and is packed full of flavor. The best part about making fried rice at home is that you can adjust the veggies based on what you have on hand. It's also a great way to use up that leftover rice you have sitting in the fridge. Serve this by itself or as a side to just about any recipe in this chapter.

PREP TIME:
10 minutes, plus prep time for rice

COOK TIME:
about 15 minutes

YIELD:
4 servings

2 tbsp (28 g) vegan butter (nut-free and/or soy-free if needed)

1 medium-sized onion, chopped small (about 1 cup [160 g])

1 cup (110 g) shredded carrots

1 cup (134 g) frozen peas

3 cloves garlic, peeled and minced, or 1 tbsp (9 g) jarred minced garlic

3 cups (500 g) Perfect White Rice (1 batch [page 350]) (see Sister Tip)

¼ cup (60 ml) low-sodium soy sauce (or tamari for gluten-free, or coconut aminos for soy-free)

1 tsp sesame oil

1 tsp garlic powder

FOR SERVING
2 green onions, chopped

Sesame seeds

In a large skillet or wok, melt the butter over medium heat. Add the onion and carrots and cook, stirring occasionally, for 5 to 7 minutes, or until the onion becomes translucent and the carrot is fork-tender.

Add the peas and garlic and cook for another minute, or until the garlic is fragrant. Add the rice and soy sauce and stir to mix well. Cook, stirring constantly, for about 3 minutes. Stir in the sesame oil and garlic powder and cook for another minute.

Serve topped with the green onions and sesame seeds.

Sister Tip

For best results, chill your prepared rice prior to using in this recipe. This makes the rice easier to separate and decreases the chances of your fried rice turning out mushy.

...ter Tofu

Inspired by the traditional Indian dish butter chicken, this veganized recipe pairs crispy tofu with a perfectly spiced coconut milk–based sauce. It's delicious and should definitely be added to your weekly dinner rotation. We love it served with Turmeric Rice (page 142) and vegan naan.

PREP TIME:
10 minutes, plus inactive time to press tofu

COOK TIME:
25 to 30 minutes

YIELD:
4 servings

1 (14- to 16-oz [396- to 453-g]) block firm or extra-firm tofu

⅓ cup (40 g) cornstarch

¼ cup (56 g) vegan butter (nut-free if needed)

1 medium-sized yellow onion, chopped small (about 1 cup [160 g])

3 cloves garlic, peeled and minced, or 1 tbsp (9 g) jarred minced garlic

1 (13.5-oz [400-ml]) can light coconut milk

1 (14.5-oz [411-g]) can crushed tomatoes

1 tbsp (15 g) tomato paste

1 tsp curry powder

1 tsp ground coriander

½ tsp ground ginger

2 tsp (5 g) ground cumin

⅛ tsp ground cinnamon

⅛ tsp ground cloves

⅛ tsp ground nutmeg

½ tsp salt

⅛ tsp freshly ground black pepper

Chopped fresh cilantro, for serving

Drain the tofu and slice lengthwise into four long, equal slices. Press the slices (see page 358 for tutorial). Use your hands to break each piece of tofu into six pieces, creating 24 roughly torn chunks. In a large bowl, combine the tofu chunks and cornstarch. Gently shake the bowl to coat all the pieces with cornstarch (alternatively, you can coat each piece separately).

In a large skillet, melt the butter over medium heat. Carefully transfer the cornstarch-coated tofu to the pan, leaving excess cornstarch in the bowl. Cook, stirring occasionally, for 7 to 10 minutes, or until the tofu pieces are crispy on all sides.

Add the onion and cook, stirring often, for 5 to 7 minutes, or until translucent. Add the garlic and cook, stirring constantly, for 30 seconds to 1 minute, or until fragrant. Stir in the coconut milk, crushed tomatoes, tomato paste, curry powder, coriander, ginger, cumin, cinnamon, cloves, nutmeg, salt and pepper. Increase the heat to medium-high and bring the mixture to a gentle boil. Lower the heat to low, bringing the mixture to a simmer.

Allow to simmer, uncovered, stirring occasionally, for about 10 minutes, or until thick and creamy. Serve topped with fresh cilantro.

Turmeric Rice
(page 142)

Turmeric Rice

This flavorful rice is easy to prepare, made in one pot and is filled with aromatic spices that are absolute perfection. It is a delicious side dish for many dishes, including our Butter Tofu (page 140).

PREP TIME:
5 minutes

COOK TIME:
about 30 minutes

YIELD:
6 to 8 servings

2 cups (360 g) uncooked basmati rice

2 tbsp (28 g) vegan butter (nut-free and/or soy-free if needed)

2 medium-sized yellow onions, peeled and chopped (about 2 cups [320 g])

3 cloves garlic, peeled and minced, or 1 tbsp (9 g) jarred minced garlic

½ tsp ground mustard

½ tsp ground coriander

¼ tsp ground turmeric

½ tsp ground cumin

¼ tsp freshly ground black pepper

½ tsp salt, plus more to taste

3 cups (720 ml) vegetable broth (see Sister Tip)

Rinse the rice in a strainer until the water runs clear. Set aside.

In a large saucepan, heat the butter over medium heat. Stir in the onions. Let cook for 5 to 7 minutes, until translucent. Stir in the garlic, ground mustard, coriander, turmeric, cumin and black pepper and cook for another minute, or until the garlic is fragrant. Stir in the rice and salt and cook for 1 minute, stirring constantly. Add the vegetable broth and cover the pot. Increase the heat to high and bring the mixture to a boil. Once boiling, stir well, then lower the heat to low, bringing it to a simmer.

Simmer, covered, for 13 to 17 minutes, or until all the broth has been absorbed. Remove from the heat and let it sit for 10 minutes with the lid on. Fluff with a fork, season with more salt, if desired, and serve.

*See in Butter Tofu image on the previous page.

Sister Tip

Don't have any vegetable broth on hand? You can use water and still yield a delicious dish. Make sure to add extra salt to taste.

Summer Rolls with Peanut Dipping Sauce

These summer rolls are light, fresh and tasty. They make the perfect appetizer, side dish or even light lunch or snack. We prefer to dip them in our peanut dipping sauce (recipe below), but you can dip them in whatever you please! The best part about these rolls is that they are easily adaptable. We loaded ours with tofu, veggies and herbs. Feel free to substitute or omit any ingredients to your liking—although we are partial to this combination of flavors and encourage you to try them.

— PREP TIME: —	— COOK TIME: —	— YIELD: —
25 minutes, plus inactive time to press tofu	*25 minutes*	*6 rolls*

BAKED TOFU
1 (14- to 16-oz [396- to 453-g]) block firm or extra-firm tofu (omit for soy-free)

Canola or olive oil (or spray version), for pan (optional)

PEANUT SAUCE
6 tbsp (90 ml) soy sauce (or tamari for gluten-free, or coconut aminos for soy-free)

¼ cup (64 g) creamy peanut butter

2 tbsp (30 ml) pure maple syrup

½ tsp garlic powder

2 tsp (10 ml) sesame oil

2 tsp (10 g) vegan sriracha

TO ASSEMBLE
6 rice paper wrappers

1¼ cups (138 g) shredded carrots

1¼ cups (94 g) shredded romaine lettuce

1 medium-sized cucumber, sliced into 12 long, thin sticks

1 large avocado, peeled, pitted and cut into 12 slices

1 tbsp (3 g) chopped fresh basil

1 tbsp (1 g) chopped fresh cilantro

1 tbsp (6 g) chopped fresh mint

Make the baked tofu: Drain the tofu and slice lengthwise into four long, equal slices. Press the slices (see page 358 for tutorial).

Preheat the oven to 400°F (200°C) and prepare a baking sheet by oiling with oil or lining with parchment paper. Cut each slice of pressed tofu into three long, equal pieces, creating twelve pieces. Place on the prepared baking sheet. Bake for 20 to 25 minutes, until lightly golden brown. Remove from the oven and set aside to cool completely.

Prepare the peanut sauce: In a small bowl, whisk together all the peanut sauce ingredients and set aside.

Assemble the summer rolls: Working 1 at a time, submerge a rice paper wrapper in lukewarm water for 5 to 10 seconds (or according to package instructions). Place the wrapper on a clean cutting board with about 1 inch (2.5 cm) of the wrapper hanging off the edge (this will help when you begin folding your summer roll). Place two pieces of tofu in the middle of the wrapper. Top with a small handful of carrots (about 3 heaping tablespoons [23 g]), a small handful of lettuce (about 3 heaping tablespoons [15 g]), 2 sticks of cucumber and 2 slices of avocado. Top with ½ teaspoon each of fresh basil, cilantro and mint. Roll your summer roll by folding over the sides first and then the bottom. Continue by rolling the wrapper upward (similar to rolling a burrito), until you have the desired shape.

Repeat with the other wrappers until you have rolled all six summer rolls. Serve with the peanut sauce.

*See in Coconut Curry image on the next page.

**Summer Rolls with
Peanut Dipping Sauce
(page 143)**

Coconut Curry

This chapter would not be complete without a coconut curry recipe. This dish has easily become a weekly staple in Emily's house. It's perfect for those nights when you want to curl up on the couch with a big bowl of warm comfort food. This recipe calls for some ingredients you may only find at an Asian market, but don't worry, you can easily substitute more widely available options as we've noted below. That being said, if you can find makrut lime leaves near you, we highly recommend using them. They add a vibrant, aromatic flavor that will transform your curry. This dish is best served over Perfect White Rice (page 350) and with a side of our Summer Rolls with Peanut Dipping Sauce (page 143).

PREP TIME:
25 minutes

COOK TIME:
30 minutes

YIELD:
6 to 8 servings

1 tbsp (15 ml) olive oil

1 acorn squash, peeled, seeded and chopped (about 3 cups [453 g])

1 Japanese or standard eggplant, chopped (about 3 cups [300 g])

1 (4-oz [113-g]) can Thai curry paste (see Sister Tip)

2 (14-oz [400-ml]) cans full-fat coconut milk

4 makrut lime leaves, chopped (about 1 tbsp [1 g]) (can substitute with 1 tsp lime zest if needed)

1 (4- to 6-oz [113- to 170-g]) package beech mushrooms, trimmed and separated, or chopped mushrooms of choice

2 cups (170 g) chopped yu choy sum, or chopped leafy greens of choice (such as bok choy or baby spinach) (chopped into about 1" [2.5-cm] pieces)

¼ cup (8 g) roughly chopped fresh basil

In a wok or large skillet, heat the oil over medium-high heat. Add the acorn squash and let cook, stirring occasionally, for 5 to 6 minutes. Add the eggplant and let cook for about 3 minutes. Add the curry paste and stir well to combine. Add the coconut milk and mix well. Increase the heat to high, bringing the mixture to a gentle boil, then lower the heat to low, bringing it to a simmer. Stir in the makrut lime leaves.

Let simmer, stirring occasionally, for about 10 minutes, or until the squash has softened. Add the mushrooms, leafy greens and basil and let simmer, stirring occasionally, for an additional 10 minutes. Serve warm.

Sister Tip

Feel free to use your favorite type of curry paste for this recipe—red, green, massaman, panang and so on; all work perfectly for this recipe. For a deliciously spicy curry, we recommend the Maesri brand of curry paste, which can typically be found at an Asian market.

Peanut Tofu and Broccoli

This dish is influenced by an old recipe of ours that we have been making for years (if you're familiar with our blog, you may remember our classic Peanut Tofu recipe). For this particular recipe, we pair tofu and broccoli with a creamy, peanutty coconut sauce that is absolutely delightful. Pair it with Perfect White Rice (page 350) or Coconut Rice (page 351).

PREP TIME:
10 minutes, plus inactive time to press tofu

COOK TIME:
15 to 20 minutes

YIELD:
4 servings

TOFU AND BROCCOLI

1 (14- to 16-oz [396- to 453-g]) block extra-firm tofu or superfirm tofu (see Sister Tip)

2 tbsp (30 ml) olive oil

3 cups (273 g) chopped broccoli

SAUCE

1½ tsp (4 g) cornstarch

1½ tsp (7 ml) water

¼ cup (60 ml) low-sodium soy sauce (or tamari for gluten-free)

¼ cup (65 g) creamy peanut butter

1 tbsp (15 ml) unseasoned rice vinegar

2 tbsp (30 ml) pure maple syrup or agave

1 tbsp (15 g) vegan sriracha

3 cloves garlic, peeled and minced, or 1 tbsp (9 g) jarred minced garlic

1 (½" [1.3-cm]) piece fresh ginger, peeled and minced

½ cup (120 ml) canned full-fat coconut milk, stirred well before measuring

FOR SERVING

Chopped green onion

Sesame seeds

Make the tofu and broccoli: Drain the tofu and slice lengthwise into four long, equal slices. Press the slices (see page 358 for tutorial). Use your hands to break each piece of tofu into six pieces, creating 24 roughly torn chunks. Heat the oil in a large sauté pan over medium heat. Add the tofu and broccoli. Cook, stirring often, for 10 to 15 minutes, or until the broccoli is fork-tender.

Meanwhile, prepare the sauce: In a small bowl, combine the cornstarch with the water, and set aside. In medium-sized bowl, whisk together the remaining sauce ingredients. Add to the tofu mixture. Increase the heat to medium-high, bringing the mixture to a gentle boil. Add the cornstarch slurry and stir to combine. Lower the heat to low, bringing the mixture to a simmer. Let cook, stirring often, for 1 to 2 minutes, or until the sauce becomes thick, then serve topped with green onion and sesame seeds.

Sister Tip

If you can get your hands on superfirm tofu, that works very well in this recipe with no need for pressing.

Sticky Sesame
Cauliflower
(page 151)

Steamed Bao Buns with Crispy Sesame Tofu

We'll be honest, this dish takes a bit of prep work and more effort than the average recipe, but trust us when we say it's 100 percent worth it. These steamed buns are soft and fluffy and pair perfectly with the crispy sesame tofu. Topped with hoisin, green onion and sesame seeds, these buns are the absolute perfect combination of flavors. Serve them as an entrée, appetizer or side dish paired with our Sticky Sesame Cauliflower (page 151). We promise, you won't be disappointed.

PREP TIME:
40 minutes, plus inactive time for rising and to press tofu

COOK TIME:
about 40 minutes

YIELD:
20 buns

STEAMED BUNS
½ cup (120 ml) warm water (heated to 100 to 110°F [37 to 43°C])

1 tsp + 1 tbsp (16 g) granulated sugar, divided

2¼ tsp (1 [7-g] packet) active dry yeast

2½ to 3 cups (312 to 375 g) all-purpose flour (spooned and leveled or weighed [see page 359 for How to Measure Flour]), plus more for kneading if needed

1 tsp salt

½ cup (120 ml) plain, unsweetened soy milk

FOR RISING
1½ tsp (7 ml) canola oil, plus more as needed for brushing

Make the bun dough: In a small bowl, whisk together the warm water with 1 teaspoon of the sugar. Sprinkle the yeast on top and whisk until it is mostly dissolved. Set aside for 5 to 10 minutes, until the mixture has foamed.

Meanwhile, in the bowl of a stand mixer fitted with the hook attachment, or in a large bowl, stir together 2½ cups (312 g) of the flour, the salt and the remaining tablespoon (12 g) of sugar. Once the yeast mixture has foamed, add it to the flour mixture along with the soy milk. Beat the mixture on low speed or stir with a rubber scraper or wooden spoon, scraping the sides as necessary, until you have a soft but manageable dough. Add more flour, up to ½ cup (62 g), as needed, to ensure the dough is not too sticky to handle.

Either beat the dough in the stand mixer on low speed for 5 to 7 minutes, or transfer the dough to a lightly floured surface and knead by hand for 5 to 7 minutes, incorporating more flour as needed so that the dough does not stick to the sides of the bowl or to your hands. The dough is ready when you gently press into it and it slowly bounces back. Coat a large bowl with the canola oil. Form the dough into a ball and place in the bowl. Turn to lightly coat the ball with the oil. Place a clean towel over the bowl. Let rest in a warm place until the dough has doubled in size, about 1 hour.

(continued)

CRISPY TOFU

1 (14- to 16-oz [396- to 453-g]) block extra-firm tofu

⅓ cup (40 g) cornstarch

¼ cup (60 ml) canola oil

SESAME SAUCE

2 tsp (5 g) cornstarch

¼ cup (60 ml) water

2 tbsp (30 ml) pure (untoasted) sesame oil

4 cloves garlic, peeled and minced, or 4 tsp (12 g) jarred minced garlic

2 tbsp (30 ml) pure maple syrup or agave

⅓ cup (80 ml) low-sodium soy sauce

1½ tsp (7 ml) chili garlic sauce

FOR SERVING

Green onion, chopped into 1" (2.5-cm) pieces

Vegan hoisin sauce

Sesame seeds

Vegan kimchi (optional)

Vegan sriracha (optional)

Begin the crispy tofu: While the dough rises, drain the tofu and slice lengthwise into four long, equal slices. Press the slices (see page 358 for tutorial).

Shape the bun dough: Once the dough has doubled in size, divide it into 20 equal-sized balls. One at a time, using a rolling pin or forming by hand, flatten each ball of dough into a circle about 4 inches (10 cm) in diameter and ¼ inch (6 mm) thick. Lightly brush the surface of each circle of dough with canola oil. Fold each circle in half, creating semicircles. For easy transfer later, place each bun on a small square of parchment paper. Once all the buns have been formed, lightly cover them with plastic wrap or a clean towel and allow to rise again until doubled in size, 30 minutes to an hour.

Finish the crispy tofu: While the dough rises again, cut each slice of pressed tofu into five long, equal slices, then cut each long slice in half (creating 40 pieces). In a large bowl, add the tofu pieces and cornstarch. Gently shake the bowl to coat all the pieces with cornstarch (alternatively, you can coat each piece separately).

In a large skillet, heat the canola oil over medium heat. Carefully transfer the cornstarch-coated tofu to the pan, leaving excess cornstarch in the bowl. Cook, stirring occasionally, for 7 to 10 minutes, or until the tofu pieces are crispy on all sides. Remove from the heat and set aside.

Make the sesame sauce: In a small bowl, combine the cornstarch with the water. Set aside. In a large sauté pan, heat the sesame oil over medium heat. Stir in the garlic and cook for 30 seconds to 1 minute, or until fragrant. Add the maple syrup, soy sauce and chili garlic sauce. Whisk to combine. Increase the heat to medium-high, bringing the mixture to a gentle boil. Add the cornstarch slurry to the saucepan and whisk to combine. Lower the heat to low, bringing the mixture to a simmer. Let simmer, whisking often, for 3 to 5 minutes, or until the sauce becomes thick and sticky. Gently stir in the crispy tofu. Remove from the heat and set aside.

Steam the buns: Once the buns have doubled in size, fill a deep skillet that can fit your bamboo steamer with about 2 inches (5 cm) of water and bring to a boil over high heat. Working in batches, if necessary, place the buns (still on their parchment paper) in the bamboo steamer, leaving 1 inch (2.5 cm) between each bun. Place the bamboo steamer in the skillet and steam for 7 minutes.

Serve each bun by carefully opening and filling with two pieces of the crispy sesame tofu, one to two pieces of chopped green onion, a drizzle of hoisin sauce and a sprinkle of sesame seeds. Top with kimchi and a drizzle of sriracha, if desired.

Sticky Sesame Cauliflower

Cauliflower is truly such a versatile, underrated vegetable that can be prepared so many different ways. For us, the best way to enjoy it is by frying it to perfection and tossing it in a flavorful sesame sauce. For this recipe, you'll batter and fry the cauliflower until crispy, then toss it in a thick, sticky sauce that comes together with just eight main ingredients. Serve it over Perfect White Rice (page 350) or as a side dish paired with Cold Peanut Noodles (page 127) or Steamed Bao Buns with Crispy Sesame Tofu (page 149).

PREP TIME:
15 minutes

COOK TIME:
30 to 35 minutes

YIELD:
6 to 8 servings

FRIED CAULIFLOWER

1 cup (125 g) all-purpose flour

1 cup (240 ml) water

½ tsp onion powder

½ tsp garlic powder

¼ tsp salt

¼ tsp freshly ground black pepper

Canola oil, for frying

1 large or 2 small heads cauliflower, chopped into bite-sized pieces (about 18 oz [510 g] chopped)

SESAME SAUCE

1 tbsp (8 g) cornstarch

1 tbsp (15 ml) water

2 tbsp (30 ml) pure (untoasted) sesame oil

3 cloves garlic, peeled and minced, or 1 tbsp (9 g) jarred minced garlic

2 tbsp (30 ml) unseasoned rice vinegar

¼ cup (60 ml) pure maple syrup or agave

¼ cup (55 g) packed light brown sugar

½ cup (120 ml) soy sauce (or coconut aminos for soy-free)

¼ cup (60 ml) sweet chili sauce

FOR TOPPING

Sesame seeds

Chopped green onion

Make the fried cauliflower: In a medium-sized bowl, whisk together the flour, water, onion powder, garlic powder, salt and pepper.

In a deep saucepan or pot, heat 2 inches (5 cm) of oil to 350°F (180°C), or use a deep fryer according to the manufacturer's instructions. Dip each piece of cauliflower into the flour mixture and place in the oil, working in batches if necessary. Fry for 6 to 10 minutes, stirring around occasionally, until golden brown. Remove from the oil and set on paper towels to absorb any extra oil.

Make the sesame sauce: In a small bowl, combine the cornstarch with the water. Set aside. In a large sauté pan, heat the sesame oil over medium heat. Stir in the garlic and cook for 30 seconds to 1 minute, or until fragrant. Add the rice vinegar, maple syrup, brown sugar, soy sauce and sweet chili sauce. Whisk to combine. Increase the heat to medium-high, bringing the mixture to a gentle boil.

Add the cornstarch slurry and whisk to combine. Lower the heat to low, bringing the mixture to a simmer. Let simmer, whisking often, for 3 to 5 minutes, or until the sauce becomes thick.

Stir in the fried cauliflower. Remove from the heat and serve topped with sesame seeds and green onions.

*See in Steamed Bao Buns with Crispy Sesame Tofu image on page 148.

Rice Bowls with Marinated Tofu and Gochujang Sauce

Inspired by the classic Korean staple bibimbap, these rice bowls are loaded with our favorite veggies, marinated tofu, vegan kimchi and a sweet and spicy gochujang sauce. Don't be afraid to create your own variation of this recipe by substituting for your favorite veggies or vegan protein—it's great for using up leftovers or getting rid of veggies that are just sitting in your fridge.

PREP TIME:

25 minutes, plus prep time for Perfect White Rice and inactive time to press and marinate tofu

COOK TIME:

about 25 minutes

YIELD:

4 bowls

MARINATED TOFU

1 (14- to 16-oz [396- to 453-g]) block extra-firm tofu

½ cup (120 ml) low-sodium soy sauce (or tamari for gluten-free)

2 tbsp (30 ml) mirin

2 tsp (10 ml) pure (untoasted) sesame oil

2 cloves garlic, peeled and minced, or 2 tsp (6 g) jarred minced garlic

1 tbsp (15 ml) olive oil

GOCHUJANG SAUCE

¼ cup (67 g) gochujang (see Sister Tips) (gluten-free if needed)

2 tbsp (30 ml) mirin

2 tsp (10 ml) sesame oil

1 tbsp (15 ml) soy sauce (or tamari for gluten-free)

1 (1½" [4-cm]) piece fresh ginger, peeled and minced

VEGGIES

2 tsp (10 ml) unseasoned rice vinegar

2 tsp (10 ml) soy sauce (or tamari for gluten-free)

Marinate the tofu: Slice the tofu lengthwise into four long, equal slices. Press the slices (see page 358 for tutorial). Cut each slice into ½- to 1-inch (1.3- to 2.5-cm) cubes (40 to 50 total). In a medium-sized bowl, whisk together the soy sauce, mirin, sesame oil and garlic. Add the tofu pieces to the marinade and mix well so that all pieces have been submerged. Let the tofu marinate for at least 30 minutes.

Make the gochujang sauce: In a small bowl, whisk together all the sauce ingredients. Set aside.

Prepare the veggies: In a small bowl, combine the rice vinegar and soy sauce and set aside.

Bring a large pot of water to a boil. Add the sweet potato to the boiling water and let cook for 5 to 7 minutes, or until fork-tender. Drain the sweet potato and set aside.

Heat a large wok (see Sister Tips) over high heat. Add 1 teaspoon of the olive oil along with the broccoli. Toss to coat the broccoli with the oil. Let the broccoli cook, tossing frequently, for 4 to 5 minutes, to lightly char but not burn (if you prefer softer broccoli, let cook for a bit longer). Remove from the wok and set aside.

Add another teaspoon of oil to the same wok (don't bother cleaning it) along with the carrot and let cook, tossing frequently, for 1 to 2 minutes. Add the rice vinegar mixture and toss to combine. Let the carrot cook, tossing occasionally, for another 1 to 2 minutes. Remove from the wok and set aside.

1 medium- to large-sized sweet potato, peeled and diced (2 heaping cups [320 g])

3 tsp (15 ml) olive oil, divided

4 cups (220 g) chopped broccoli

1 cup (110 g) shredded carrot

1 (4- to 6-oz [113- to 170-g]) package shiitake mushrooms, chopped

4 green onions, cut into 1 to 2" (2.5- to 5-cm) pieces

FOR SERVING

4½ cups (750 g) Perfect White Rice (1½ batches [page 350])

1 cup (224 g) vegan kimchi

Sesame seeds

Sister Tips

We prefer the Haechandle brand of gochujang. You can usually find it at an Asian market, in a red container. If you can't find that particular brand, any more widely available option will work.

If you don't have a wok, you can use a large skillet over medium-high heat. The veggies and tofu may take slightly longer to cook, so adjust the cook time accordingly.

Add the remaining 1 teaspoon of oil to the wok along with the shiitake mushrooms and toss to combine. Let the mushrooms cook, tossing frequently, for about 2 minutes. Remove from the wok and set aside.

Add the green onions to the wok. Cook for 1 to 2 minutes, then flip the green onions and allow to cook for another minute. Remove from the heat and set aside.

Prepare the tofu: Add 1 tablespoon (15 ml) of olive oil to the wok and add the tofu along with the excess marinade. Let the tofu cook, stirring frequently so that it does not stick, for 4 to 5 minutes, or until the sauce reduces and the tofu turns a deep brown. Remove from the wok and set aside.

If any of the dishes are now cold, you can microwave them to warm them. Assemble your bowls by evenly splitting the rice, veggies and tofu among them. Top evenly with the gochujang sauce, kimchi and a sprinkle of sesame seeds.

HANDHELDS

We've always loved creating different sandwiches with ingredients we have on hand. From a fresh Pesto Mozzarella Melt (page 160) in the summer to a crispy Garlic Bread Grilled Cheese (page 163) in the winter, we have developed a variety of comforting recipes, no matter the season. Encompassing sliders, wraps and sandwiches, this chapter is packed full of recipes meant to be eaten with your hands. Whether you're looking for Crispy Buffalo Tofu Sliders (page 173), Hannah's favorite, or a Seitan Gyro with Tzatziki Sauce (page 182), we've got you covered. These handhelds are great served on their own or paired with Fries (Baked or Fried) (page 259) or any recipe found in our Not Your Average Soups and Salads chapter (pages 189 to 211).

Tofu Parm Melt

This melt combines crispy breaded tofu with marinara sauce and vegan Mozzarella (page 340). It's a favorite in our house because it's easy and downright delicious. Serve it with a side of Fries (Baked or Fried) (page 259) and White Jackfruit Chili (page 197).

PREP TIME:
15 minutes, plus inactive time to press tofu

COOK TIME:
45 to 47 minutes

YIELD:
4 sandwiches

1 (14- to 16-oz [396- to 453-g]) block firm or extra-firm tofu

Nonstick cooking spray

FLOUR COATING
¼ cup (31 g) all-purpose flour

⅓ cup (80 ml) plain, unsweetened soy milk

PANKO COATING
1 cup (60 g) vegan panko bread crumbs

½ tsp onion powder

½ tsp garlic powder

½ tsp dried oregano

⅛ tsp dried thyme

¼ tsp dried rosemary

¼ tsp dried sage

¼ tsp dried basil

¼ tsp salt

Pinch of black pepper

FOR ASSEMBLING
4 (6" [15-cm]) baguette slices, sliced in half lengthwise, or vegan hoagie rolls

1 cup (240 g) vegan marinara sauce, divided

1 cup (113 g) vegan Mozzarella shreds (page 340) or store-bought, divided (nut-free if needed)

¼ cup (25 g) vegan Parmesan Cheese (page 342) or store-bought, divided (nut-free if needed)

Press the tofu: Drain the tofu and slice into eight long, equal slices. Press the slices (see page 358 for tutorial).

Coat and bake the tofu: Preheat the oven to 400°F (200°C) and spray a baking sheet with nonstick cooking spray or line it with parchment paper. In a small bowl, mix together the flour and milk. In a separate small bowl, stir together all the panko coating ingredients. Dip each slice of tofu into the flour coating, then the panko coating, entirely coating each slice, then place on the prepared baking sheet.

Spray the tofu with nonstick spray. Bake for 40 minutes, flipping halfway through and spraying both sides with nonstick cooking spray. Once done, remove from the oven, keeping the oven on, and set aside.

Assemble the sandwiches: Coat the insides of each baguette slice with ¼ cup (60 g) of marinara sauce, then evenly sprinkle ¼ cup (28 g) of mozzarella and 1 tablespoon (6 g) of Parmesan on top. Add two slices of baked tofu to each sandwich. Place, open-faced, on an ungreased baking sheet and bake until the bread is crispy and the cheese has melted, 5 to 7 minutes. Serve immediately.

Tofu Patty Melt

Gluten-free option,
Nut-free option

This melt is absolute perfection. It's loaded with flavorful baked tofu, with caramelized onions, vegan cheese and homemade Thousand Island dressing, all served between crispy bread. This recipe calls for slices of bread, but feel free to use whatever you have on hand—vegan hoagie rolls, burger buns and pita bread all work just as great.

PREP TIME:
20 minutes, plus inactive time to press tofu

COOK TIME:
1 hour

YIELD:
4 sandwiches

BASTED TOFU
1 (14- to 16-oz [396- to 453-g]) block firm or extra-firm tofu

¼ cup (60 ml) low-sodium soy sauce (or tamari for gluten-free)

1 tbsp (15 ml) pure maple syrup

1 tbsp (15 ml) Worcestershire sauce (gluten-free if needed)

½ tsp garlic powder

½ tsp onion powder

½ tsp paprika

⅛ tsp freshly ground black pepper

1 tbsp (15 ml) olive oil, plus more as needed, to panfry

CARAMELIZED ONION
2 tbsp (28 g) vegan butter (nut-free if needed)

1 medium-sized white onion, sliced into long, thin slices (about 1 cup [160 g])

THOUSAND ISLAND DRESSING
½ cup (120 g) vegan Mayo (page 353) or store-bought

2 tbsp (30 g) ketchup

1 tbsp (15 ml) apple cider vinegar

1½ tsp (6 g) granulated sugar

1 tbsp (15 g) sweet relish

1 tsp minced sweet onion

Pinch of salt and freshly ground black pepper

FOR ASSEMBLING
Vegan butter (nut-free if needed)

8 slices thick-cut vegan bread, such as Texas toast (gluten-free if needed)

4 slices store-bought vegan Cheddar cheese or desired amount of Cheddar shreds (page 341) (nut-free if needed)

Bake the tofu: Drain the tofu and slice into eight long, equal slices. Press the slices (see page 358 for tutorial). Preheat the oven to 400°F (200°C) and line a baking sheet with parchment paper. In a small bowl, stir together the soy sauce, maple syrup, Worcestershire sauce, garlic powder, onion powder, paprika and pepper. Dip each slice of tofu into the sauce and place the pieces in a single later on the prepared baking sheet. Reserve the extra sauce for basting. Bake for 40 minutes, using a pastry brush to baste with the sauce every 10 minutes. At 20 minutes, baste, then flip and baste again.

Caramelize the onion: Meanwhile, in a large skillet, melt the butter over medium heat. Add the onion slices and cook, stirring often, for about 5 minutes. Lower the heat to low and cook, stirring occasionally, for 45 minutes, or until deeply golden brown. Set aside.

Make the dressing: In a small bowl, stir together the mayo, ketchup, vinegar, sugar, relish and onion. Add salt and pepper to taste and set aside.

Panfry the tofu: In a large skillet, heat the olive oil over medium heat. Place the baked tofu in the pan and sauté for 2 to 3 minutes on each side, or until crispy. Remove from the heat and set aside.

Assemble the sandwiches: Butter one side of each slice of bread. For each sandwich, place 1 slice of bread, butter side down, in a skillet over medium heat. Top with two pieces of panfried tofu, a slice of cheese, caramelized onion and another slice of bread, butter side up. Cook for 3 to 5 minutes on each side, or until the bread is golden brown and the cheese is melted. Remove from the heat, open carefully and add Thousand Island dressing to taste. Repeat to make the rest of the sandwiches. Slice and serve immediately.

Pesto Mozzarella Melt

Pesto and mozzarella really is the best combination, especially when melted between toasted, garlicky, buttery ciabatta. This melt is so easy to make—just throw some mozzarella, pesto and tomato between two slices of bread and get cooking. Pair it with "Chicken" Noodle Soup (page 198) or Creamy Tomato Soup (page 194).

PREP TIME:
5 minutes

COOK TIME:
10 minutes

YIELD:
4 sandwiches

4 vegan ciabatta rolls, sliced in half horizontally, or 8 slices vegan bread of choice (gluten-free if needed)

Vegan butter, as needed (nut-free and/or soy-free if needed)

Garlic Salt (page 356) or store-bought, as needed

½ cup (125 g) vegan Pesto (page 352) or store-bought, divided (nut-free if needed)

1 cup (113 g) vegan Mozzarella shreds (page 340) or store-bought, divided (nut-free and/or soy-free if needed)

1 medium-sized beefsteak tomato, sliced into 8 slices

For each half of the ciabatta, spread a thin layer of butter on the outside and sprinkle with your desired amount of garlic salt.

Place a large sauté pan with a lid over medium-low heat. Place the bottom four halves of ciabatta, buttered side down, in the sauté pan (you may need to do this in two batches, depending on the size of the pan). Spread about 2 tablespoons (31 g) of pesto on each piece and sprinkle with about ¼ cup (28 g) of mozzarella. Top each with 2 slices of tomato and place a top of the ciabatta on each, butter side up.

Cover and cook for about 5 minutes, or until the bottom side is golden brown. Flip and cook the other side for 3 to 5 minutes, until the mozzarella is melted and the bread is golden brown. Slice and serve immediately.

*See in "Chicken" Noodle Soup image on page 199.

Spicy Crispy Tofu Pita

This recipe combines crispy tofu (which is baked, not fried!) with homemade Coleslaw (page 258) and spicy ranch. Pair it with our Baked Mac and Cheese (page 86) or Caesar Salad (page 206).

PREP TIME:
15 minutes, plus inactive time to press tofu and prep time for Coleslaw

COOK TIME:
42 minutes

YIELD:
6 pitas

1 (14- to 16-oz [396- to 453-g]) block firm or extra-firm tofu

FLOUR COATING
¼ cup (31 g) all-purpose flour

MAYO COATING
¼ cup (60 g) vegan Mayo (page 353) or store-bought

2 tbsp (30 ml) plain, unsweetened rice milk

1 tbsp (15 ml) hot sauce

PANKO COATING
1 cup (60 g) vegan panko bread crumbs

1 tsp salt

2 tsp (4 g) paprika

¼ tsp cayenne pepper

1½ tsp (4 g) garlic powder

1 tsp onion powder

SPICY RANCH
½ cup (120 ml) vegan Ranch Dressing (page 345) or store-bought (nut-free if needed)

1 tbsp (15 ml) hot sauce, plus more as desired

FOR ASSEMBLING
6 vegan pitas or flour tortillas

1 batch Coleslaw (page 258)

Prepare the tofu: Drain the tofu and slice lengthwise into four long, equal slices. Press the slices (see page 358 for tutorial). Use your hands to break each piece of tofu into six pieces, creating 24 roughly torn chunks.

Coat and bake the tofu: Preheat the oven to 400°F (200°C) and line a large baking sheet with parchment paper. Prepare three medium-sized bowls. Place the flour for the flour coating in one bowl. In the second, stir together the Mayo, rice milk and hot sauce for the mayo coating. In the third, stir together the bread crumbs, salt, paprika, cayenne, garlic powder and onion powder for the panko coating.

Add all the tofu pieces to the flour coating and toss to coat evenly. Using tongs or your hands, transfer the tofu to the bowl of mayo coating and carefully toss to coat each piece evenly. Finally, dip each piece of tofu individually in the panko mixture to coat evenly. Place the pieces in a single layer on the prepared baking sheet.

Bake for 40 minutes, flipping halfway through. Broil on high for 1 to 2 minutes, if desired, to make extra crispy.

Make the spicy ranch: Meanwhile, in a small bowl, mix together the Ranch Dressing and hot sauce.

Assemble the pitas: Crisp up your pitas by placing them on a skillet over medium-high heat until crispy, 1 to 2 minutes on each side. Place four pieces of tofu and an even amount of coleslaw down the center of each toasted pita. Drizzle with about 2 tablespoons (30 ml) of the prepared spicy ranch. If you want more spice, drizzle with extra hot sauce. Fold in the sides, secure each with a toothpick and serve immediately.

*See in Caesar Salad image on page 207.

"Chicken Bacon" Ranch Pita

Homemade seitan is one of our favorite go-to meat substitutes, and it works perfectly in these vegan pita sandwiches. The Steamed Seitan (page 332), Tofu "Bacon" (page 335), avocado and Ranch Dressing (page 345) make for a delicious combination. Serve these pitas with our Fries (Baked or Fried) (page 259) or White Jackfruit Chili (page 197).

PREP TIME:
5 minutes

COOK TIME:
10 minutes

YIELD:
6 pitas

1 batch Steamed Seitan (page 332) or 1 (14-oz [396-g]) bag store-bought vegan chicken strips (gluten-free and/or soy-free if needed)

1 tbsp (15 ml) olive oil

12 slices Tofu "Bacon" (page 335) or store-bought alternative, chopped (gluten-free and/or soy-free if needed)

3 medium-sized ripe avocados, peeled, pitted and sliced

6 vegan pitas (gluten-free if needed)

Shredded iceberg lettuce, for serving

Vegan Ranch Dressing (page 345) or store-bought, for serving (nut-free and/or soy-free if needed)

Slice the Steamed Seitan into strips that are ½ inch (1.3 cm) thick and 1 to 2 inches (2.5 to 5 cm) long.

In a large skillet, heat the oil over medium heat. Add the seitan and cook, stirring occasionally, for 2 to 3 minutes, or until lightly crispy.

Add the chopped "bacon" to the pan and cook, stirring often, for another 2 to 3 minutes, or until crispy. Assemble the pitas by adding an even amount of seitan, "bacon" and avocado slices down the center of each pita. Top with your desired amount of shredded lettuce and ranch dressing. Serve immediately.

*See in White Jackfruit Chili image on page 196.

Garlic Bread Grilled Cheese

Ever since we were kids, we've been making our grilled cheeses like this—by slathering the bread with butter and topping it with garlic salt before slowly cooking it to crispy perfection. In our opinion, this is the only acceptable way to make a grilled cheese—it's just *so* good. Pair this with our Creamy Tomato Soup (page 194) for the ultimate combination.

PREP TIME:
5 minutes

COOK TIME:
10 minutes

YIELD:
4 sandwiches

Vegan butter, as needed (nut-free and/or soy-free if needed)

8 slices thick-cut vegan bread, such as Texas toast, or bread of choice (gluten-free if needed)

Garlic salt (page 356) or store-bought, as needed

1 cup (113 g) vegan Mozzarella shreds (page 340) or store-bought (nut-free and/or soy-free if needed)

1 cup (112 g) vegan Cheddar shreds (page 341) or store-bought (nut-free and/or soy-free if needed)

Butter one side of each slice of bread. Sprinkle your desired amount of garlic salt over the buttered sides of the bread.

Assemble the sandwiches by placing 4 slices of bread, butter side down, in a large, lidded skillet over medium heat (you may need to do this in batches, depending on the size of your pan). Place about ¼ cup (28 g) of mozzarella and ¼ cup (28 g) of Cheddar on each slice of bread. Place the remaining 4 slices of bread, butter side up, evenly over the sandwiches. Cook, covered, for about 5 minutes on each side, or until the shreds are melted and the bread is lightly browned and crispy. Remove from the skillet and slice each grilled sandwich in half. Serve.

*See in Creamy Tomato Soup image on page 195.

Philly Cheesesteak

This veganized version of a classic recipe combines panfried Simmered Seitan (page 333) with caramelized onion, sautéed peppers and vegan cheese sauce—it's perfection served in a fresh hoagie roll. Don't be intimidated by the number of steps; this recipe is absolutely worth the effort. While the onions are caramelizing, you can prepare the other elements, but make sure to keep everything warm for assembling the sandwiches at the end! Pair these with our Baked Seasoned Fries (page 251).

PREP TIME:	COOK TIME:	YIELD:
10 minutes plus, prep time for Simmered Seitan	*50 minutes*	*6 sandwiches*

CARAMELIZED ONION
2 tbsp (28 g) vegan butter (nut-free and/or soy-free if needed)

1 medium-sized white onion, sliced into long, thin slices (about 1 cup [160 g])

SAUTÉED PEPPER
1 tbsp (15 ml) olive oil

1 large red bell pepper, seeded and sliced (about 1½ cups [223 g])

CHEESE SAUCE
1½ tbsp (21 g) vegan butter (nut-free and/or soy-free if needed)

1½ tbsp (12 g) all-purpose flour

¾ cup (180 ml) plain, unsweetened rice milk

¾ cup (84 g) vegan Mozzarella shreds (page 340) or store-bought (nut-free and/or soy-free if needed)

PANFRIED SEITAN
1 batch Simmered Seitan (page 333) (soy-free if needed)

2 tbsp (30 ml) olive oil, plus more as needed

FOR ASSEMBLING
6 vegan hoagie rolls

Caramelize the onion: In a large skillet, melt the butter over medium heat. Add the onion and cook, stirring often, for about 5 minutes. Lower the heat to low and cook, stirring occasionally, for 45 minutes, or until deeply golden brown. Remove from the heat and set aside.

Meanwhile, sauté the pepper: In a small sauté pan, heat the oil over medium heat. Add the red bell pepper and cook, stirring occasionally, for 5 to 7 minutes, or until fork-tender. If the slices are beginning to burn or stick to the pan before they are done, add a little water.

Make the cheese sauce: In a small saucepan, melt the butter over medium-low heat. Whisk in the flour until it is completely incorporated. Slowly pour in the rice milk, whisking constantly. Increase the heat to medium-high and bring the mixture to a gentle boil, whisking constantly. Lower the heat to low, bringing the mixture to a simmer. Let simmer, whisking occasionally, for 3 to 5 minutes, or until thickened. Stir in the Mozzarella shreds until melted. Remove from the heat and set aside.

Panfry the seitan: Slice the seitan into about 24 long, thin pieces. In a large skillet, heat the olive oil over medium heat and, working in batches, lightly fry the seitan slices for 2 to 3 minutes, or until crispy. Repeat until all the slices are panfried, adding more oil as necessary.

Assemble the cheesesteaks: For each hoagie roll, add about four pieces of crispy seitan, some caramelized onion, sautéed peppers and a big drizzle of cheese sauce.

BBQ Seitan Sandwich

Nut-free, Soy-free option

These sandwiches combine BBQ sauce–smothered seitan with homemade Coleslaw (page 258). They're easy to prepare, so not only are they perfect for weekend gatherings or barbecues, they're great for busy weeknights when you need a quick meal for the whole family. Serve them with Macaroni Salad (page 84) and extra coleslaw on the side.

PREP TIME:
5 minutes, plus prep time for Simmered Seitan and Coleslaw

COOK TIME:
6 minutes

YIELD:
6 burgers

1 batch Simmered Seitan (page 333) (soy-free if needed)

2 tbsp (30 ml) olive oil, plus more as needed

1 cup (240 ml) vegan BBQ sauce, divided, plus more if desired

6 vegan burger buns

1 batch Coleslaw (page 258) (soy-free if needed)

Slice the seitan into about 24 thin slices. In a large skillet, heat the olive oil over medium-high heat. Place the seitan slices in the pan and evenly spread ½ cup (120 ml) of BBQ sauce over the slices (depending on the size of pan, you may need to do this in batches, adding more oil as needed). Sauté for 2 to 3 minutes, or until the bottoms are crispy, then flip and evenly spread the other ½ cup (120 ml) of BBQ sauce over the slices. Sauté for another 2 to 3 minutes, or until the seitan is crispy.

Serve each burger by topping each bun with about four slices of seitan, your desired amount of coleslaw and a drizzle of BBQ sauce, if desired.

Macaroni Salad
(page 84)

Coleslaw
(page 258)

BLTA

If you don't know what BLTA stands for—it's bacon (vegan for us, of course!), lettuce, tomato and avocado. The addition of avocado takes the classic BLT up a notch. We recommend using our homemade Tofu "Bacon" (page 335) for this recipe, but store-bought is also delicious in a pinch.

PREP TIME:
10 minutes

COOK TIME:
none

YIELD:
4 sandwiches

8 slices thick-cut vegan bread, such as Texas toast, or bread of choice (gluten-free if needed)

24 slices Tofu "Bacon" (page 335), or prepared store-bought alternative (gluten-free and/or soy-free if needed)

1 medium-sized beefsteak tomato, sliced into 8 slices

2 medium-sized ripe avocados, peeled, pitted and smashed

16 pieces iceberg lettuce

Vegan Mayo (page 353) or store-bought, for serving (soy-free if needed)

If desired, toast each slice of bread until golden brown.

Assemble each sandwich with 6 slices of "bacon," 2 slices of tomato, some smashed avocado, 4 pieces of lettuce and your desired amount of mayo, all between 2 slices of bread. Slice and serve immediately.

Tofu Banh Mi

Banh mi means "bread" in Vietnamese and typically refers to a type of baguette that's filled with meat, pickled veggies and garnishes. For our version, we replace meat with flavorful baked tofu and also fill the baguettes with pickled veggies, vegan Mayo (page 353), fresh jalapeño and cilantro. Serve these sandwiches with our Crunchy Cabbage Peanut Salad (page 201) or Summer Rolls with Peanut Dipping Sauce (page 143).

PREP TIME:
15 minutes, plus inactive time to press tofu and pickle veggies

COOK TIME:
40 minutes

YIELD:
4 sandwiches

BASTED TOFU
1 (14- to 16-oz [396- to 453-g]) block firm or extra-firm tofu

2 tbsp (34 g) vegan hoisin sauce (gluten-free if needed)

2 tbsp (30 ml) soy sauce (or tamari for gluten-free)

¼ cup (60 ml) unseasoned rice vinegar

3 cloves garlic, peeled and minced, or 1 tbsp (9 g) jarred minced garlic

1½ tsp (7 g) vegan sriracha

PICKLED VEGGIES
1 cup (110 g) shredded carrot

¼ large daikon radish, sliced into matchsticks (about 1 heaping cup [169 g])

1 cup (240 ml) water

1 cup (240 ml) white vinegar

3 tbsp (37 g) granulated sugar

2 tsp (12 g) salt

FOR ASSEMBLING
1 (24" [60-cm]) baguette, sliced into four 6" (15-cm) pieces (gluten-free if needed)

Vegan Mayo (page 353) or store-bought, as needed

1 large jalapeño pepper, thinly sliced into rounds

Fresh cilantro leaves

Press the tofu: Slice the tofu into eight long, equal slices. Press the slices (see page 358 for tutorial).

Meanwhile, pickle the veggies: In a large mason jar, add the carrot and daikon. In a medium-sized microwave-safe bowl if using a microwave, or in a small saucepan if using a stovetop, combine the water, vinegar, sugar and salt. Heat in the microwave or on the stovetop over medium heat until hot but not yet boiling—the sugar and salt should dissolve into the mixture. Pour over the veggies. Allow to sit at room temperature for about 30 minutes, then put on the lid and place in the fridge for at least 30 more minutes (see Sister Tip).

Bake the tofu: Preheat the oven to 400°F (200°C) and line a large baking sheet with parchment paper. In a small bowl, whisk together the hoisin sauce, soy sauce, rice vinegar, garlic and sriracha. Dip each slice of tofu into the sauce, then place on the prepared baking sheet. Reserve the extra sauce for basting. Bake for 40 minutes, using a pastry brush to baste with the sauce every 10 minutes. At 20 minutes, baste, then flip and baste again on the other side.

Assemble the sandwiches: Slice open the baguette pieces horizontally, spread evenly with your desired amount of mayo and top each with two slices of baked tofu, some pickled veggies and a few slices of jalapeño. Sprinkle the fresh cilantro on top and serve immediately.

Sister Tip

These pickled veggies will keep in the fridge for at least 2 weeks, so feel free to prep them ahead of time or save extra for later use.

Crunchy Cabbage Peanut
Salad (page 201)

Baked Seasoned Fries
(page 251)

Crispy Buffalo Tofu Sliders

We're completely obsessed with this recipe—Hannah makes these any chance she gets. We stack crispy buffalo tofu, pickles, lettuce and mayo between fresh slider buns. The trick to obtaining the perfect texture is to freeze the tofu beforehand (see page 358 for tutorial). These sliders are perfect in the summer with Macaroni Salad (page 84) or Baked Seasoned Fries (page 251). Double the recipe to serve a crowd.

PREP TIME:
20 minutes, plus inactive time for pressing and marinating tofu

COOK TIME:
30 minutes

YIELD:
8 sliders

---

1 (14- to 16-oz [396- to 453-g]) block firm or extra-firm tofu

MARINADE
1 cup (240 ml) plain, unsweetened soy milk

2 tbsp (30 ml) white or apple cider vinegar

1 tsp paprika

1 tsp garlic powder

1 tsp onion powder

1 tbsp (15 ml) hot sauce

BUFFALO SAUCE
¼ cup (56 g) vegan butter (nut-free if needed)

⅓ cup (80 ml) hot sauce

Prepare the tofu: Remove the tofu from the packaging and drain any excess liquid. If a meatier texture is desired, freeze the tofu overnight, then thaw (you can repeat this once more; see page 358 for tutorial). Slice the tofu into eight long, equal slices. Press the slices (see page 358 for tutorial).

Make the marinade: In a small bowl, whisk together the milk and vinegar, then set aside for 10 to 15 minutes, until curdled. Once curdled, stir in the rest of the marinade ingredients. Pour the marinade into a large resealable plastic bag and add the tofu slices. Release any air in the bag and seal tightly so that the marinade covers the tofu as much as possible. Place in the fridge to marinate for at least 4 hours, flipping over occasionally to fully submerge the tofu in the marinade.

Make the buffalo sauce: In a small saucepan, heat the butter over medium heat. Allow it to melt, then whisk in the hot sauce. Remove from the heat and set aside for later.

(continued)

Crispy Buffalo Tofu Sliders (Continued)

FLOUR COATING
¾ cup (94 g) all-purpose flour

2 tsp (4 g) smoked paprika

½ tsp cayenne pepper

1 tsp garlic powder

½ tsp salt

Pinch of freshly ground black pepper

FOR FRYING
Canola oil

FOR ASSEMBLING
Vegan Mayo (page 353) or store-bought

8 vegan slider buns

Bread-and-butter pickles

Lettuce

Coat and fry the tofu: In a small, wide bowl, whisk together the flour coating ingredients. Remove the tofu from the marinade and dredge each piece in the flour mixture, then set on a nonstick wire rack. Save the excess flour mixture for later. Pour 1 to 2 inches (2.5 to 5 cm) of canola oil into a deep saucepan or pot or use a deep fryer according to the manufacturer's instructions, and bring the oil to 325°F (162°C). Once the oil is hot, dredge each piece of tofu again in the flour mixture and place it into the hot oil (frying one or two pieces at a time). Fry on each side until crispy, 3 to 4 minutes per side. Once fried, place on paper towels to remove any excess oil, then submerge in the buffalo sauce.

Assemble the sliders: Spread your desired amount of vegan mayo on the bottom of a bun, place a piece of buffalo tofu on top, then add your desired amount of pickles and lettuce. Spread more mayo on the top bun and sandwich the buns together. Repeat to assemble all 8 sliders and serve.

Peanut Seitan Wrap

We've been making a version of this recipe as a go-to quick and easy lunch for years. Whether you make your own seitan or use store-bought vegan "chicken" strips, this recipe is delicious thanks to the homemade Peanut Vinaigrette (page 346). Obsessed with peanut dishes? Check out our Peanut Vegetables (page 249), Crunchy Cabbage Peanut Salad (page 201) and Cold Peanut Noodles (page 127).

PREP TIME:
5 minutes, plus prep time for Peanut Vinaigrette

COOK TIME:
8 minutes

YIELD:
6 wraps

1 batch Steamed Seitan (page 332) or 1 (14-oz [396-g]) bag store-bought vegan "chicken" strips (gluten-free and/or soy-free if needed)

1 tbsp (15 ml) canola oil

1 batch Peanut Vinaigrette (page 346), divided (gluten-free and/or soy-free if needed)

1 cup (110 g) shredded carrot

2 cups (94 g) shredded iceberg lettuce

½ cup (28 g) vegan fried wonton strips or vegan chow mein noodles (crunchy variety; see Sister Tip) (gluten-free and/or soy-free if needed)

6 medium-sized vegan flour tortillas (gluten-free if needed)

Cut the seitan into strips that are ½ inch (1.3 cm) thick and 1 to 2 inches (2.5 to 5 cm) long. In a large skillet, heat the oil over medium heat. Stir in the seitan strips and cook, stirring often, for 4 to 6 minutes, or until crispy.

Lower the heat to medium-low. Reserving ¼ cup (60 ml) of Peanut Vinaigrette, add the remaining vinaigrette to the seitan and cook, stirring often, for 1 to 2 minutes. Remove from the heat.

For each wrap, place an equal amount of peanut seitan, carrot, lettuce and wonton strips down the center of the tortilla. Drizzle your desired amount of the reserved Peanut Vinaigrette on top. Fold in the sides and secure with a toothpick. Serve immediately.

Sister Tip

Here we're calling for the chow mein noodles that are crispy, crunchy and ready to eat, normally found in a can. You should not be using the variety that is raw and used in noodle dishes.

Crispy "Chicken" Caesar Melt

This recipe is inspired by our love for Caesar Salad (page 206). It combines breaded and fried Crispy Seitan (page 336) with Mozzarella (page 340), lettuce and Creamy Caesar Dressing (page 348). Yes, it is as good as it sounds. Pair it with Garlic Dill Smashed Potatoes (page 256) or Creamy Tomato Soup (page 194).

PREP TIME:
5 minutes, plus prep time for Crispy Seitan

COOK TIME:
18 minutes

YIELD:
6 sandwiches

12 slices thick-cut vegan bread, such as Texas toast, or bread of choice

Vegan butter, as needed (nut-free and/or soy-free if needed)

Garlic Salt (page 356) or store-bought, as needed

1½ cups (170 g) vegan Mozzarella shreds (page 340) or store-bought, divided (nut-free and/or soy-free if needed)

1 batch Crispy Seitan (page 336) (soy-free if needed)

1½ cups (70 g) shredded iceberg lettuce, divided

6 tbsp (90 ml) vegan Creamy Caesar Dressing (page 348) or store-bought, divided, plus more if desired (soy-free if needed)

On one side of each slice of bread, spread a thin layer of butter and sprinkle with some garlic salt. Working in batches, place 2 to 3 slices of the bread, butter side down, in a large, lidded skillet over medium-low heat. Sprinkle about ¼ cup (28 g) of mozzarella on each slice. Place an additional slice of bread on top of each sandwich, butter side up. Cover and cook for 3 to 5 minutes, or until lightly browned and crispy on the bottom.

Flip each sandwich, then carefully open and add a piece of Crispy Seitan to each sandwich, then place the top piece of bread back on top. Cook, uncovered, for another 3 to 5 minutes, or until the bread is golden brown and the cheese is melted.

Remove the sandwiches from the pan. Carefully open and add ¼ cup (11 g) of shredded lettuce and 1 tablespoon (15 ml) of Caesar dressing to each sandwich, plus more dressing to taste, if desired. Repeat for the remaining sandwiches.

Crispy "Chicken" Ranch Sandwich

We know we shouldn't pick favorites, but this sandwich is definitely in the running. The combination of Crispy Seitan (page 336), vegan cheese, lettuce, pickles and vegan Ranch Dressing (page 345) is just too good, especially when served on a fresh hamburger bun. Seitan's chewy, meaty texture makes it the perfect substitute for chicken. Pair this with Fries (Baked or Fried) (page 259) or Orzo and Rice Salad (page 261).

PREP TIME:
10 minutes, plus prep time for Crispy Seitan

COOK TIME:
14 minutes

YIELD:
6 sandwiches

1 batch Crispy Seitan (page 336) (soy-free if needed)

6 slices store-bought vegan Cheddar cheese (nut-free and/or soy-free if needed)

6 vegan hamburger buns

18 sandwich pickles

18 pieces iceberg lettuce

6 tbsp (90 g) vegan Ranch Dressing (page 345) or store-bought, plus more if desired (nut-free and/or soy-free if needed)

Working in batches if necessary, place each piece of Crispy Seitan in a large, lidded sauté pan over medium-low heat. Top each with a slice of cheese. Cover and cook for 5 to 7 minutes, or until the cheese is melted, checking occasionally to ensure the bottom of the seitan is not burning and lowering the heat to low if needed.

Assemble each sandwich by adding a piece of cheese-topped seitan to each bun, along with 3 pickles, 3 pieces of lettuce and 1 tablespoon (15 ml) of ranch dressing, plus more dressing to taste, if desired.

"Chicken Bacon" Caesar Salad Wrap

A vegan chicken bacon Caesar salad wrap may seem like an oxymoron, but trust us, this wrap is perfectly plant-based; no animal ingredients necessary! Just like our Crispy "Chicken" Caesar Melt (page 176), this wrap is inspired by our love for Caesar Salad (page 206). Loaded with lettuce, Steamed Seitan (page 332), Tofu "Bacon" (page 335), Parmesan Cheese (page 342) and Creamy Caesar Dressing (page 348), this wrap has an amazing combination of flavors. Pair it with Macaroni Salad (page 84) or Roasted Garlic Potatoes (page 253).

PREP TIME:
10 minutes

COOK TIME:
3 to 5 minutes

YIELD:
6 wraps

1 batch Steamed Seitan (page 332) or 1 (14-oz [396-g]) bag store-bought vegan "chicken" strips (gluten-free and/or soy-free if needed)

12 slices Tofu "Bacon" (page 335) or store-bought alternative (gluten-free and/or soy-free if needed)

1 tbsp (15 ml) olive oil

4 packed cups (300 g) chopped romaine lettuce

¼ cup (25 g) vegan Parmesan Cheese (page 342) or store-bought (nut-free and/or soy-free if needed)

¾ cup (180 ml) vegan Creamy Caesar Dressing (page 348) or store-bought (soy-free if needed)

6 medium-sized vegan flour tortillas (gluten-free if needed)

Chop the steamed seitan and "bacon" into small pieces. In a large skillet, heat the olive oil over medium-low heat. Add the seitan and "bacon" and cook, stirring often, for 3 to 5 minutes, or until crispy.

Remove the seitan and "bacon" from the pan and transfer to a medium-sized bowl along with the romaine lettuce, Parmesan and Caesar dressing. Toss to combine. Serve by evenly distributing the salad into the centers of the tortillas, then folding up the sides and securing with toothpicks.

Hummus Ranch Wrap

This wrap is loaded with Hummus (page 243), Perfect White Rice (page 350), black beans, Roasted Tomato Salsa (page 217), avocado, Cheddar shreds (page 341), lettuce and Ranch Dressing (page 345). It's hearty, filling and great served on its own, but it's also delicious paired with Fries (Baked or Fried) (page 259).

PREP TIME:
10 minutes, plus inactive time for pickling onions and prep time for Perfect White Rice

COOK TIME:
3 minutes

YIELD:
6 wraps

PICKLED ONION

½ medium-sized red onion, thinly sliced (about ½ cup [80 g])

½ cup (120 ml) water

½ cup (120 ml) white vinegar

2 tbsp (25 g) granulated sugar

2 tsp (12 g) salt

HUMMUS RANCH WRAPS

1 cup (236 g) Hummus (page 243) or store-bought

1 cup (166 g) Perfect White Rice (⅓ batch [page 350]) (see Sister Tips)

¾ cup (129 g) canned black beans, drained and rinsed

¾ cup (180 g) Roasted Tomato Salsa (page 217) or store-bought salsa of choice

2 medium-sized ripe avocados, peeled, pitted and sliced

¾ cups (80 g) vegan Cheddar shreds (page 341) or store-bought (nut-free and/or soy-free if needed)

1½ cups (108 g) shredded iceberg lettuce

1 cup (240 ml) vegan Ranch Dressing (page 345) or store-bought (nut-free and/or soy-free if needed)

6 large burrito vegan flour tortillas (gluten-free if needed)

Place the red onion in a mason jar. In a small microwave-safe bowl if using a microwave, or in a small saucepan if using a stovetop, combine the water, vinegar, sugar and salt. Heat in the microwave or on the stovetop until hot but not yet boiling; the sugar and salt should dissolve into the mixture. Pour over the onion. Allow to sit at room temperature for about 30 minutes, then put on the lid and place in the fridge for at least 30 more minutes (see Sister Tips).

Assemble the wraps by adding an even amount of hummus, rice, black beans, salsa, avocado, Cheddar shreds, lettuce and ranch dressing to each tortilla. For each wrap, fold in the bottom, fold in the sides, then roll tightly to form a burrito shape. Serve immediately.

Sister Tips

These pickled onions will stay good for at least 2 weeks in the refrigerator, so feel free to prep ahead of time and save leftovers for later.

Don't have white rice on hand? Feel free to substitute cooked brown rice or quinoa.

Seitan Gyro with Tzatziki Sauce

Vegan gyros are hard to come by, so stay home and make your own. This recipe combines a flavorful seitan gyro "meat" with lettuce, tomato, onion and vegan tzatziki sauce, all stuffed into a fresh pita. Serve these gyros with a side of Fries (Baked or Fried) (page 259).

PREP TIME:
15 minutes

COOK TIME:
1 hour 45 minutes

YIELD:
6 gyros

SEITAN

1 cup (120 g) vital wheat gluten (spooned and leveled or weighed [see page 359 for tutorial])

¼ cup (20 g) nutritional yeast

½ tsp garlic powder

½ tsp onion powder

1½ tsp (1 g) dried marjoram

¼ tsp ground rosemary

½ tsp dried oregano

½ tsp salt

¼ tsp freshly ground black pepper

¾ cup (180 ml) vegetable broth

1 tbsp (15 ml) vegan Worcestershire sauce (soy-free if needed)

FOR SIMMERING

2 cups (480 ml) vegetable broth

2 cups (480 ml) water

1 tbsp (15 ml) low-sodium soy sauce (or coconut aminos for soy-free)

1 tbsp (15 ml) pure maple syrup

Make the seitan: In a large bowl or the bowl of a stand mixer fitted with a hook attachment, mix together the vital wheat gluten, nutritional yeast, garlic powder, onion powder, marjoram, rosemary, oregano, salt and pepper. Add the vegetable broth and Worcestershire sauce and stir well to form a ball of dough. Either transfer to a flat surface and knead by hand for 5 minutes, or beat in the stand mixer on low speed for 5 minutes. Form into a large patty.

Simmer the seitan: In a large saucepan over high heat, whisk together the vegetable broth, water, soy sauce and maple syrup and bring to a boil. Place the seitan patty in the boiling liquid. Lower the heat to low and bring the liquid to a simmer. Let simmer, covered, for an hour, flipping halfway through. Remove from the heat, remove the lid and let the seitan patty cool in the liquid for about 30 minutes.

(continued)

Seitan Gyro with Tzatziki Sauce (Continued)

TZATZIKI SAUCE

½ medium-sized to large cucumber

1 cup (226 g) plain, unsweetened vegan yogurt (we suggest cashew or coconut) (nut-free and/or soy-free if needed)

1 clove garlic, peeled and minced, or 1 tsp jarred minced garlic

1½ tsp (7 ml) olive oil

½ tsp white vinegar

½ tsp salt

⅛ tsp freshly ground black pepper

1 tbsp (2 g) minced fresh dill

FOR PANFRYING

2 tbsp (30 ml) canola oil, plus more as needed

FOR ASSEMBLING

6 vegan pitas

¼ medium-sized red onion, sliced (about ¼ cup [40 g])

1 large beefsteak tomato, sliced

1 cup (72 g) shredded iceberg lettuce

Make the tzatziki sauce: Using a cheese grater, shred the cucumber. Place in a cheesecloth or clean, thin towel and squeeze out as much water as you can. In a small bowl, whisk together all the sauce ingredients, including the shredded cucumber. Cover and set in the fridge for later.

Panfry the seitan: Remove the seitan from the liquid and place on a clean, absorbent towel. Pat it dry, then place on a cutting board. Slice into long, thin strips. In a large skillet, heat the canola oil over medium heat. Sauté the seitan strips, stirring occasionally, for 5 to 7 minutes, or until crispy. You may need to do this in batches, adding more oil as necessary. Remove from the heat and set aside.

Assemble the gyros: Lightly crisp the pitas by placing them in a large skillet over medium heat for 1 to 2 minutes on each side. Place an equal amount of seitan, onion, tomato, shredded lettuce and tzatziki in each warm pita, then fold up the sides and wrap the bottom two-thirds tightly in foil. Serve immediately.

Loaded Burritos

This is our vegan version of classic loaded burritos. They're stuffed with Easy Taco "Meat" (page 332), Cilantro Lime Rice (page 350), black beans, Roasted Tomato Salsa (page 217), Fresh and Easy Guacamole (page 242), lettuce and Cheddar (page 341)—did we mention they're loaded? If you love these, check out our Loaded Nachos (page 98).

PREP TIME:
15 minutes, plus prep time for Easy Taco "Meat" and Perfect White Rice

COOK TIME:
1 to 6 minutes

YIELD:
6 burritos

6 large burrito flour tortillas (gluten-free if needed)

½ cup (120 g) Fresh and Easy Guacamole (page 242) or store-bought

2 cups (333 g) Perfect White Rice, Cilantro Lime Variation (about ⅔ batch [page 350])

1 batch Easy Taco "Meat" (page 332) (gluten-free, nut-free and/or soy-free if needed)

1 (15-oz [424-g]) can black beans, drained and rinsed

1 cup (264 g) Roasted Tomato Salsa (page 217) or store-bought salsa of choice

2 cups (144 g) shredded iceberg lettuce

¾ cup (85 g) vegan Cheddar shreds (page 341) or store-bought (nut-free and/or soy-free if needed)

Warm the tortillas by microwaving them, wrapped in a damp paper towel, until warm, 10 to 20 seconds, or by heating one at a time in a large skillet over medium-low heat for 15 to 30 seconds per side.

For each burrito, spread 1 heaping tablespoon (20 g) of guacamole along the center of the tortilla, leaving room around the edges. Sprinkle ⅓ cup (60 g) of rice in each wrap, on top of the guacamole. Top with one-sixth of the taco "meat" and one-sixth of the black beans. Top with 2 heaping tablespoons (44 g) of salsa, ⅓ cup (24 g) of shredded lettuce and 2 tablespoons (14 g) of Cheddar shreds. To form each burrito, fold in the bottom, fold in the sides, then roll tightly. Serve immediately.

Fried Avocado Tacos

Take your taco night to the next level with these fried avocado tacos. Once you try them, you'll be wondering why people don't swap out the fish for avocado more often. These tacos are stuffed with fried avocado, red onion, lettuce and Chipotle Ranch (page 347). Serve with a side of tortilla chips and Roasted Tomato Salsa (page 217) or Nacho Cheese (page 218).

PREP TIME:
10 minutes, plus prep time for Chipotle Ranch

COOK TIME:
20 to 25 minutes

YIELD:
12 tacos

FRIED AVOCADO

3 large avocados

¾ cup (93 g) all-purpose flour

1 tsp salt

¾ cup (180 ml) soda water, ice cold

Canola oil, for frying

FOR ASSEMBLING

12 small corn or flour tortillas

1 cup (72 g) shredded iceberg lettuce

¼ medium-sized red onion, chopped small (about ¼ cup [40 g])

¾ cup (180 ml) Chipotle Ranch (page 347), plus more if desired

Peel, pit and slice each avocado into eight slices. Set aside. Whisk together the flour, salt and soda water in a medium-sized bowl. Set aside.

Pour 2 inches (5 cm) of canola oil into a deep saucepan or pot, or use a deep fryer according to the manufacturer's instructions, and bring the oil to 350°F (175°C). Using a fork or tongs, dip each slice of avocado into the flour mixture and let any excess drip off. Place in the hot oil, adding as many as can fit without touching, and fry for 3 to 4 minutes on each side, or until crispy. Remove from the oil and place on paper towels to drain. Repeat, in batches, until all the avocado is fried.

In batches of four, heat the tortillas by wrapping them in a damp paper towel and heating in a microwave until warm, 10 to 20 seconds. Assemble the tacos by placing two pieces of fried avocado in each tortilla, along with 1 heaping tablespoon (6 g) of lettuce, 1 teaspoon of onion and 1 tablespoon (15 ml) of Chipotle Ranch, plus more ranch to taste, if desired. Fold up the sides and serve immediately.

NOT YOUR AVERAGE SOUPS AND SALADS

We know what you're thinking: Of course this vegan cookbook would have a chapter dedicated to salads (and soups). After all, it's a common misconception that vegans only eat salad. But, if you haven't realized it yet, that's far from the truth—just take a look at our Crowd-Pleasing Pasta and Pizza chapter (page 59). Plus, these salads are anything but boring. They're loaded with veggies, proteins, Homemade Croutons (page 349) and homemade dressings—which we can all agree are always better than store-bought. Carrie's go-to is the Kale Tahini Salad with Baked Tempeh (page 210), but you'll also find a fresh Crunchy Cabbage Peanut Salad (page 201) and a flavorful Caesar Salad (page 206) in this chapter.

Okay, enough about salads; let's get to the soups. This chapter includes seven hearty soup recipes perfect for chilly winter nights. They're easy enough for when you're in a time crunch and they can even be prepped ahead of time. From Broccoli Cheddar Soup (page 191) to White Jackfruit Chili (page 197), there's something for everyone.

Not only are soups and salads the perfect complement for one another, but they are also great paired with many dishes in this cookbook, including Pesto Pasta (page 62), Garlic Bread Grilled Cheese (page 163) and Crispy "Chicken" Ranch Sandwich (page 179).

Breadsticks
(page 266)

Broccoli Cheddar Soup

Growing up, Panera's broccoli cheddar soup was our absolute favorite. So, naturally, we had to make it vegan. Bonus: it's even gluten-free! Our version is creamy, cheesy and isn't missing any flavor. Pair this with our Breadsticks (page 266) or Dinner Rolls (page 271).

PREP TIME:
10 minutes, plus inactive time to soak cashews

COOK TIME:
25 minutes

YIELD:
8 servings

¼ cup (32 g) cornstarch

¾ cup (180 ml) water, divided

1 tbsp (15 ml) canola oil

1½ medium-sized white onions, chopped (about 1½ cups [240 g])

2 cups (220 g) shredded carrot

5 packed cups (500 g) finely chopped broccoli

3 cloves garlic, peeled and minced, or 1 tbsp (9 g) jarred minced garlic

3 cups (720 ml) vegetable broth

3 cups (720 ml) plain, unsweetened rice milk

½ cup (40 g) nutritional yeast

1 tsp garlic powder

½ tsp dried parsley

¼ tsp freshly ground black pepper, plus more to taste

1½ tsp (9 g) salt, plus more to taste

1 cup (146 g) raw unsalted whole cashews, soaked (see Sister Tip)

2 cups (226 g) vegan Cheddar shreds (page 341) or store-bought, plus more for topping if desired (soy-free if needed)

In a small bowl, combine the cornstarch with ¼ cup (60 ml) of the water. Set aside.

In a large stockpot, heat the canola oil over medium-low heat. Stir in the onions, carrot and broccoli. Cook, stirring often, for 15 minutes. Stir in the garlic and cook for another 30 seconds to 1 minute, or until fragrant. Stir in the vegetable broth and rice milk. Increase the heat to high, bring the soup to a boil and stir in the cornstarch slurry. Lower the heat to low, bringing the soup to a simmer, and stir in the nutritional yeast, garlic powder, parsley, pepper and salt. Simmer, covered, for 10 minutes.

In a high-speed blender, combine the cashews, the remaining ½ cup (120 ml) of water and 1 cup (240 ml) of the soup, and blend until smooth. Add back to the pot and stir. Stir in the cheese and cook over low heat until melted. Taste and add more salt and pepper, if desired. Serve hot, topped with more Cheddar shreds, if desired.

Sister Tip

To soak cashews, place them in a bowl and cover completely with water. Let sit for at least 2 hours, then drain, rinse and pat dry (see page 358 for more options and tips).

Corn Chowder

Our version of chowder is lighter than most. The trick to getting this soup creamy (without the need for dairy cream) is to blend half of it. This soup is great to enjoy throughout the week, so no need to worry about wasting any leftovers. Pair this chowder with our Pesto Mozzarella Melt (page 160) or Buttermilk Biscuits (page 265).

PREP TIME:
15 minutes

COOK TIME:
30 minutes

YIELD:
6 to 8 servings

1 tbsp (15 ml) olive oil

1 medium-sized white onion, chopped (about 1 cup [160 g])

3 cloves garlic, peeled and minced, or 1 tbsp (9 g) jarred minced garlic

3 cups (720 ml) vegetable broth

3 cups (720 ml) plain, unsweetened rice milk

4 green onions, minced (just the white bulbs)

3 cups (450 g) peeled and diced white potatoes

1 red bell pepper, seeded and chopped (about 1 cup [149 g])

2 cups (220 g) shredded carrots

2 cups (202 g) diced celery

4 cups (544 g) frozen corn

½ tsp paprika

2 tsp (12 g) salt, plus more to taste

¼ tsp freshly ground black pepper, plus more to taste

Dried or chopped fresh parsley, for topping (optional)

In a large stockpot, heat the olive oil over medium-low heat. Stir in the onion and let cook for 5 to 7 minutes, or until translucent. Add the garlic and cook for 30 seconds to 1 minute, or until fragrant. Stir in the vegetable broth and rice milk. Increase the heat to high, stir in the green onions, potatoes, red bell pepper, carrots, celery and corn and bring the soup to a boil. Lower the heat to low, bringing the soup to a simmer. Simmer, covered, for 15 to 20 minutes, or until the potatoes are fork-tender.

Remove about half of the soup and carefully transfer it to a blender. Blend until smooth and creamy, then pour back into the pot.

Stir in the paprika, salt and black pepper. Taste and add more salt and black pepper, if desired. Serve hot, topped with parlsey, if desired.

*See in Buttermilk Biscuits image on page 264.

Sweet Potato Chili

This chili recipe is hearty, slightly sweet and perfect for serving at get-togethers, tailgates or holidays. We love it served with a dollop of Cashew Cream (page 343) and a sprinkle of fresh parsley. Pair it with our Garlic Bread Grilled Cheese (page 163), tortilla chips or Kale Tahini Salad with Baked Tempeh (page 210).

PREP TIME:
15 minutes

COOK TIME:
about 25 minutes

YIELD:
8 servings

1 tbsp (15 ml) canola oil

1 medium-sized white onion, chopped (about 1 cup [160 g])

1 red bell pepper, chopped (about 1 cup [149 g])

3 cloves garlic, peeled and minced, or 1 tbsp (9 g) jarred minced garlic

1½ tbsp (12 g) ground cumin

2½ tbsp (21 g) chili powder

2 tsp (5 g) garlic powder

4 cups (568 g) peeled and diced sweet potato (diced small)

1 (28-oz [793-g]) can diced tomatoes

1 cup (240 ml) tomato sauce

2 cups (480 ml) vegetable broth

2 tbsp (27 g) packed light brown sugar

1 (16-oz [453-g]) can pinto beans, drained and rinsed

1 (16-oz [453-g]) can great northern beans, drained and rinsed

1 (16-oz [453-g]) can kidney beans, drained and rinsed

1 tsp dried parsley

2 tsp (12 g) salt

¼ tsp freshly ground black pepper

FOR TOPPING
Cashew Cream (page 343) or vegan sour cream (nut-free and/or soy-free if needed)

Dried or chopped fresh parsley

In a large stockpot, heat the oil over medium-low heat. Stir in the onion and bell pepper and cook, stirring often, for 5 to 7 minutes, or until the onion becomes translucent and the pepper is fork-tender. Stir in the garlic, cumin, chili powder and garlic powder. Cook for 30 seconds to 1 minute, or until the garlic is fragrant.

Increase the heat to high, stir in the sweet potato, diced tomatoes, tomato sauce, vegetable broth and brown sugar and bring to a boil. Lower the heat to low, bringing the mixture to a simmer. Simmer, covered, for 20 minutes.

Stir in the pinto beans, great northern beans, and kidney beans, parsley, salt and black pepper. Simmer, covered, for another 10 minutes, or until the sweet potato is fork-tender.

Serve hot, topped with Cashew Cream and parsley.

*See in Kale Tahini Salad with Baked Tempeh image on page 211.

Creamy Tomato Soup

We've got to give credit where credit is due—this is our mom's classic recipe that she's been perfecting for years. It's creamy, flavorful and easy to whip up. Pair this with our Garlic Bread Grilled Cheese (page 163), of course. After all, what's tomato soup without a grilled cheese sandwich?

PREP TIME:
5 minutes, plus prep time for Cashew Cream and Homemade Croutons

COOK TIME:
20 minutes

YIELD:
6 to 8 servings

1 tbsp (15 ml) olive oil

1 medium-sized white onion, chopped (about 1 cup [160 g])

6 cloves garlic, peeled and minced, or 2 tbsp (18 g) jarred minced garlic

1 (28-oz [793-g]) can crushed tomatoes

1 heaping cup (270 g) Cashew Cream (1 batch [page 343])

3 cups (720 ml) vegetable broth

2 tbsp (30 ml) pure maple syrup

1 tsp onion powder

1 tsp garlic powder

2 tsp (1 g) dried basil, plus more for topping

½ tsp salt, plus more to taste

¼ tsp freshly ground black pepper, plus more to taste

Homemade Croutons (page 349), for topping (gluten-free if needed)

In a large stockpot, heat the olive oil over medium-low heat. Add the onion and cook, stirring often, for 5 to 7 minutes, or until translucent. Stir in the garlic and cook for 30 seconds to 1 minute, or until fragrant. Add the crushed tomatoes, Cashew Cream, vegetable broth, maple syrup, onion powder and garlic powder, stir and let cook, stirring occasionally, for another 5 minutes.

Carefully transfer the soup to a high-speed blender and blend until smooth, then pour back into the pot. Stir in the basil, salt and pepper, then increase the heat to high and bring the soup to a boil. Lower the heat to low and simmer for 5 minutes. Season with more salt and pepper to taste, if desired.

Serve hot, topped with croutons and more basil.

Garlic Bread Grilled
Cheese (page 163)

"Chicken Bacon"
Ranch Pita (page 162)

Fries (Baked or Fried)
(page 259)

White Jackfruit Chili

This chili uses jackfruit in place of chicken. If you've never had jackfruit before, it's a fruit that has a meatlike texture and is great for vegan cooking. The resulting chili is hearty and delicious. We love serving it with tortilla chips, Dinner Rolls (page 271) or with a side of Fries (Baked or Fried) (page 259) and pairing it with a "Chicken Bacon" Ranch Pita (page 162).

PREP TIME:
10 minutes

COOK TIME:
25 minutes

YIELD:
8 servings

2 (20-oz [566-g]) cans young jackfruit in brine

2 tbsp (28 g) vegan butter (nut-free and/or soy-free if needed)

1 medium-sized onion, chopped (about 1 cup [160 g])

3 cloves garlic, peeled and minced, or 1 tbsp (9 g) jarred minced garlic

1½ tsp (3 g) dried oregano

2 tsp (4 g) paprika

1 tbsp (6 g) ground cumin

2 tbsp (17 g) chili powder

⅓ cup (41 g) all-purpose flour

3 cups (720 ml) plain, unsweetened rice milk

2 cups (480 ml) vegetable broth

2 (15.5-oz [439-g]) cans cannellini beans, drained and rinsed

1 (14.5-oz [411-g]) can diced tomatoes

2 tbsp (30 g) canned chopped green chiles

1½ cups (204 g) frozen corn

2 cups (224 g) vegan Mozzarella shreds (page 340) or store-bought (nut-free and/or soy-free if needed)

2 tsp (12 g) salt, plus more to taste

½ tsp freshly ground black pepper, plus more to taste

FOR SERVING
Cashew Cream (page 343) or vegan sour cream (nut-free and/or soy-free if needed)

Dried or chopped fresh parsley

Drain and rinse the jackfruit and squeeze out as much water as possible, using a cheesecloth or clean towel. Chop it into small pieces and set aside.

In a large stockpot, melt the butter over medium heat. Add the onion and cook for 5 to 7 minutes, or until translucent. Stir in the jackfruit and cook for another 5 minutes. Stir in the garlic, oregano, paprika, cumin and chili powder and cook for 30 seconds to 1 minute, or until the garlic is fragrant. Stir in the flour until it is well mixed with the vegetables. Slowly pour in the rice milk, stirring constantly. Stir in the vegetable broth, cannellini beans, diced tomatoes, green chiles and corn. Increase the heat to high and bring the chili to a boil, stirring often. Lower the heat to low, bringing the chili to a simmer. Simmer, covered, for 20 minutes, or until thickened, stirring occasionally.

Stir in the cheese until melted, then stir in the salt and pepper, adding more to taste if desired. Serve hot, topped with Cashew Cream and parsley.

"Chicken" Noodle Soup

Remember that canned chicken noodle soup you ate growing up? This is like that, but much better. For this chicken-less recipe, you'll use Steamed Seitan (page 332) or your favorite vegan store-bought alternative. This "Chicken" Noodle Soup is a family favorite; it's even approved by our picky, nonvegan brothers. Pair it with our Garlic Bread Grilled Cheese (page 163) or Pesto Mozzarella Melt (page 160).

PREP TIME:
15 minutes

COOK TIME:
20 to 25 minutes

YIELD:
8 to 10 servings

1 tbsp (14 g) vegan butter (nut-free and/or soy-free if needed)

1 large sweet onion, chopped (about 1 heaping cup [200 g])

2 cups (202 g) diced celery

2 cups (256 g) chopped carrot

10 oz (283 g) Steamed Seitan (page 332), chopped (about 2 cups), or 1 (10-oz [283-g]) bag vegan "chicken" strips, chopped (gluten-free and/or soy-free if needed)

6 cloves garlic, peeled and minced, or 2 tbsp (18 g) jarred minced garlic

12 cups (2.8 L) vegetable broth, plus more as needed (see Sister Tips)

1 tsp dried oregano

1 tsp garlic powder

1 tbsp dried parsley, or 3 tbsp (11 g) chopped fresh parsley, plus more for topping

1 tsp salt, plus more to taste

¼ tsp freshly ground black pepper, plus more to taste

2 bay leaves

8 oz (226 g) uncooked fusilli pasta or pasta of choice (gluten-free if needed)

In a large stockpot, melt the butter over medium-low heat. Add the onion, celery and carrot. Cook, stirring often, for 5 to 7 minutes. Stir in the chopped seitan. Cook, stirring often, for 5 to 7 more minutes. Stir in the garlic and cook for 30 seconds to 1 minute, or until fragrant.

Stir in the broth, oregano, garlic powder, parsley, salt, pepper and bay leaves. Increase the heat to high and cover, bringing the mixture to a boil. Add the pasta and boil, uncovered, for 7 to 12 minutes, or until al dente (this will vary depending on the type of pasta—you can check the package for an estimated time).

Once the noodles are done cooking, remove the pot from the heat. Remove and discard the bay leaves. Taste and add more salt and pepper, if desired. Serve hot topped with more parsley (see Sister Tips).

Sister Tips

Our favorite broth for this recipe is Better Than Bouillon Vegetarian No Chicken Base plus water, prepared according to the package instructions.

Once the soup is done and begins to sit, the noodles will absorb some of the broth. You may want to add extra broth, as needed, if you don't eat the soup right away.

Pesto Mozzarella Melt (page 160)

Butternut Squash Soup with Sautéed Pepitas

This sweet and savory soup combines butternut squash and maple syrup with onion, garlic and cashews. It's topped with sautéed pepitas, making it perfect for fall. Serve it with Garlic and Herb Focaccia (page 272) (for dippin'!) and Roasted Veggie and Quinoa Salad (page 203).

PREP TIME:
5 minutes, plus inactive time for soaking cashews

COOK TIME:
1 hour

YIELD:
6 to 8 servings

SOUP

1 (2½-lb [1.1-kg]) butternut squash

2 tbsp (30 ml) olive oil, divided, plus more for pan if needed

1 medium-sized onion, chopped (about 1 cup [160 g])

3 cloves garlic, peeled and minced, or 1 tbsp (9 g) jarred minced garlic

3 tbsp (45 ml) pure maple syrup

½ cup (73 g) raw unsalted whole cashews, soaked (see Sister Tip)

3 cups (720 ml) vegetable broth

SAUTÉED PEPITAS

1½ tsp (7 g) coconut oil

½ cup (60 g) pepitas

Make the soup: Preheat the oven to 400°F (200°C). Oil a baking sheet or line it with parchment paper. Slice the squash in half, scrape out and discard the seeds and brush the insides with 1 tablespoon (15 ml) of the olive oil. Place cut side down on the prepared baking sheet. Bake for 50 minutes.

In a large stockpot, heat the remaining tablespoon (15 ml) of olive oil over medium-low heat. Add the onion and cook, stirring often, for 5 to 7 minutes, or until translucent. Stir in the garlic and cook for another 30 seconds to 1 minute, or until fragrant. Once the squash is done cooking, remove the skins and add the flesh to a high-speed blender, along with the remaining soup ingredients, including the cooked onion and garlic. Blend until smooth, then add back to the pot. Heat over medium-low heat for 5 to 7 minutes, stirring occasionally, or until hot.

Sauté the pepitas: In a small skillet, heat the coconut oil over medium heat. Add the pepitas and cook, stirring often, for 7 to 10 minutes, until browned. Serve hot, topped with the sautéed pepitas.

*See in Roasted Veggie and Quinoa Salad image on page 202.

Sister Tip

To soak cashews, place them in a bowl and cover completely with water. Let sit for at least 2 hours, then drain, rinse and pat dry (see page 358 for more options and tips).

Crunchy Cabbage Peanut Salad

This easy cabbage salad combines fresh vegetables with crunchy cashews and a creamy Peanut Vinaigrette (page 346). The combination of flavors is nothing short of perfection. Serve this salad with Sesame Noodles (page 125) and Tofu Banh Mi (page 170).

PREP TIME: **COOK TIME:**   **YIELD:**

15 minutes   *none*   *4 servings*

2 cups (140 g) chopped red cabbage (chopped small)

3 cups (216 g) shredded iceberg lettuce

1 cup (110 g) shredded carrots

2 tbsp (11 g) sliced green onion

¼ cup (10 g) fresh cilantro leaves, chopped

½ cup (65 g) chopped roasted cashews

½ cup (28 g) chow mein noodles (crunchy variety; see Sister Tip) (gluten-free if needed)

1 tbsp (9 g) toasted sesame seeds

½ cup (120 ml) Peanut Vinaigrette (page 346) or store-bought (gluten-free and/or soy-free if needed)

In a large salad bowl, add the red cabbage, lettuce, carrots, green onion and cilantro and toss.

Mix in the cashews, chow mein noodles and toasted sesame seeds. Pour in the peanut vinaigrette and toss again, then serve.

*See in Tofu Banh Mi image on page 171.

Sister Tip

Here we're calling for the chow mein noodles that are crispy, crunchy and ready to eat, normally found in a can. You should not be using the variety that is raw and used in noodle dishes.

**Butternut Squash Soup with
Sautéed Pepitas (page 200)**

Roasted Veggie and Quinoa Salad

This salad is loaded with tofu, veggies and quinoa and tossed in a slightly spicy tahini dressing. The addition of dates and cashews adds a delicious sweet and salty twist. Serve this with our Pesto Mozzarella Melt (page 160), Spicy Crispy Tofu Pita (page 161) or Butternut Squash Soup with Sautéed Pepitas (page 200).

PREP TIME:
20 minutes, plus prep time for Baked Tofu

COOK TIME:
about 15 minutes, plus time to cook quinoa

YIELD:
6 to 8 servings

QUINOA
¼ cup (43 g) uncooked quinoa

FOR SAUTÉEING
1 tbsp (15 ml) olive oil

1 cup (110 g) shredded carrot

2 cups (170 g) thinly sliced Brussels sprouts

1 cup (134 g) peeled and diced sweet potato

1½ cups (150 g) diced cauliflower florets

¼ cup (60 ml) water

½ cup (85 g) chopped dates (chopped small)

Make the quinoa: Cook the quinoa according to the package instructions. Remove from the heat and set aside.

Meanwhile, sauté the vegetables and dates: In a large, lidded sauté pan, heat the olive oil over medium-low heat. Add the carrot, Brussels sprouts, sweet potato and cauliflower and stir. Cook, stirring often, for 5 minutes. Stir in the water, cover and cook for another 7 to 10 minutes, until the vegetables are fork-tender. Stir in the dates and cook, uncovered, stirring for 1 minute, to lightly cook the dates.

(continued)

DRESSING

½ cup (120 g) tahini

¼ cup (60 ml) water, plus more as needed

1 tsp garlic powder

2 tbsp (30 ml) lemon juice

1½ tbsp (22 g) vegan sriracha

1 tbsp (15 ml) pure maple syrup

1 tsp salt

⅛ tsp freshly ground black pepper

FOR TOSSING

4 cups (4 oz [120 g]) baby spinach, chopped small

5 packed cups (13 oz [375 g]) chopped romaine lettuce

1 batch Baked Tofu (page 334) (omit for soy-free)

½ cup (65 g) chopped roasted and salted cashews (omit for nut-free)

Make the dressing: In a small bowl, whisk together all the dressing ingredients. Add more water, as necessary, to reach your desired consistency.

Toss the salad: Add the spinach, romaine, Baked Tofu, cashews, prepared quinoa and sautéed veggies to a large mixing bowl and toss well. Add the dressing and toss well, then serve.

Simple Ranch Salad

Although this recipe is simple, it's loaded with flavor and is an amazing side to almost anything and everything. If you're a (vegan) ranch lover like us, this is the recipe for you. The combination of fresh veggies, Homemade Croutons (page 349) and flavorful Ranch Dressing (page 345) is just too good. Serve it with our Pesto Seitan Pizza (page 82) or BBQ Seitan Pizza (page 81) and Garlic Knots (page 267).

PREP TIME:	COOK TIME:	YIELD:
15 minutes	*none*	*6 to 8 servings*

5 to 6 cups (360 to 432 g) chopped iceberg lettuce (about ½ large head)

3 cups (210 g) chopped red cabbage

1 cup (110 g) shredded carrot

2 cups (360 g) cherry tomatoes, halved

½ large cucumber, sliced into quarters or half-moons

½ cup (80 g) cubed vegan Cheddar (page 341) or store-bought (nut-free and/or soy-free if needed)

2 heaping cups (115 g) Homemade Croutons, Rosemary Variation (page 349) or store-bought (gluten-free if needed)

1 cup (240 ml) vegan Ranch Dressing (page 345) or store-bought (nut-free and/or soy-free if needed)

In a large bowl, combine the lettuce, cabbage, carrot, tomatoes and cucumber and toss well.

Mix in the Cheddar cubes and croutons. Add the ranch dressing, toss well and serve.

*See in Pesto Seitan Pizza image on page 80.

Caesar Salad

Gluten-free option, Nut-free option, Soy-free option

Between the fish and dairy, traditional Caesar salads are far from vegan, which is why we created a cruelty-free version. It has all of the flavor with none of the animal ingredients. We love serving this salad with our Spicy Crispy Tofu Pita (page 161).

PREP TIME:
10 minutes

COOK TIME:
none

YIELD:
6 to 8 servings

12 packed cups (2 lb [907 g]) chopped romaine lettuce

2 heaping cups (115 g) Homemade Croutons, Caesar Variation (1 batch [page 349]) or store-bought (gluten-free if needed)

1 cup (240 ml) Creamy Caesar Dressing (½ batch [page 348]) or store-bought, plus more if desired (soy-free if needed)

¾ cup (75 g) vegan Parmesan Cheese (page 342) or store-bought, plus more for serving (nut-free and/or soy-free if needed)

Freshly ground black pepper, for serving

In a large bowl, combine the chopped lettuce, croutons, Caesar dressing and Parmesan, and toss well. Add more dressing to taste, if desired.

Serve topped with more Parmesan and freshly ground black pepper.

Spicy Crispy Tofu Pita (page 161)

Easy Taco "Meat"
(page 332)

Taco Salad

Turn any night into taco night with this delicious salad. It's loaded with veggies, fresh cilantro, black beans, Easy Taco "Meat" (page 332) and tortilla chips, all tossed in a homemade Chipotle Ranch (page 347). Love this taco-inspired dish? Try our Taco Pasta (page 112) or Fried Avocado Tacos (page 187).

PREP TIME:
15 minutes, plus prep time for Easy Taco "Meat" and Chipotle Ranch

COOK TIME:
none

YIELD:
6 to 8 servings

8 packed cups (19 oz [540 g]) chopped romaine lettuce

2 tbsp (20 g) chopped red onion (chopped small)

¾ cup (135 g) cherry tomatoes, quartered

1 avocado, peeled, pitted and diced

2 tbsp (5 g) chopped fresh cilantro leaves

1 (15-oz [425-g]) can black beans, drained and rinsed

¾ cup (116 g) corn (fresh [cooked], frozen [defrosted] or canned [drained and rinsed])

½ cup (120 ml) Chipotle Ranch (page 347), plus more for topping if desired

½ batch Easy Taco "Meat" (page 332) (gluten-free and/or nut-free if needed)

½ cup (14 g) broken tortilla chips, plus more for topping

In a large bowl, combine the lettuce, red onion, cherry tomatoes, avocado, cilantro, black beans and corn, and toss well.

Add the Chipotle Ranch and toss again to mix well. Add the taco "meat" and broken tortilla chips. Lightly toss. Serve topped with extra tortilla chips and Chipotle Ranch, if desired.

Kale Tahini Salad with Baked Tempeh

This salad has been known to change the minds of kale-haters. The tahini dressing softens the kale and complements the baked tempeh, tomatoes and Homemade Croutons (page 349) perfectly. Serve this salad with our Sweet Potato Chili (page 193) or "Chicken Bacon" Ranch Pita (page 162).

PREP TIME:
20 minutes, plus inactive time to marinate tempeh

COOK TIME:
20 minutes

YIELD:
6 servings

MARINADE
3 tbsp (45 ml) low-sodium soy sauce (or tamari for gluten-free)

2 tbsp (30 ml) unseasoned rice vinegar

1 tsp maple syrup or agave

½ tsp garlic powder

1 tsp vegan sriracha

½ tsp liquid smoke

TEMPEH
1 (8-oz [226-g]) block tempeh

DRESSING
½ cup (120 g) tahini

¼ cup (60 ml) water, plus more as needed

3 tbsp (45 ml) lemon juice

1 tbsp (15 ml) maple syrup or agave

1 tsp garlic powder

1 tsp salt

⅛ tsp freshly ground black pepper

SALAD
8 cups (240 g) de-stemmed and chopped kale

1½ cups (300 g) cherry tomatoes, quartered

1 to 2 heaping cups (57 to 115 g) Homemade Croutons (½ to 1 batch [page 349]) or store-bought (gluten-free if needed)

Marinate the tempeh: In a large bowl, mix together the marinade ingredients. Dice the tempeh and add to the marinade. Allow to marinate for at least 2 hours, stirring occasionally to fully submerge all the tempeh pieces in the marinade.

Bake the tempeh: Preheat the oven to 375°F (190°C). Line a baking sheet with parchment paper. Remove the tempeh from the marinade and spread on the baking sheet. Bake for 20 minutes, flipping halfway through.

Prepare the dressing: In a small bowl, whisk together the tahini, water, lemon juice, maple syrup, garlic powder, salt and pepper. Add more water, as needed, to reach your desired consistency.

Prepare the salad: Place the kale in a large bowl. Pour the dressing on top and toss well. Let sit for 5 to 10 minutes to soften the kale. Add the marinated tempeh, quartered tomatoes and croutons (starting with 1 heaping cup [57 g] and adding more, up to 2 heaping cups [115 g], if preferred). Toss gently and serve immediately.

Sweet Potato Chili (page 193)

SCRUMPTIOUS
STARTERS

In our opinion, no get-together is complete without a few appetizers. We've also been known to skip the entrée altogether and serve a spread of appetizers instead. We have always (and we mean always) been obsessed with dips, which is why you'll notice there are a lot of mouthwatering dip recipes in this chapter—including Classic Spinach Dip (page 215), Artichoke Parmesan Dip (page 229) and Sour Cream and Onion Dip (page 225), all inspired by versions our mom made for us growing up. Aside from the abundance of dips, you'll find that this chapter is packed with many other delicious appetizers. From our Seitan Fried "Chicken" Nuggets with Sweet BBQ Dipping Sauce (page 223) to Bruschetta with Tofu Cashew Cheese and Balsamic Drizzle (page 239), there's something for everyone.

Classic Spinach Dip

Looking for an easy appetizer that takes less than 30 minutes to whip up? Look no further than this spinach dip recipe that uses minimal ingredients but is packed full of flavor. We prefer to use our homemade vegan Cream Cheese (page 344) and homemade vegan Mayo (page 353) recipes for this, but if you're in a time crunch, store-bought works perfectly. Serve this hot or cold and with anything you'd like—we love pita bread, carrots, tortilla chips or vegan crackers.

PREP TIME:
5 minutes

COOK TIME:
20 to 25 minutes

YIELD:
6 to 8 servings

Canola or olive oil (or spray version), for baking dish

1 cup (226 g) vegan Cream Cheese (page 344) or store-bought (nut-free and/or soy-free if needed)

½ cup (113 g) vegan Mayo (page 353) or store-bought (soy-free if needed)

4½ packed cups (135 g) fresh spinach, chopped

¼ cup (20 g) nutritional yeast

1½ tsp (7 ml) lemon juice

1 tsp garlic powder

½ tsp onion powder

½ tsp salt

⅛ tsp freshly ground black pepper

Preheat the oven to 350°F (180°C) and oil an 8 x 8–inch (20 x 20–cm) baking dish with canola or olive oil.

In a large bowl, combine the cream cheese, mayo, spinach, nutritional yeast, lemon juice, garlic powder, onion powder, salt and pepper. Mix well.

Spread the spinach dip in the prepared dish and bake for 20 to 25 minutes, or until hot and bubbly.

Avocado Bean Dip

Inspired by cowboy caviar, our Avocado Bean Dip is easy, fresh and a perfect dish to bring to a party or barbecue. We prefer to serve it as a dip with tortilla chips, but it can also be served as a side dish or salad topping. The best part is that you can easily adjust it with any ingredients you have on hand.

PREP TIME:
15 minutes

COOK TIME:
none

YIELD:
6 to 8 servings

1 cup (154 g) corn (fresh [cooked], frozen [defrosted] or canned [drained and rinsed])

1 cup (180 g) baby tomatoes, quartered

2 cups (300 g) peeled, pitted and chopped avocado

¼ cup (40 g) diced red onion (diced small)

1 tbsp (1 g) chopped fresh cilantro leaves

1 cup (172 g) black beans, drained and rinsed

DRESSING
Juice of 1 lime (about 2 tbsp [30 ml])

1 tbsp (15 ml) olive oil

1 tsp chili powder

1 tsp ground cumin

1 tsp garlic powder

¼ tsp onion powder

¼ tsp crushed red pepper flakes

¼ tsp freshly ground black pepper

½ tsp salt

In a large bowl, combine the corn, tomatoes, avocado, onion, cilantro and beans. Mix well, then set aside.

In a small bowl, whisk together all the dressing ingredients. Pour the dressing into the bean mixture and mix well. Serve immediately.

Roasted Tomato Salsa

While it may seem intimidating to make your own salsa at home, we promise it's worth it—this salsa is flavorful and fresh, making it much better than store-bought. Serve it as is with tortilla chips or use it in our Nacho Cheese recipe (page 218) or Loaded Burritos (page 185).

PREP TIME:	COOK TIME:	CHILL TIME:	YIELD:
15 minutes	20 minutes	2 hours	6 servings

4 Roma tomatoes, cut in half

1 jalapeño pepper, cut in half, seeds removed

½ large red onion, peeled and quartered

4 cloves garlic, unpeeled

¼ cup (4 g) fresh cilantro leaves

1 tsp granulated sugar

Juice of ½ lime (about 1 tbsp [15 ml])

1 tsp ground cumin

1½ tsp (9 g) salt, plus more to taste

Preheat the oven to 400°F (200°C). Line a baking sheet with parchment paper.

Place the tomato and jalapeño halves, skin side up, as well as the red onion and unpeeled garlic on the prepared baking sheet and roast in the oven for 20 minutes. Remove from the oven and allow to cool slightly.

Peel the roasted garlic and add it to a food processor or blender, along with the remaining roasted vegetables and the cilantro, sugar, lime juice, cumin and salt. Process or blend until lightly pureed, leaving some small chunks. Season with more salt to taste, if desired. Chill for at least 2 hours, as this salsa is best served cold.

Nacho Cheese

This flavorful Nacho Cheese is the perfect go-to cheese sauce to drizzle on just about anything. It's also really easy to make—just blend all the ingredients, heat to thicken and serve. Use it on our Loaded Nachos (page 98), drizzle it over veggies or serve it as a dip with tortilla chips.

PREP TIME:
5 minutes, plus inactive time to soak cashews

COOK TIME:
5 to 7 minutes

YIELD:
8 to 10 servings

3 tbsp (24 g) tapioca flour

1½ cups (219 g) raw unsalted whole cashews, soaked (see Sister Tips)

1 tbsp (15 ml) lemon juice

⅓ cup (26 g) nutritional yeast

½ cup (130 g) Roasted Tomato Salsa (page 217) or store-bought salsa of choice

1½ tsp (9 g) salt

1½ tsp (3 g) paprika (see Sister Tips)

½ tsp chili powder

½ tsp onion powder

1 tsp garlic powder

1 chipotle pepper in adobo sauce + 1 tbsp (15 ml) adobo sauce (see Sister Tips)

3 cups (720 ml) water

In a blender, combine all the ingredients and blend until smooth and creamy.

Transfer to a medium-sized saucepan and cook over medium-low heat, whisking constantly, for 5 to 7 minutes, until thick and creamy. Serve.

*See in Loaded Nachos image on page 99.

Sister Tips

To soak cashews, place them in a bowl and cover completely with water. Let sit for at least 2 hours, then drain, rinse and pat dry (see page 358 for more options and tips).

If you like smoky flavor, replace the paprika with smoked paprika.

Chipotle peppers normally come in a small can with adobo sauce.

Soy-Miso Edamame

It's hard to beat finger food that serves as a snack, side dish or appetizer, and this recipe provides just that. Plus, it's the perfect combination of garlic, soy sauce and miso. If you're not familiar with miso, it's a fermented soybean paste that's salty, tangy and savory, and is widely used in Japan. Serve this dish with our Sweet and Sour Tofu (page 128), Tofu Lettuce Wraps (page 220) or any recipes found in the Travel-Inspired Eats chapter (page 123).

PREP TIME:
5 minutes

COOK TIME:
about 10 minutes

YIELD:
2 to 4 servings

1 tsp cornstarch

2 tbsp (30 ml) water

2 tbsp (34 g) white miso paste (gluten-free if needed)

4 cloves garlic, peeled and minced, or 4 tsp (12 g) jarred minced garlic

2 tbsp (30 ml) soy sauce (or tamari for gluten-free) (low-sodium if desired)

1 tsp pure (untoasted) sesame oil

2 tsp (10 ml) olive oil

2 cups (326 g) frozen edamame (in the pod)

Sesame seeds, for topping

In a small bowl, combine the cornstarch with the water. Whisk in the miso, garlic, soy sauce and sesame oil. Set aside.

Heat a wok over high heat, or a large skillet over medium heat. Once hot, add the olive oil and edamame. Let cook, stirring occasionally, for 6 to 8 minutes, allowing the edamame to char a bit on the outside.

Lower the heat to medium if using a wok, or medium-low heat if using a skillet, and add the miso mixture. Cook, stirring constantly, for another 1 to 2 minutes, or until the sauce thickens. Serve topped with sesame seeds.

*See in Tofu Lettuce Wraps image on page 221.

Tofu Lettuce Wraps

We have always been obsessed with lettuce wraps, so of course this recipe deserves a spot in this cookbook. These lettuce wraps pair crispy butter lettuce with flavorful tofu filling and they are served with a soy-vinegar dipping sauce. Serve them with Soy-Miso Edamame (page 219) and Gochujang Brussels Sprouts (page 133).

PREP TIME:
10 minutes, plus inactive time to press tofu

COOK TIME:
about 15 minutes

YIELD:
4 servings

TOFU FILLING

3 tbsp (45 ml) hoisin sauce (gluten-free if needed)

3 tbsp (45 ml) low-sodium soy sauce (or tamari for gluten-free)

1½ tsp (7 ml) pure (untoasted) sesame oil

½ tsp chili garlic sauce

½ tsp ground ginger

1 tbsp (15 ml) olive oil

1 medium-sized white onion, chopped (about 1 cup [160 g])

3 cloves garlic, peeled and minced, or 1 tbsp (9 g) jarred minced garlic

1 (14- to 16-oz [396- to 453-g]) block firm or extra-firm tofu, pressed (see page 358 for tutorial)

1 (8-oz [226-g]) can water chestnuts, drained, rinsed and chopped small

DIPPING SAUCE

2 tbsp (30 ml) low-sodium soy sauce (or tamari for gluten-free)

1½ tsp (7 ml) sesame oil

2 tbsp (30 ml) water

2 tbsp (30 ml) unseasoned rice vinegar

1 tsp granulated sugar

1½ tsp (7 ml) chili garlic sauce

1 tbsp (5 g) minced green onion

1½ tsp (6 g) sesame seeds

FOR SERVING

1 head butter lettuce, separated into whole pieces

Chopped green onion

Sesame seeds

Make the tofu filling: In a small bowl, stir together the hoisin sauce, soy sauce, sesame oil, chili garlic sauce and ginger and set aside.

In a large skillet, heat the olive oil over medium-low heat. Stir in the onion and cook for 5 to 7 minutes, or until translucent. Stir in the garlic and cook for another 30 seconds to 1 minute, or until fragrant. Crumble the pressed tofu into the pan and stir well. Cook, stirring often, for another 3 minutes.

Stir the prepared hoisin mixture into the tofu mixture, coating the tofu evenly. Stir in the chopped water chestnuts. Cook, stirring often, for another 5 minutes.

Make the dipping sauce: In a small bowl, whisk together all the dipping sauce ingredients.

Assemble the wraps: Serve by placing your desired amount of the tofu filling down the center of each piece of butter lettuce and topping with green onions and sesame seeds. Serve with the dipping sauce.

Soy-Miso Edamame
(page 219)

Gochujang Brussels
Sprouts (page 133)

Seitan Fried "Chicken" Nuggets with Sweet BBQ Dipping Sauce

For this alternative to fried chicken, we use Steamed Seitan (page 332)—it has a chewy, meatlike texture, making it perfect for vegan fried chicken. The seitan is battered and fried to crispy perfection. Don't want to deep-fry these? Check out our Sister Tip to make them in an air fryer. Dip these nuggets in the sweet BBQ sauce and serve with a side of homemade Fries (Baked or Fried) (page 259).

PREP TIME:
20 minutes, plus prep time for Steamed Seitan

COOK TIME:
20 minutes

YIELD:
30 nuggets

SWEET BBQ DIPPING SAUCE
½ cup (113 g) vegan Mayo (page 353) or store-bought (soy-free if needed)

¼ cup (60 g) Dijon mustard

¼ cup (72 g) vegan BBQ sauce

2 tbsp (30 ml) maple syrup or agave

FLOUR COATING
½ cup (62 g) all-purpose flour

½ cup (120 ml) water

¼ tsp salt

PANKO COATING
½ cup (62 g) all-purpose flour

½ cup (30 g) vegan panko bread crumbs

1 tsp paprika

1 tsp garlic powder

1 tsp onion powder

½ tsp cayenne pepper

½ tsp salt

⅛ tsp freshly ground black pepper

FRIED SEITAN
Canola oil

1 batch Steamed Seitan (page 332), chopped into about 30 bite-sized pieces (soy-free if needed)

Prepare the dipping sauce: In a small bowl, combine the mayo, mustard, BBQ sauce and maple syrup. Mix well and refrigerate until serving.

Prepare the flour coating and panko coating: In a small bowl, whisk together the ingredients for the flour mixture. In a separate small bowl, mix together the panko coating ingredients.

Coat and fry the seitan: Pour 2 inches (5 cm) of canola oil into a deep saucepan or pot, or use a deep fryer according to the manufacturer's instructions, and bring the oil to 350°F (180°C). For each piece of seitan, dip into the flour coating, allowing excess to drip off, then coat with the panko coating. Place in the hot oil, working in batches, if necessary. Fry for about 6 minutes, or until crispy, flipping halfway through. Remove from the oil and place on a large, paper towel–lined plate to absorb any excess oil.

Serve warm with the sweet BBQ dipping sauce.

Sister Tip

You can air fry these! Evenly place the seitan pieces in your air fryer (without touching). Spray with canola oil and air fry at 370 to 380°F (187 to 193°C) for 10 to 14 minutes (timing can vary based on your air fryer), flipping and spraying with more canola oil halfway through.

Baked Tofu Nuggets

These nuggets are cruelty-free and baked, not fried. Growing up, before we were vegan, nuggets (with a side of ranch dressing, of course) were our go-to order at restaurants. So, naturally, we wanted to create a simple plant-based alternative. They are perfectly seasoned and surprisingly easy to whip up. They pair deliciously with vegan Ranch Dressing (page 345), ketchup or vegan BBQ sauce.

PREP TIME:
20 minutes, plus inactive time to press tofu

COOK TIME:
40 minutes

YIELD:
24 nuggets

TOFU
1 (14- to 16-oz [396- to 453-g]) block firm or extra-firm tofu

4 tbsp (60 ml) canola oil, divided

Cooking oil spray, as needed

FLOUR COATING
¼ cup (31 g) all-purpose flour

¼ cup (20 g) nutritional yeast

1 tsp garlic powder

1 tsp onion powder

⅛ tsp ground turmeric

1 tsp paprika

1 tsp salt

⅛ tsp freshly ground black pepper

Prepare the tofu: Slice the tofu into four long, equal pieces. Press the slices (see page 358 for tutorial).

Preheat the oven to 400°F (200°C). Oil a large baking sheet with 1 tablespoon (15 ml) of the canola oil, brushing to cover the surface.

Break each piece of tofu into six pieces, creating 24 bite-sized chunks. Place the tofu in a medium-sized bowl and drizzle with the remaining 3 tablespoons (45 ml) of canola oil. Gently toss the tofu in the oil, evenly coating each piece.

Coat and bake the tofu: In a small bowl, stir together all the ingredients for the flour coating, then add to the bowl of tofu. Toss the tofu in the flour coating, liberally coating each piece. Place each piece of tofu on the prepared baking sheet and spray them liberally with cooking oil.

Bake for 40 minutes, flipping and spraying both sides with oil halfway through. Remove from the oven and serve warm.

*See in BBQ Jackfruit Sliders image on page 2.

Sour Cream and Onion Dip

This dip will always remind us of our childhood. It was the one dish we could always count on our grandparents to serve us when we visited their house or had family parties. Lucky for us (and you!), we have perfected this plant-based variation that's not only delicious, but lightened up (as it's made primarily from cashews) and ready in just five minutes. Serve this dip with classic potato chips, pretzels or anything you'd like.

PREP TIME:
5 minutes

COOK TIME:
none

YIELD:
4 to 6 servings

1 heaping cup (270 g) Cashew Cream (1 batch [page 343]) (can substitute for 1 cup [240 g] store-bought vegan sour cream, nut-free and/or soy-free if needed)

2 tbsp (16 g) dried minced onion, plus more for topping

½ tsp onion powder

¼ tsp garlic powder

⅛ tsp freshly ground black pepper

Chopped green onion, for topping

In a small bowl, mix together the Cashew Cream, dried minced onion, onion powder, garlic powder and pepper. Refrigerate until ready to serve (see Sister Tip). Serve topped with green onion and more dried minced onion.

*See in Cashew and Herb Cheese Wheel image on page 227.

Sister Tip

We recommend chilling for at least 1 to 2 hours if your Cashew Cream is at room temperature.

Cashew and Herb Cheese Wheel

Gluten-free, Soy-free

Impress your guests with this creamy, flavorful cheese that's perfect for a gathering. Serve a spread of apps by setting out this cheese wheel along with Sour Cream and Onion Dip (page 225), Pub Cheese (page 228) and your favorite combination of chips, crackers, pretzels and vegetables.

PREP TIME:
5 minutes, plus inactive time to soak cashews

CHILL TIME:
2 hours

YIELD:
6 to 8 servings

1½ cups (219 g) raw unsalted whole cashews, soaked (see Sister Tips)

1 tbsp (15 ml) lemon juice

3 tbsp (40 g) refined coconut oil

⅓ cup (80 ml) water

½ tsp garlic powder

½ tsp onion powder

1½ tsp (1 g) dried parsley

1 tbsp (0.2 g) dried chives

1½ tbsp (7 g) nutritional yeast

½ tsp salt

½ tsp freshly ground black pepper

SERVING IDEAS
Vegan crackers

Pretzels

Chips

Veggies

Line a 4-inch (10-cm) circular mold with plastic wrap (see Sister Tips).

In a food processor or high-speed blender, combine all the ingredients. Process or blend until creamy, occasionally stopping to scrape the sides as necessary. Transfer to the prepared circular mold, cover and refrigerate for at least 2 hours.

After 2 hours, pull out the cheese—it should be pretty solid—by pulling at the edges of the plastic wrap and flipping onto a plate. Slowly peel off the wrap to reveal your cheese wheel. Serve with your choice of crackers, pretzels, chips or veggies.

Sister Tips

To soak cashews, place them in a bowl and cover completely with water. Let sit for at least 2 hours, then drain, rinse and pat dry (see page 358 for more options and tips).

Any 1-cup (240-ml) circular container will work.

Pub Cheese (page 228)

**Sour Cream and
Onion Dip (page 225)**

Pub Cheese

Growing up, it was tradition that we would go to our grandparents' house the day before Thanksgiving to help them get ready for the holiday. (Beer-less) pub cheese was the one thing we could always count on our grandparents having for us—it was our favorite. So, this recipe is reminiscent of that memory, and is (of course!) now vegan, making it the perfect alternative to the snack we all remember.

PREP TIME:
5 minutes, plus inactive time to soak cashews

COOK TIME:
none

CHILL TIME:
2 hours

YIELD:
6 to 8 servings

⅓ cup (72 g) refined coconut oil

⅓ cup (80 ml) plain, unsweetened rice milk

1½ cups (219 g) raw unsalted whole cashews, soaked and drained (see Sister Tip)

⅓ cup (80 ml) light beer (gluten-free if needed)

¼ cup (20 g) nutritional yeast

1 tbsp (17 g) white miso paste (gluten-free if needed)

1 clove garlic, peeled, or 1 tsp (3 g) jarred minced garlic

1 tbsp (15 ml) vegan Worcestershire sauce (gluten-free if needed)

½ tsp dry mustard

1 tsp hot sauce

1 tsp paprika

½ tsp salt

SERVING IDEAS
Pretzels

Vegan crackers

In a food processor or blender, combine all the ingredients. Process or blend until creamy, occasionally stopping to scrape the sides. Pour into a medium-sized container and refrigerate, covered, for at least 2 hours. We love to serve this with pretzels or vegan crackers.

*See in Cashew and Herb Cheese Wheel image on the previous page.

Sister Tip

To soak cashews, place them in a bowl and cover completely with water. Let sit for at least 2 hours, then drain, rinse and pat dry (see page 358 for more options and tips).

Artichoke Parmesan Dip

Artichoke dip has always been our mom's go-to appetizer to serve at parties, barbecues and family gatherings. Not only is this vegan version downright delicious, but it takes just five minutes to prepare. Even though it's made with only five ingredients, it's super flavorful and sure to please everyone, vegans and nonvegans alike. This dip is best served hot with tortilla chips. You can also slather it on a piece of pita bread for a delicious handheld that can be served as an appetizer, a side or a full meal.

PREP TIME:
5 minutes

COOK TIME:
21 to 22 minutes

YIELD:
6 to 8 servings

Canola or olive oil (or spray version), for baking dish

2 (14-oz [397-g]) cans artichoke hearts

1½ cups (340 g) vegan Mayo (page 353) or store-bought (soy-free if needed)

1½ cups (160 g) vegan Parmesan Cheese (2 batches [page 342]) or store-bought (nut-free and/or soy-free if needed)

2 tsp (10 ml) lemon juice

1 tsp Garlic Salt (page 356) or store-bought

Preheat the oven to 350°F (180°C) and oil a 9 x 13-inch (23 x 33-cm) baking dish with canola or olive oil. Set aside.

Drain and rinse the artichoke hearts. Pat them dry, chop into very small pieces and place in a large bowl. Add the mayo, Parmesan, lemon juice and garlic salt and mix well.

Spread in the prepared baking dish and place on the top oven rack. Bake for 20 minutes. Then, broil on high for another 1 to 2 minutes, or until the top is nice and bubbly. Serve warm.

Kale Artichoke Dip

Gluten-free, Nut-free option, Soy-free option

This is a spin on our Classic Spinach Dip (page 215). It combines vegan Cream Cheese (page 344), vegan Mayo (page 353) and vegan Mozzarella (page 340) with artichokes, baby kale and a handful of seasonings. It has all the creamy, cheesy deliciousness of the nonvegan dip you're probably familiar with, but is made better without all the dairy. We love to serve it with fresh bread slices and tortilla chips.

PREP TIME:
5 minutes

COOK TIME:
20 to 22 minutes

YIELD:
8 servings

Canola or olive oil (or spray version), for baking dish

2 (14-oz [396-g]) cans artichoke hearts

2 packed cups (85 g) baby kale, chopped small

1 cup (226 g) vegan Cream Cheese (page 344) or store-bought (nut-free and/or soy-free if needed)

1 cup (226 g) vegan Mayo (page 353) or store-bought (soy-free if needed)

2 cloves garlic, peeled and minced, or 2 tsp (6 g) jarred minced garlic

1 tbsp (12 g) Garlic Salt (page 356) or store-bought

1 tsp dried parsley

1½ tsp (7 ml) lemon juice

2 cups (226 g) vegan Mozzarella shreds (page 340) or store-bought, divided (nut-free and/or soy-free if needed)

Preheat the oven to 400°F (200°C) and grease a 9 x 13-inch (23 x 33-cm) baking dish with canola or olive oil. Set aside.

Drain and rinse the artichoke hearts. Pat dry, chop into very small pieces and place in a medium-sized bowl. Add the kale, cream cheese, mayo, garlic, garlic salt, parsley, lemon juice and 1 cup (113 g) of the mozzarella and mix well.

Spread the mixture evenly in the prepared baking dish. Sprinkle the remaining cup (113 g) of mozzarella on top. Bake for 20 minutes, or until the top is melted and bubbly. Then, broil on high for 1 to 2 minutes, if desired, to get the top extra bubbly. Serve warm.

Creamy Spinach Queso

This is the creamiest, dreamiest queso recipe ever. The fire-roasted tomatoes and jalapeño really kick the flavor up a notch, making this one of our favorite appetizers in this chapter (but really, how can we pick just one?). It's also made in just one pot and ready in less than 15 minutes. Trust us, you'll want to serve this at just about any party, gathering or barbecue; your guests will not be disappointed. We prefer it served with tortilla chips, but feel free to serve it with whatever you'd like.

PREP TIME:
5 minutes

COOK TIME:
7 to 10 minutes

YIELD:
6 to 8 servings

½ medium-sized jalapeño pepper, seeded and minced

1 (14.5-oz [411-g]) can fire-roasted diced tomatoes

2 cups (226 g) vegan Cheddar shreds (page 341) or store-bought (nut-free and/or soy-free if needed)

1 cup (226 g) vegan Cream Cheese (page 344) or store-bought (nut-free and/or soy-free if needed)

1 tbsp (12 g) Garlic Salt (page 356) or store-bought

1 tbsp (2 g) dried parsley

1½ cups (50 g) chopped fresh spinach

½ cup (120 ml) vegetable broth

Salt and freshly ground black pepper

In a medium-sized saucepan, mix together all of the ingredients, except the salt and black pepper.

Cook, stirring often, for 7 to 10 minutes, or until the Cheddar is melted and the mixture is smooth and creamy. Season with salt and pepper to taste. Serve warm.

Jackfruit Taquitos

Gluten-free, Nut-free option, Soy-free option

You know those premade taquitos you can buy in the freezer section of the grocery store? Well, we grew up on those, and to be honest, this homemade recipe puts them to shame. Seasoned jackfruit and homemade Mozzarella (page 340) stuffed inside crispy corn tortillas make for the perfect appetizer. Dunk these into homemade Cashew Cream (page 343), Fresh and Easy Guacamole (page 242) or Roasted Tomato Salsa (page 217).

PREP TIME: 15 minutes

COOK TIME: 20 to 25 minutes

YIELD: 8 taquitos

1 (20-oz [567-g]) can young jackfruit in brine

1 tbsp (15 ml) olive oil

½ medium-sized white onion, chopped (about ½ cup [80 g])

2 cloves garlic, peeled and minced, or 2 tsp (6 g) jarred minced garlic

1 tbsp (6 g) Taco Seasoning (page 357) or store-bought

1 tbsp (5 g) nutritional yeast

2 tbsp (17 g) canned chopped green chiles

2 tbsp (30 ml) plain, unsweetened rice milk

½ cup (56 g) vegan Mozzarella shreds (page 340) or store-bought (nut-free and/or soy-free if needed)

8 fresh corn tortillas

Canola oil, for frying

FOR SERVING (OPTIONAL)
Diced tomatoes

Chopped fresh cilantro

Roasted Tomato Salsa (page 217) or store-bought salsa of choice

Cashew Cream (page 343) or store-bought vegan sour cream, for serving (nut-free and/or soy-free if needed)

Fresh and Easy Guacamole (page 242) or store-bought

Drain and rinse the jackfruit and squeeze out as much water as possible, using a cheesecloth or clean towel. Chop it into small pieces and set aside.

In a medium-sized skillet, heat the olive oil over medium-low heat. Add the jackfruit and onion and cook, stirring often, for 5 to 7 minutes, or until the onion becomes translucent. Stir in the garlic and cook for another 30 seconds to 1 minute, or until fragrant.

Stir in the taco seasoning, nutritional yeast, green chiles and rice milk until fully incorporated. Stir in the cheese shreds until completely melted. Remove from the heat and set aside. Run a paper towel lightly under water to dampen. Wrap the tortillas in the damp paper towel, place them on a plate and microwave for 1 minute. This will make the tortillas pliable so they do not break when rolling.

Pour 1 to 2 inches (2.5 to 5 cm) of canola oil into a deep saucepan or pot, or use a deep fryer according to the manufacturer's instructions, and bring the oil to 350°F (175°C).

Lay the tortillas on a flat surface and equally distribute the taquito mixture among the tortillas, spreading the mixture along the centers, coming just short of the edges. Roll up each tortilla tightly and secure with a toothpick. Using tongs, place each taquito in the hot oil. Fry for 3 to 5 minutes, or until they are lightly browned and crispy, flipping halfway through if necessary to fry completely. Serve garnished with the tomatoes and cilantro and dipped into the salsa, Cashew Cream and guacamole.

Crispy and Melty Mozzarella Sticks

There's a common misconception that vegan cheese doesn't melt. This recipe proves otherwise. These restaurant-style mozzarella sticks are fairly simple to make and will have you thinking, they can't possibly be vegan! Serve them dunked into vegan marinara sauce or Ranch Dressing (page 345).

PREP TIME:
20 minutes, plus prep time for Mozzarella and inactive time for freezing

COOK TIME:
about 12 minutes

YIELD:
12 to 15 sticks

MOZZARELLA
6 oz (170 g) vegan Mozzarella (¼ batch [page 340]) (see Sister Tips)

BATTER
½ cup (62 g) all-purpose flour

⅔ cup (160 ml) water

BREAD CRUMB COATING
1 cup (108 g) vegan standard bread crumbs

½ tsp dried oregano

⅛ tsp ground thyme

⅛ tsp ground rosemary

¼ tsp ground sage

½ tsp dried basil

1 tsp garlic powder

1½ tsp (9 g) salt

FOR FRYING
Canola oil

Prepare the mozzarella: Slice the mozzarella into 12 to 15 sticks, each about 2 inches (5 cm) long and ½ inch (1.3 cm) thick.

Coat the mozzarella sticks: In a medium-sized bowl, mix together the flour and water to create the batter. In a separate medium-sized bowl, mix together the bread crumb coating ingredients. Use a fork or tongs to dip a piece of mozzarella into the batter, then coat with the bread crumb mixture. Repeat, creating a double dip on the mozzarella stick. Place on a large, wax paper–lined plate and repeat with all the remaining sticks. Place in the freezer for about an hour.

Fry the mozzarella sticks: When ready to fry, pour 1 to 2 inches (2.5 to 5 cm) of canola oil into a deep saucepan or pot, or use a deep fryer according to the manufacturer's instructions, and bring the oil to 350°F (180°C). Working in batches, if necessary, place the frozen mozzarella sticks into the hot oil and fry for about 4 minutes, until lightly browned and crispy, flipping halfway through. Remove from the oil and place on a large, paper towel–lined plate to absorb any excess oil. Serve immediately.

Sister Tips

We recommend making the full batch of Mozzarella and saving the rest in the fridge for later.

You can use an air fryer! Once the mozzarella sticks are frozen, spread them in the air fryer, ensuring they aren't touching. Spray with nonstick cooking spray. Air fry at 370 to 380°F (188 to 193°C) for 10 to 14 minutes, or until crispy (timing can vary based on your air fryer).

Bruschetta with Tofu Cashew Cheese and Balsamic Drizzle

This recipe has four moving parts, so get ready. It may sound intimidating, but it is actually pretty quick and oh so worth it. Bring this to a gathering and surprise guests with a cheese that is made from tofu and cashews. Toasted bread, vegan cheese, tomato and sweet balsamic glaze make up a bruschetta that will have everyone coming back for more.

PREP TIME:
20 minutes, plus inactive time to press tofu and soak cashews

COOK TIME:
10 minutes

YIELD:
about 26 pieces

TOFU CASHEW CHEESE
8 oz (226 g [about ½ block]) firm or extra-firm tofu, pressed (see page 358 for tutorial)

¼ cup (56 g) refined coconut oil

½ cup (73 g) raw unsalted whole cashews, soaked (see Sister Tip)

¼ tsp onion powder

½ tsp garlic powder

2 tbsp (10 g) nutritional yeast

1½ tsp (7 ml) lemon juice

1½ tsp (7 ml) apple cider vinegar

½ tsp salt

BAGUETTE
1 (26-inch [66-cm]) vegan baguette (gluten-free if needed)

3 tbsp (45 ml) olive oil

TOMATO MIXTURE
¼ medium-sized red onion, chopped small (about ¼ cup [40 g])

5 Roma tomatoes, chopped (about 2 cups [360 g])

10 large fresh basil leaves, chopped

3 cloves garlic, peeled and minced, or 1 tbsp (9 g) jarred minced garlic

½ tsp salt

Make the tofu cashew cheese: In a high-speed blender, add all the cheese ingredients and blend until smooth. Place in the refrigerator to chill while making the rest of the bruschetta.

Prepare the baguette: Preheat the oven to 425°F (220°C). Slice the baguette into about 1-inch (2.5-cm) slices and lay flat onto an ungreased baking sheet. Brush the tops with the olive oil. Bake for 5 to 7 minutes, until crispy.

Make the tomato mixture: In a medium-sized bowl, mix together the red onion, tomatoes, basil, garlic and salt. Place in the refrigerator while you make the balsamic glaze.

(continued)

BALSAMIC GLAZE

1½ tsp (4 g) cornstarch

1½ tsp (7 ml) water

⅓ cup (80 ml) balsamic vinegar

2 tbsp (27 g) packed light brown sugar

Make the balsamic glaze: In a small bowl, whisk together the cornstarch and water. Set aside. In a small saucepan, combine the balsamic vinegar and brown sugar and place over medium heat. Bring to a gentle boil, whisking constantly, allowing the sugar to dissolve. Whisk in the cornstarch slurry and lower the heat to low, bringing the mixture to a simmer. Simmer, whisking constantly, until the mixture thickens, then remove from the heat.

Assemble the bruschetta: Spread the tofu cashew cheese evenly among the surfaces of the baked baguette slices. Top each slice with an equal amount of the tomato mixture and a drizzle of the balsamic glaze. Serve immediately.

Sister Tip

To soak cashews, place them in a bowl and cover completely with water. Let sit for at least 2 hours, then drain, rinse and pat dry (see page 358 for more options and tips).

Fried Pickles with Spicy Mayo

Vegan fried pickles can be hard to come by—eggs are often used in the batter. Skip the eggs with this simple recipe that uses a seasoned flour-and-water–based batter. Even if you're not a pickle lover, this recipe is one to try. Pair these fried pickles with the spicy mayo dip or dunk them into vegan Ranch Dressing (page 345)—or both!

PREP TIME:
10 minutes

COOK TIME:
about 20 minutes

YIELD:
about 40 fried pickles

SPICY MAYO
1 cup (226 g) vegan Mayo (page 353) or store-bought (soy-free if needed)

3 tbsp (45 g) vegan sriracha, plus more as desired

FRIED PICKLES
1 (24-oz [680-g]) jar hamburger dill chips (about 40 pickle chips)

⅔ cup (83 g) all-purpose flour

⅔ cup (160 ml) water

½ tsp paprika

1 tsp garlic powder

1 tsp onion powder

¼ tsp dried oregano

⅛ tsp freshly ground black pepper

⅛ tsp cayenne pepper

½ tsp salt

FOR FRYING
Canola oil

Make the spicy mayo: In a small bowl, stir together the mayo and sriracha. Stir in more sriracha to taste, if desired.

Set aside in the fridge until ready to serve.

Fry the pickles: Drain, rinse and pat dry the pickle chips. In a small bowl, mix together the flour, water, paprika, garlic powder, onion powder, oregano, black pepper, cayenne and salt.

Pour 2 inches (5 cm) of canola oil into a deep saucepan or pot, or use a deep fryer according to the manufacturer's instructions, and bring the oil to 350°F (175°C). Using a fork or tongs, dip each pickle slice in the flour mixture, letting the extra batter drip off. Working in batches, place in the hot oil and fry for 4 to 5 minutes, or until crispy, flipping halfway through. Remove from the oil and place on a large, paper towel–lined plate to absorb any excess oil.

Serve immediately with the spicy mayo.

Fresh and Easy Guacamole

We can all agree that homemade guacamole is much better than store-bought—it's fresh and easy to make. This recipe comes together in ten minutes and is great to serve in the summertime. Check out our sweet and spicy variation for a fun twist on traditional guac. Serve this dip with tortilla chips or on our Loaded Nachos (page 98).

PREP TIME:
10 minutes

COOK TIME:
none

YIELD:
4 to 6 servings

3 large ripe avocados, peeled and pitted

1 medium-sized beefsteak tomato or 2 Roma tomatoes, diced

¼ medium-sized red onion, chopped small (about ¼ cup [40 g])

1 jalapeño pepper, seeded and chopped small

2 tbsp (2 g) finely chopped fresh cilantro leaves

1 clove garlic, peeled and minced, or 1 tsp jarred minced garlic

½ tsp ground cumin

½ tsp crushed red pepper flakes

½ tsp salt, plus more to taste

¼ tsp freshly ground black pepper, plus more to taste

Juice of ¼ lime (about 1½ tsp [7 ml])

SWEET AND SPICY VARIATION
1 serrano (for spicier version) or jalapeño pepper, seeded and chopped small

1 medium-sized ripe mango, pitted and chopped small

1½ tsp (2 g) crushed red pepper flakes, plus more to taste

In a large bowl, mash the avocado flesh with a fork. Add the tomato, red onion, jalapeño, cilantro and garlic and mix well. Add the cumin, crushed red pepper flakes, salt and black pepper and mix again. Squeeze in the fresh lime juice and mix well. Add more salt and pepper to taste. Serve fresh.

If making the sweet and spicy variation: Add the serrano pepper (or additional jalapeño), mango and the additional crushed red pepper flakes, and mix to combine. Add more crushed red pepper flakes as desired, for a spicier guacamole.

*See in Loaded Nachos image on page 99.

Hummus

Gluten-free, Nut-free, Soy-free

Never made your own hummus? Well, it's surprisingly easy and much tastier than store-bought versions. This is a great basic hummus that is delicious on vegan crackers, sandwiches or veggies and can also be transformed into a roasted red pepper or roasted garlic hummus. Make a double batch and serve at a party—your guests will be impressed. Have leftovers? Make our Hummus Ranch Wrap (page 181).

PREP TIME:
10 minutes

COOK TIME:
none (or 15 to 40 minutes if making a variation)

YIELD:
about 2½ cups (600 g)

1 (15.5-oz [439-g]) can chickpeas, drained (reserve the chickpea liquid) and rinsed

2 tbsp (30 ml) lemon juice

¼ cup (60 g) tahini

3 cloves garlic, peeled, or 1 tbsp (9 g) jarred minced garlic

½ tsp ground cumin

2 tbsp (30 ml) olive oil, plus more for topping

¾ tsp salt

Paprika, for topping (optional)

ROASTED RED PEPPER VARIATION

2 tsp (10 ml) olive oil, plus more for pan

1 red bell pepper, seeded and sliced into 1″ (2.5-cm) slices

ROASTED GARLIC VARIATION

1 head garlic

1 tsp olive oil

In a food processor, add the chickpeas, lemon juice, tahini, garlic, cumin, olive oil, salt and 3 tablespoons (45 ml) of the reserved chickpea liquid. If making a variation, add the roasted red pepper or garlic (directions for roasting vegetables are below). Puree until completely blended. Add more chickpea liquid until your desired consistency is reached. If a cold hummus is desired, chill for at least 2 hours, then top with a drizzle of olive oil and a sprinkle of paprika, if desired, and serve.

If making the roasted red pepper variation: Preheat the oven to 450°F (230°C) and oil a baking sheet with olive oil. In a small bowl, toss the red pepper slices with the oil to lightly coat. Place the slices on the baking sheet so that they are not touching. Roast in the oven for 15 to 20 minutes, or until fork-tender and lightly blackened. Remove from the oven and set aside to cool slightly.

If making the roasted garlic variation: Preheat the oven to 400°F (200°C). Slice off the top of the garlic head, exposing some of the insides of the cloves. Place the garlic head on a piece of foil (cut large enough to be wrapped around the whole head), cut side up. Drizzle with olive oil, then wrap completely in the foil. Place on a baking sheet and roast in the oven for 40 minutes, then remove from the oven and allow to cool slightly. Squeeze as much of the roasted garlic out of the skins as you can.

Poutine

If you're not familiar with poutine, it's a Canadian dish typically made of French fries, cheese curds and gravy. For our vegan version, we use homemade Fries (Baked or Fried) (page 259), vegan Mozzarella (page 340) and a mushroom-based gravy. Even if you've never had poutine before, we highly recommend you try this dish.

PREP TIME:
5 minutes, plus prep time for Mozzarella

COOK TIME:
about 15 minutes

YIELD:
6 to 8 servings

GRAVY

3 tbsp (42 g) vegan butter (soy-free if needed)

½ cup (40 g) minced crimini mushrooms

½ medium-sized white onion, chopped small (about ½ cup [80 g])

3 cloves garlic, peeled and minced, or 1 tbsp (9 g) jarred minced garlic

¼ cup (31 g) all-purpose flour

2 cups (480 ml) vegetable broth

1 tsp garlic powder

1½ tsp (5 g) onion powder

POUTINE

1 batch Fries (Baked or Fried) (page 259), hot, or 2½ lb (1.1 kg) store-bought fries, prepared according to the package instructions

6 oz (170 g) vegan Mozzarella (page 340), chopped into small cubes and at room temperature

Make the gravy: In a large skillet, melt the butter over medium-low heat. Add the mushrooms and onion and cook, stirring often, for 5 to 7 minutes, or until the onion becomes translucent. Stir in the garlic and cook for 30 seconds to 1 minute, or until fragrant.

Whisk in the flour until it is completely incorporated. Slowly pour in the vegetable broth, whisking constantly. Increase the heat to high and bring the mixture to a gentle boil, whisking constantly. Lower the heat to low, bringing the mixture to a simmer. Whisk in the garlic powder and onion powder. Let simmer, whisking occasionally, for 3 to 5 minutes, or until thickened. Remove from the heat and set aside.

Assemble the poutine: Place the hot fries on a serving tray. Top with the room-temperature cubed cheese. Pour the hot gravy on top and serve immediately.

GO-TO
SIDES

For us, dinner is never complete without a few sides (after all, we've got to have options!). This chapter will show you that vegan sides are anything but boring. From Peanut Vegetables (page 249) to Orzo and Rice Salad (page 261), these sides can transform any meal. Pair them with an entrée from our Crowd-Pleasing Pasta and Pizza chapter (page 59) or our Travel-Inspired Eats chapter (page 123), or any dish that needs a great pairing.

Peanut Vegetables

Gluten-free option,
Soy-free option

We love having simple go-to recipes that we can whip up any night of the week. This is a delicious side to serve with almost any dish; we especially love it on a bed of Coconut Rice (page 351).

PREP TIME:
10 minutes

COOK TIME:
about 15 minutes

YIELD:
4 servings

PEANUT SAUCE
1 tsp pure (untoasted) sesame oil

3 tbsp (48 g) creamy peanut butter (soy-free if needed)

3 tbsp (45 ml) soy sauce (or tamari for gluten-free, or coconut aminos for soy-free)

1 tsp chili garlic sauce

1 tbsp (15 ml) unseasoned rice vinegar

1 tsp agave or pure maple syrup

VEGETABLES
2 tbsp (30 ml) olive oil

½ medium-sized red onion, sliced (about ½ cup [80 g])

2 cups (256 g) chopped carrot

3 cups (165 g) chopped broccoli

2 cloves garlic, peeled and minced, or 2 tsp (6 g) jarred minced garlic

1 packed cup (37 g) baby spinach

FOR TOPPING
Sesame seeds

Make the peanut sauce: In a small bowl, whisk together all the peanut sauce ingredients. Set aside.

Prepare the vegetables: In a large sauté pan, heat the olive oil over medium-low heat. Add the onion, carrot and broccoli. Cook, stirring often, for 13 to 15 minutes, or until the vegetables are fork-tender. Add water, as necessary, to ensure the vegetables don't stick to the pan. Stir in the garlic and spinach and cook for 30 seconds to 1 minute, or until the spinach has wilted and the garlic is fragrant.

Stir in the peanut sauce, then remove from the heat. Serve immediately, topped with sesame seeds.

"Bacon" Balsamic Brussels Sprouts

This dish combines Tofu "Bacon" (page 335) with crispy Brussels sprouts and a balsamic drizzle. It's the perfect combination of salty and sweet. Serve it with our Fettuccine Alfredo (page 71) or Creamy Roasted Garlic Pasta (page 85).

PREP TIME: 5 minutes

COOK TIME: about 30 minutes

YIELD: 4 to 6 servings

BRUSSELS SPROUTS

1½ tbsp (22 ml) olive oil, plus more for pan

5 cups (775 g) trimmed and halved Brussels sprouts (see Sister Tip)

BALSAMIC DRIZZLE

1 tsp cornstarch

1½ tsp (7 ml) water

¼ cup (60 ml) balsamic vinegar

1 tbsp (15 ml) olive oil

2 tbsp (25 g) granulated sugar

"BACON"

1 tbsp (15 ml) olive oil

5 slices Tofu "Bacon" (page 335) or store-bought alternative, chopped (gluten-free and/or soy-free if needed)

1 clove garlic, peeled and minced, or 1 tsp jarred minced garlic

¼ tsp salt

Roast the Brussels sprouts: Preheat the oven to 400°F (200°C) and oil a large baking sheet with olive oil.

In a large bowl, toss the Brussels sprouts in the olive oil to evenly coat. Spread on the prepared baking sheet and bake for 20 to 25 minutes, or until fork-tender, flipping halfway through; the time will depend on the size of the Brussels sprouts, as larger ones will take longer to cook.

Make the balsamic drizzle: In a small bowl, combine the cornstarch with the water to make a slurry. Set aside. In a small saucepan, combine the balsamic vinegar, olive oil and sugar and place over medium heat. Bring to a gentle boil, whisking constantly, allowing the sugar to dissolve. Whisk in the cornstarch slurry and lower the heat to low, bringing the mixture to a simmer. Simmer, whisking constantly, until the mixture thickens, then remove from the heat and set aside.

Finish and serve: In a large skillet, heat the olive oil over medium-low heat. Stir in the chopped "bacon" and cook, stirring occasionally, for 3 to 5 minutes, or until lightly crispy. Add the garlic and cook for another 30 seconds to 1 minute, or until fragrant. Lower the heat to low and stir in the roasted Brussels sprouts and salt. Drizzle with the balsamic drizzle, lightly stir to coat and serve.

Sister Tip

If your Brussels sprouts are very large, quarter them so they are bite-sized.

Baked Seasoned Fries

These perfectly seasoned fries are actually baked, not fried. Serve them with a side of ketchup, spicy mayo, smashed avocado or your favorite dip. We love to pair these with our Crispy Buffalo Tofu Sliders (page 173), "Chicken Bacon" Caesar Salad Wrap (page 180) or BBQ Seitan Sandwich (page 166).

PREP TIME:
10 minutes, plus inactive time to soak potatoes

COOK TIME:
45 to 50 minutes

YIELD:
4 to 6 servings

4 to 5 russet potatoes, peeled and sliced into long, ½ to 1″ (1.3- to 2.5-cm)-thick slices

2 tbsp (30 ml) canola oil, plus more for pan if needed

1 tsp Garlic Salt (page 356) or store-bought

1 tsp onion powder

1 tsp paprika

1 tbsp (8 g) cornstarch

1 tsp dried parsley

½ tsp salt

⅛ tsp freshly ground black pepper

2 cloves garlic, peeled and minced, or 2 tsp (6 g) jarred minced garlic

2 tbsp (14 g) vegan Parmesan Cheese (page 342) or vegan Mozzarella shreds (page 340), or store-bought (nut-free and/or soy-free if needed)

Place the potato slices in a strainer and run under cold water for at least 30 seconds. Transfer to a large bowl and cover completely with cold water. Allow them to soak for 1 to 3 hours (see Sister Tip).

Once the potatoes are done soaking, preheat the oven to 425°F (220°C). Oil a large baking sheet with canola oil or line it with parchment paper.

Drain, rinse and pat the potatoes dry, then place them in a large bowl. Add the canola oil and toss to coat evenly. In a small bowl, mix together the garlic salt, onion powder, paprika and cornstarch. Pour over the potatoes and toss to coat evenly.

Spread the potatoes evenly on the prepared baking sheet, making sure they are not overlapping or touching—you may need a second baking sheet if they don't all fit. Bake for 40 to 45 minutes, or until your desired crispiness is reached, flipping halfway through. If desired, broil on high for 1 to 2 minutes, for extra crispiness.

Once the fries are finished baking, transfer them to a large bowl and toss with the parsley, salt, pepper, garlic and Parmesan until evenly coated. Serve immediately.

*See in Crispy Buffalo Tofu Sliders image on page 172.

Sister Tip

Soaking the potatoes is optional, but it leads to crispier fries because it removes some of the starch; the longer you soak them, the crispier the fries will be.

Tahini Green Beans

Transform plain ol' green beans into a delicious side dish by smothering them in a simple tahini sauce. This recipe comes together with just five main ingredients and in less than 15 minutes. We love this dish on the side of just about anything, but especially our Fettuccine Alfredo (page 71) or Easy Creamy Mac and Cheese (page 83).

PREP TIME:
5 minutes

COOK TIME:
5 to 7 minutes

YIELD:
4 to 6 servings

¼ cup (60 g) tahini

2 tbsp (30 ml) water

1 tsp lemon juice

1 tbsp (15 ml) pure maple syrup

¼ tsp salt

¼ tsp freshly ground black pepper

1 tbsp (15 ml) olive oil

3 cups (330 g) green beans

In a small bowl, whisk together the tahini, water, lemon juice, maple syrup, salt and pepper. Set aside.

Heat the olive oil in a large wok over medium-high heat (see Sister Tip). Add the green beans and sauté, stirring constantly, for 5 to 7 minutes, or until crisp-tender. Once the green beans are finished cooking, remove from the heat and stir in the tahini mixture. Serve immediately.

Sister Tip

If you don't have a wok, you can use a large skillet over medium heat. The beans may take slightly longer to cook, so adjust the cook time accordingly.

Roasted Garlic Potatoes

These potatoes are roasted to perfection with fresh garlic and spices. The nutritional yeast adds a slight cheesy flavor, bringing this dish up a notch. Serve with our BBQ Seitan Sandwich (page 166) or Crispy "Chicken" Ranch Sandwich (page 179).

PREP TIME:
10 minutes

COOK TIME:
40 minutes

YIELD:
4 servings

3 tbsp (45 ml) olive oil, plus more for pan

2 tsp (8 g) Garlic Salt (page 356) or store-bought

1 tsp dried parsley

1 tsp onion powder

1 tbsp (0.2 g) dried chives

2 tbsp (10 g) nutritional yeast

1 lb (453 g) baby potatoes, quartered or halved (about 4 cups)

5 cloves garlic, peeled and minced, or 5 tsp (13 g) jarred minced garlic

Salt and freshly ground black pepper

FOR SERVING (OPTIONAL)
Dried or finely chopped fresh chives

Dried or finely chopped fresh parsley

Preheat the oven to 400°F (200°C) and oil a large baking sheet with olive oil.

In a large bowl, stir together the olive oil, garlic salt, parsley, onion powder, chives and nutritional yeast. Stir in the potatoes.

Spread the potato mixture evenly on the prepared baking sheet and bake for 35 minutes, stirring at the 20-minute mark. Then, remove from the oven, stir in the garlic and place back in the oven for about 3 more minutes, or until your desired crispiness is reached. Season with salt and pepper to taste, and serve topped with chives and parsley, if desired.

Miso Sweet Potato

Gluten-free option,
Nut-free

This recipe combines diced sweet potato with a creamy miso sauce. If you're not familiar with miso, it's a paste made from fermented soybeans that's popular in Japanese cooking—its flavor can be described as salty, earthy and savory. For this recipe, we use white miso, which is a bit sweeter and milder than dark miso. You will also come across this ingredient in our Soy-Miso Edamame (page 219) and Cheddar (page 341).

PREP TIME:
10 minutes

COOK TIME:
15 minutes

YIELD:
4 servings

¼ cup (60 ml) low-sodium soy sauce (or tamari for gluten-free)

¼ cup (68 g) white miso paste (gluten-free if needed)

1 tsp vegan sriracha

2 tbsp (30 ml) pure maple syrup

1 tsp unseasoned rice vinegar

2 cloves garlic, peeled and minced, or 2 tsp (6 g) jarred minced garlic

4 cups (568 g) diced sweet potato

1 tbsp (15 ml) olive oil

In a large bowl, whisk together the soy sauce, miso paste, sriracha, maple syrup, rice vinegar and garlic. Stir the sweet potato cubes into the sauce.

In a large skillet, heat the olive oil over medium-low heat. Using a slotted spoon, remove the sweet potato cubes from the sauce and place in the oil, reserving the remaining sauce for later. Cook, stirring occasionally, for about 15 minutes, or until the sweet potato is fork-tender.

Lower the heat to low and pour in the rest of the sauce. Cook for another minute to heat the sauce, stirring to coat evenly, and serve immediately.

"Chicken" Curry Salad

Say hello to your new favorite side dish. Once you try this flavorful "chicken" salad, you'll be wondering why you didn't make it sooner. Make a double batch and serve it at your next barbecue—it's great on the side of our BBQ Jackfruit Sliders (page 94) and Baked Mac and Cheese (page 86).

PREP TIME:	COOK TIME:	CHILL TIME:	YIELD:
15 minutes	*none*	*1 hour*	*4 servings*

10 oz (283 g) Steamed Seitan (page 332), chopped into bite-sized pieces (about 2½ cups), or 10 oz (283 g) store-bought vegan "chicken" strips, prepared according to the package instructions, cooled and chopped into bite-sized pieces (gluten-free and/or soy-free if needed)

¾ cup (76 g) chopped celery

2 tbsp (6 g) chopped green onion

¼ cup (40 g) chopped red onion (chopped small)

¼ cup (27 g) slivered almonds (omit for nut-free)

⅓ cup (48 g) raisins

⅓ cup (80 g) vegan Mayo (page 353) or store-bought (soy-free if needed)

3 tbsp (45 g) mango chutney

1½ tsp (7 ml) lemon juice

1 tsp granulated sugar

2 tsp (3 g) curry powder

¼ tsp salt

⅛ tsp freshly ground black pepper

In a large bowl, combine the seitan with the celery, green onion, red onion, almonds and raisins.

In a small bowl, mix together the mayo, chutney, lemon juice, sugar, curry powder, salt and pepper. Add the mayo mixture to the seitan mixture and mix everything together thoroughly. Chill for at least an hour before serving.

Garlic Dill Smashed Potatoes

If you've never tried smashed potatoes, you're missing out. For this recipe, you'll boil the potatoes, smash them and then bake them covered with (vegan) garlic-herb butter. Using this method allows them to get crispy on the outside while staying soft on the inside. Serve these at a gathering with our Macaroni Salad (page 84) and Crispy Buffalo Tofu Sliders (page 173).

PREP TIME:
10 minutes

COOK TIME:
40 to 45 minutes

YIELD:
6 servings

Canola or olive oil (or spray version), for pan (optional)

2 lb (907 g) baby gold potatoes

2 tbsp (28 g) vegan butter, melted (nut-free and/or soy-free if needed)

1 tbsp (4 g) minced fresh dill

2 cloves garlic, peeled and minced, or 2 tsp (6 g) jarred minced garlic

½ tsp garlic powder

½ tsp dried parsley

1 tsp salt, plus more for topping

Freshly ground black pepper, for topping

Preheat the oven to 400°F (200°C) and prepare a baking sheet with parchment paper or by lightly oiling with canola or olive oil.

Fill a large stockpot three-quarters full with water and bring to a boil. Once boiling, add the potatoes and allow them to boil for 20 to 25 minutes, or until fork-tender.

In a small bowl, stir together the melted butter, dill, garlic, garlic powder, parsley and salt. Once the potatoes are finished boiling, drain, rinse and pat dry. Place them on the prepared baking sheet. Using the back of a fork, the bottom of a cup or a potato masher, lightly smash each potato. Brush each potato with the butter mixture, then bake for about 20 minutes, or until crispy on the outside.

Serve topped with more salt and pepper.

Coleslaw

This recipe *literally* takes 5 minutes to whip up. It has all the workings of classic coleslaw, but none of the egg or dairy. If you'd like, you can replace the coleslaw mixture with 1¼ cups (113 g) of shredded carrot and 4 cups (340 g) of shredded cabbage. Enjoy this simple dish as is or use it in our BBQ Seitan Sandwich (page 166) or Spicy Crispy Tofu Pita (page 161).

PREP TIME:
5 minutes

COOK TIME:
none

YIELD:
6 to 8 servings

½ cup (113 g) vegan Mayo (page 353) or store-bought (soy-free if needed)

1 tbsp (12 g) granulated sugar

1 tbsp (15 ml) lemon juice

1 tbsp (15 ml) white vinegar

¼ tsp salt

¼ tsp freshly ground black pepper

1 (16-oz [453-g]) bag coleslaw mixture

In a large bowl, whisk together the mayo, sugar, lemon juice, vinegar, salt and pepper. Add the coleslaw mixture and stir until well combined.

Serve immediately or chill until you are ready to serve. We recommend serving on the same day.

*See in BBQ Jackfruit Sliders image on page 2.

Easy Steamed Broccoli

This recipe may seem really simple (which it is!), but it's the perfect recipe to have in your back pocket for when you're looking for a veggie to round out a meal. This recipe is great paired with our Easy Creamy Mac and Cheese (page 83), Orange Tofu (page 131) or Creamy Tomato Pasta (page 67).

PREP TIME:
5 minutes

COOK TIME:
12 minutes

YIELD:
4 servings

1 tbsp (15 ml) olive oil

4 cups (250 g) chopped broccoli

¼ cup (60 ml) water

3 cloves garlic, peeled and minced, or 1 tbsp (9 g) jarred minced garlic

½ tsp Garlic Salt (page 356) or store-bought

In a large sauté pan with a lid, heat the olive oil over medium-low heat. Stir in the broccoli and cook, uncovered, stirring often, for 5 to 7 minutes. Stir in the water, cover and cook for another 5 minutes, or until the broccoli is fork-tender.

Stir in the garlic and cook for 30 seconds to 1 minute, or until fragrant. Remove from the heat, stir in the garlic salt and serve warm.

*See in Orange Tofu image on page 130.

Fries (Baked or Fried)

This recipe gives you two different foolproof ways to cook your fries—whether you're a fan of frying or baking, we've got you covered. These fries are very lightly seasoned so that they can be used as a base for other recipes, but if you're eating them on their own, feel free to add seasoning to taste—we love to add some Garlic Salt (page 356) or a dash of paprika, cayenne and garlic powder for a spicy and flavorful kick. Use this classic fries recipe in Poutine (page 244), Loaded Cheese Fries (page 118) or as a side to any burger or sandwich recipe you'll find in this cookbook.

PREP TIME:
5 minutes, plus inactive time for soaking potatoes

COOK TIME:
45 minutes if baking, 10 to 12 minutes (plus 10 minutes rest time) if frying

YIELD:
4 to 6 servings

2½ lb (40 oz [1.1 kg]) russet potatoes, peeled and sliced into long, ½" to 1" (1.3- to 2.5-cm)-thick slices (3 to 4 large potatoes)

Canola oil (1 tbsp [15 ml] if baking, plus more for pan if needed, or enough to fry if frying)

1 tsp salt, plus more to taste

¼ tsp freshly ground black pepper, plus more to taste

Sister Tip

Soaking the potatoes is optional, but leads to crispier fries as it removes some of the starch.

Place the potato slices in a strainer and run under cold water for at least 30 seconds. Transfer to a large bowl and cover completely with cold water. Allow them to soak for 1 to 3 hours (see Sister Tip). Once they are done soaking, drain, rinse and pat dry.

To bake: Preheat the oven to 400°F (200°C) and oil a large baking sheet with canola oil or line it with parchment paper. Transfer the potatoes to a large bowl. Add 1 tablespoon (15 ml) of canola oil to the potatoes and toss to coat evenly. Stir in the salt and pepper. Spread evenly on the prepared baking sheet, making sure they are not overlapping or touching—you may need a second baking sheet if they don't all fit. Bake for 40 to 45 minutes, or until your desired crispiness is reached, flipping halfway through. Once they are done, add more salt and pepper to taste, if desired.

To fry: Pour 3 inches (7.5 cm) of canola oil into a deep saucepan or pot, or use a deep fryer according to the manufacturer's instructions, and bring the oil to 300°F (150°C). In batches, fry the potatoes for 5 minutes, stirring and flipping occasionally. Remove from the oil and place on paper towels to absorb excess oil. Allow them to sit for 10 minutes, and in the meantime, increase the oil's temperature to 375°F (190°C). Fry the potatoes again, in batches, for 5 to 7 minutes, or until crispy, stirring and flipping occasionally. Place on paper towels to absorb excess oil. Toss with the salt and pepper, adding more to taste, if desired.

Orzo and Rice Salad

This cold salad is a perfect dish to make on a warm summer's day. It's easy, delicious and packed full of veggies and grains. The addition of raisins and a touch of maple syrup lends the perfect amount of sweetness to this otherwise savory dish. Pair it with our Pesto Mozzarella Melt (page 160), Tofu Patty Melt (page 158) or BLTA (page 169).

PREP TIME:
10 minutes

COOK TIME:
time to cook orzo and rice

YIELD:
4 to 6 servings

ORZO MIXTURE

1 cup (84 g) uncooked orzo (gluten-free if needed)

½ cup (90 g) uncooked brown or wild rice

3 tbsp (27 g) chopped red onion (chopped small)

⅓ cup (53 g) raisins, dried cranberries or currants

½ cup (74 g) seeded and chopped red bell pepper (chopped small)

1 cup (170 g) sweet corn (fresh [cooked], frozen [defrosted] or canned [drained and rinsed])

2 tbsp (8 g) chopped fresh parsley, plus more for topping

2 tbsp (6 g) chopped fresh basil

DRESSING

¼ cup (60 ml) canola oil

1 tbsp (15 ml) white balsamic or regular balsamic vinegar

1 tbsp (15 ml) pure maple syrup or agave

1½ tsp (7 g) Dijon mustard

½ tsp garlic powder

¼ tsp salt

¼ tsp freshly ground black pepper

Make the orzo and rice mixture: Cook the orzo and rice separately according to their package instructions. Let cool completely, then transfer them to a large bowl and add the red onion, raisins, bell pepper, corn, parsley and basil. Stir well.

Make the dressing: In a small bowl, whisk together all the dressing ingredients (see Sister Tip). To serve immediately, pour the dressing over the orzo mixture and stir well. To chill and serve later, keep the dressing and orzo mixture separate and refrigerate. Combine when ready to serve and serve topped with more parsley, if desired.

Sister Tip

You can use a mason jar to easily mix the dressing. Add all the ingredients, shut tightly and shake vigorously prior to pouring onto the orzo mixture.

Garlic Cheese Bread
(page 270)

Dinner Rolls (page 271)

Buttermilk Biscuits
(page 265)

Breadsticks (page 266)

Garlic Cheese Pull-Apart
Bread (page 275)

FRESHLY BAKED
BREADS

We know bread can seem intimidating to make at home, but lucky for you (and us), we created eight easy bread recipes that require no eggs or dairy. Most of these recipes do require allotting yourself a bit of time to wait for the bread to rise, but other than that, they are very simple and will have you wondering why you don't make homemade bread more often. Pair any of these breads with an entrée from our Crowd-Pleasing Pasta and Pizza chapter (page 59) or with any of the dips in our Scrumptious Starters chapter (page 213)—the possibilities are endless.

Corn Chowder
(page 192)

Buttermilk Biscuits

These biscuits are light, fluffy and buttery. For this recipe, you'll make a vegan buttermilk using soy milk and vinegar. To ensure flaky and perfect biscuits every time, keep the buttermilk and butter cold until you use them and make sure not to overwork the dough. Serve these in the morning smothered with jam or at dinner paired with Corn Chowder (page 192).

PREP TIME:	COOK TIME:	YIELD:
25 minutes	*16 to 20 minutes*	*6 biscuits*

¾ cup (180 ml) plain, unsweetened soy milk

2 tsp (10 ml) apple cider vinegar, white vinegar or lemon juice

6 tbsp (¾ stick [84 g]) vegan butter (see Sister Tips) (nut-free if needed)

2 cups (250 g) all-purpose flour (spooned and leveled or weighed [see page 359 for How to Measure Flour]), plus more as needed

1 tbsp (12 g) granulated sugar

2 tsp (9 g) baking powder

¼ tsp baking soda

½ tsp salt

TOPPING
2 tbsp (28 g) vegan butter, melted (nut-free if needed)

Preheat the oven to 425°F (220°C). Line a baking sheet with parchment paper and set aside.

In a small bowl, whisk together the milk and vinegar. Place in the fridge to curdle, for later use. Place the butter in the freezer to get cold for later use.

In a large bowl, whisk together the flour, sugar, baking powder, baking soda and salt. Use a cheese grater to shred the cold butter into the flour mixture, then stir until well mixed (see Sister Tips). Add the cold milk mixture and mix to incorporate. Transfer to a floured surface. Incorporate a bit of flour into the dough until it's workable.

Using your hands, press the dough into a rectangle that is about 1 inch (2.5 cm) thick. Fold the dough in half widthwise and press back into a rectangle. Repeat this four times, creating layers of dough. Then, press into a rectangle that is ¾ to 1 inch (2 to 2.5 cm) thick. Using a biscuit cutter that is 2¾ to 3 inches (7 to 7.5 cm) in diameter, cut out six circles (cut straight down without wiggling the cutter) and place on the prepared baking sheet.

Bake for 16 to 20 minutes, until golden brown. When done, brush the melted butter on top of the baked biscuits.

Sister Tips

For this recipe, we recommend using vegan buttery sticks, rather than from the tub.

Using a cheese grater is a simple way to cut the cold butter into the flour mixture without the need for much handling of the dough. However, you can also use a pastry cutter or fork to cut the butter into the flour mixture (see page 359 for tutorial).

Breadsticks

This recipe is reminiscent of the crazy bread from Little Caesars that we grew up eating (shout out to our fellow Michiganders!). As much as we love pizza, it just isn't complete without a side of breadsticks. Serve these with our Detroit-Style Cheese Pizza (page 77) and a side of marinara sauce or Ranch Dressing (page 345) for dipping.

PREP TIME:
30 minutes, plus inactive time for rising

COOK TIME:
10 to 12 minutes

YIELD:
20 breadsticks

BREAD
1 cup (240 ml) warm water (heated to 100 to 110°F [37 to 43°C])

1 tbsp (15 g) granulated sugar

2¼ tsp (1 [7-g] packet) active dry yeast

2¾ to 3¼ cups (343 to 406 g) all-purpose flour (spooned and leveled or weighed [see page 359 for How to Measure Flour]), plus more for kneading if needed

1 tsp salt

2½ tbsp (37 ml) olive oil, divided, plus more for pan if needed

TOPPING
¼ cup (56 g) vegan butter, melted (nut-free and/or soy-free if needed)

3 tbsp (19 g) vegan Parmesan Cheese (page 342) or store-bought (nut-free and/or soy-free if needed)

In a small bowl, whisk together the warm water and sugar. Sprinkle the yeast on top and whisk until it is mostly dissolved. Set aside for 5 to 10 minutes, until the mixture has foamed.

Meanwhile, in the bowl of a stand mixer fitted with the hook attachment, or in a large bowl, stir together 2¾ cups (343 g) of the flour and the salt. Once the yeast mixture is foamy, add it and 2 tablespoons (30 ml) of the olive oil to the flour mixture. Beat the mixture on low speed or stir using a rubber scraper or wooden spoon, scraping the sides as necessary, until you have a soft but manageable dough. Add more flour as needed, up to ½ cup (62 g), to ensure the dough is not too sticky to handle.

Either beat the dough in the stand mixer on low speed for 5 to 7 minutes, or transfer the dough to a lightly floured surface and knead by hand for 5 to 7 minutes, incorporating more flour as needed so that the dough does not stick to the sides of the bowl or to your hands. The dough is ready when you gently press into it and it slowly bounces back. Coat a large bowl with the remaining 1½ teaspoons (7 ml) of olive oil. Form the dough into a ball and place in the bowl. Turn to lightly coat the ball with oil. Place a clean towel over the bowl. Let rest in a warm place until the dough has doubled in size, about 1 hour.

Meanwhile, oil a large baking sheet with olive oil or line it with parchment paper. Set aside. Once the dough has doubled in size, gently punch into it to release any air bubbles. Place on a lightly floured surface and roll out into a rectangle that is about 8 x 12 inches (20 x 30 cm). Cut vertically into ten equal-sized pieces, then cut once horizontally, creating 20 long pieces. Place on the prepared baking sheet, leaving room between the pieces for expanding. Lightly cover with a large clean towel or plastic wrap and let rest in a warm place until the pieces have doubled in size, 30 minutes to an hour.

Once the pieces are close to being doubled in size, preheat the oven to 400°F (200°C). Once the pieces are doubled in size, bake for 10 to 12 minutes, until the bottoms are lightly golden brown. Brush the melted butter evenly over the top, then sprinkle evenly with Parmesan. Serve warm.

*See in Broccoli Cheddar Soup image on page 190.

Garlic Knots

You know those perfect, buttery garlic knots you can get at your local pizza joint? Well, this recipe is reminiscent of those, but better (and vegan). Don't be discouraged by the rise time; they are absolutely worth the wait. Serve them with our Pesto Seitan Pizza (page 82) or BBQ Seitan Pizza (page 81). They're great dunked into vegan marinara sauce or homemade Ranch Dressing (page 345).

PREP TIME:	COOK TIME:	YIELD:
35 minutes, plus inactive time for rising	*12 to 16 minutes*	*36 knots*

DOUGH

1½ cups (360 ml) warm water (heated to 100 to 110°F [37 to 43°C])

1 tbsp (12 g) granulated sugar

2¼ tsp (1 [7-g] packet) active dry yeast

4 to 4½ cups (500 to 562 g) all-purpose flour (spooned and leveled or weighed [see page 359 for How to Measure Flour]), plus more for kneading if needed

1½ tsp (9 g) salt

4½ tbsp (67 ml) olive oil, divided, plus more for pan if needed

In a small bowl, whisk together the warm water and sugar. Sprinkle the yeast on top and whisk until it is mostly dissolved. Set aside for 5 to 10 minutes, until the mixture has foamed.

Meanwhile, in the bowl of a stand mixer fitted with the hook attachment, or in a large bowl, stir together 4 cups (500 g) of the flour and the salt. Once the yeast mixture is foamy, add it and 2 tablespoons (30 ml) of the olive oil to the flour mixture. Beat on low speed or stir with a rubber scraper or wooden spoon, scraping the sides as necessary, until you have a soft but manageable dough. Add more flour as needed, up to ½ cup (62 g), to ensure the dough is not too sticky to handle.

Either beat the dough in the stand mixer on low speed for 5 to 7 minutes, or transfer the dough to a lightly floured surface and knead by hand for 5 to 7 minutes, incorporating more flour as needed so that the dough does not stick to the sides of the bowl or to your hands. The dough is ready when you gently press into it and it slowly bounces back. Coat a large bowl with ½ tablespoon (7 ml) of the olive oil. Form the dough into a ball and place in the bowl. Turn to lightly coat the ball with oil. Place a clean towel over the bowl. Let rest in a warm place until the dough has doubled in size, about 1 hour.

Meanwhile, oil two large baking sheets with olive oil or line them with parchment paper. Set aside. Once the dough has doubled in size, gently punch into it to release any air bubbles. Place on a lightly floured surface and roll out into a rectangle that is about 10 x 12 inches (25 x 30 cm). Cut the dough vertically to create 12 equal strips that are approximately 1 inch (2.5 cm) wide. Cut the dough twice horizontally, creating about 36 small, equal strips.

(continued)

BUTTER TOPPING

¼ cup (56 g) vegan butter, melted (nut-free and/or soy-free if needed)

1½ tsp (5 g) garlic salt

½ tsp dried oregano

½ tsp dried parsley

FOR SERVING

Vegan Parmesan Cheese (page 342) or store-bought (nut-free and/or soy-free if needed)

Vegan marinara sauce or dip of choice

Gently roll and stretch each strip of dough until it is 6 to 7 inches (15 to 18 cm) long, then gently tie into a knot. Place on the prepared baking sheets, leaving room between the knots for expanding. Once you have prepared all of the dough knots, gently cover with plastic wrap or a clean towel, then set aside to double again, 30 minutes to an hour.

Once the dough knots are close to being doubled, preheat the oven to 400°F (200°C).

Once the dough knots have doubled in size, use the remaining 2 tablespoons (30 ml) of olive oil to gently brush the top of each dough knot with oil.

Bake for 12 to 16 minutes, until the bottoms are lightly golden brown, swapping the pans halfway through. Meanwhile, prepare the butter topping by stirring together the melted butter, garlic salt, oregano and parsley in a small bowl. When the knots are done baking, remove from the oven and brush with the butter topping. Transfer to a serving platter and top with Parmesan. Serve with marinara sauce or the dip of your choice.

*See in BBQ Seitan Pizza image on page 80.

Classic Garlic Bread

Growing up, we rarely ate stuffed shells or lasagna without a side of garlic bread. For this recipe, all you need is a loaf of your favorite bread, vegan butter, garlic salt and about 20 minutes. Serve it with our Classic Stuffed Shells (page 89) or Cashew Tofu Sweet Potato Lasagna (page 61) for the perfect pairing.

PREP TIME:
5 minutes

COOK TIME:
10 to 15 minutes

YIELD:
20 slices

1 (16-oz [453-g]) vegan French loaf or your favorite loaf of unsliced vegan bread (gluten-free, nut-free and/or soy-free if needed)

⅓ cup (75 g) vegan butter, at room temperature (nut-free and/or soy-free if needed)

1 tbsp (10 g) Garlic Salt (page 356) or store-bought

Preheat the oven to 400°F (200°C) and set aside a baking sheet.

Slice the loaf of bread in half lengthwise. Spread the butter evenly over both of the cut sides. Sprinkle the garlic salt evenly over the butter. Place both halves, butter side up, on the baking sheet.

Bake for 10 to 15 minutes, until golden brown. Slice each half into 10 slices and serve immediately.

*See in Cashew Tofu Sweet Potato Lasagna image on page 60.

Garlic Cheese Bread

Nut-free option,
Soy-free option

This bread is made using our homemade Pizza Dough (page 355), topped with vegan butter, garlic salt and vegan cheese shreds; we prefer to use our homemade Mozzarella (page 340) and Cheddar (page 341). It's the perfect complement to our Detroit-Style Cheese Pizza (page 77) and Caesar Salad (page 206).

PREP TIME:
10 minutes, plus prep time for Pizza Dough

COOK TIME:
20 to 25 minutes

YIELD:
16 slices

1 tbsp (15 ml) olive oil, for baking dish

1 batch Pizza Dough (page 355) (see Sister Tip)

3 tbsp (42 g) vegan butter, melted (nut-free and/or soy-free if needed)

1½ tsp (5 g) Garlic Salt (page 356) or store-bought

1½ cups (170 g) vegan Mozzarella shreds (page 340) or store-bought (nut-free and/or soy-free if needed)

1½ cups (170 g) vegan Cheddar shreds (page 341) or store-bought (nut-free and/or soy-free if needed)

TOPPINGS (OPTIONAL)
Dried basil

Dried oregano

Vegan Parmesan Cheese (page 342) or store-bought (nut-free and/or soy-free if needed)

Drizzle the olive oil on the bottom of a 9 x 13–inch (23 x 33–cm) baking dish. Brush to evenly coat the bottom and sides of the dish. Press the dough evenly into the dish.

In a small bowl, stir together the melted butter and the garlic salt. Brush the butter mixture over the dough. Sprinkle the mozzarella and cheddar shreds evenly over the dough. Bake for 20 to 25 minutes, until the crust is crispy and the shreds are melted.

Remove from the oven and sprinkle the dried basil, dried oregano and Parmesan on top, if desired. Let cool for 3 to 5 minutes, then use a spatula to carefully remove the bread from the dish. Place it on a cutting board and slice once horizontally and seven times vertically to create sixteen equal pieces. Serve immediately.

*See in chapter opener image (page 262) (top left).

Sister Tip

If in a time crunch, you can use 16-ounce (453-g) store-bought vegan pizza dough; note that the cook time may vary.

Dinner Rolls

Growing up, we spent many dinners with our grandparents and they always served light and fluffy dinner rolls, which were the inspiration behind this recipe. These simple rolls are made easy with accessible ingredients that you can find at just about any grocery store. Serve them with any recipe in our Not Your Average Soups and Salads chapter (page 189) or Crowd-Pleasing Pasta and Pizza chapter (page 59), especially Classic Stuffed Shells (page 89).

PREP TIME:
25 minutes, plus inactive time for rising

COOK TIME:
20 to 24 minutes

YIELD:
12 rolls

½ cup (120 ml) warm water (heated to 100 to 110°F [37 to 43°C])

1 tsp + 1 tbsp (16 g) granulated sugar, divided

2¼ tsp (1 [7-g] packet) active dry yeast

2¾ to 3¼ cups (343 to 406 g) all-purpose flour (spooned and leveled or weighed [see page 359 for How to Measure Flour]), plus more for kneading if needed

1 tsp salt

¼ cup (56 g) vegan butter, cut into 4 pieces, at room temperature (nut-free if needed)

½ cup (120 ml) plain, unsweetened soy milk

FOR RISING
1½ tsp (7 ml) canola oil

FOR PAN
Vegan butter or nonstick cooking spray (nut-free if needed)

TOPPING
2 tbsp (28 g) vegan butter, melted (nut-free if needed)

Flaky sea salt (optional)

In a small bowl, whisk together the warm water and 1 teaspoon of the sugar. Sprinkle the yeast on top and whisk until it is mostly dissolved. Set aside for 5 to 10 minutes, until the mixture has foamed.

Meanwhile, in the bowl of a stand mixer fitted with the hook attachment, or in a large bowl, stir together 2¾ cups (343 g) of the flour, the salt and the remaining tablespoon (12 g) of sugar. Add the butter and beat until it is incorporated into the flour. Alternatively, you can mix it with a rubber scraper or large wooden spoon—the butter should slightly break up into the flour, but it's okay if large pieces remain. Once the yeast mixture is foamy, add it and the soy milk to the flour mixture. Beat the mixture on low speed or stir with the rubber scraper or wooden spoon, scraping the sides as necessary, until you have a soft but manageable dough. Add more flour as needed, up to ½ cup (62 g), to ensure the dough is not too sticky to handle.

Either beat the dough in the stand mixer on low speed for 5 to 7 minutes, or transfer the dough to a lightly floured surface and knead by hand for 5 to 7 minutes, incorporating more flour as needed so that the dough does not stick to the sides of the bowl or to your hands. The dough is ready when you gently press into it and it slowly bounces back. Coat a large bowl with the canola oil. Form the dough into a ball and place in the bowl. Turn to lightly coat the ball with oil. Place a clean towel over the bowl. Let rest in a warm place until the dough has doubled in size, about 1 hour.

Meanwhile, grease a 9 x 13–inch (23 x 33–cm) baking dish with vegan butter or nonstick spray. Once the dough has doubled, punch into the dough to release any air bubbles. Divide into 12 equal-sized balls. Evenly distribute the balls in the prepared pan. Lightly cover with a clean towel or plastic wrap and set aside until the balls of dough have doubled in size, 30 minutes to 1 hour.

Once the balls of dough are close to being doubled in size, preheat the oven to 375°F (190°C). Once the balls of dough have doubled in size, bake for 20 to 24 minutes, until lightly golden brown on top. Brush the melted butter over the warm rolls. Sprinkle with flaky sea salt, if desired.

Garlic and Herb Focaccia

This focaccia is extra fluffy and absolutely delicious. After the soft, yeasted dough goes through two rises, you'll use your fingers to press dimples into it, which is satisfying and fun. It's a great addition to your weekly dinners. Serve it with Pesto Pasta (page 62), Classic Stuffed Shells (page 89) or slathered with Kale Artichoke Dip (page 231).

PREP TIME:
30 minutes, plus inactive time for rising

COOK TIME:
22 to 26 minutes

YIELD:
12 slices

1½ cups (360 ml) warm water (heated to 100 to 110°F [37 to 43°C])

1 tbsp (12 g) granulated sugar

2¼ tsp (1 [7-g] packet) active dry yeast

4½ to 5 cups (562 to 625 g) all-purpose flour (spooned and leveled or weighed [see page 359 for How to Measure Flour]), plus more for kneading if needed

1½ tsp (9 g) salt

⅓ cup plus ¼ cup (140 ml) olive oil, divided

FOR RISING
1½ tsp (7 ml) olive oil

In a small bowl, whisk together the warm water and sugar. Sprinkle the yeast on top and whisk until it is mostly dissolved. Set aside for 5 to 10 minutes, until the mixture has foamed.

In the bowl of a stand mixer fitted with the hook attachment, or in a large bowl, stir together 4½ cups (562 g) of the flour and the salt. Once the yeast mixture is foamy, add it and ⅓ cup (80 ml) of the olive oil to the flour mixture. Beat the mixture on low speed or stir with a rubber scraper or wooden spoon, scraping the sides as necessary, until you have a soft but manageable dough. Add more flour, up to ½ cup (62 g), as needed, to ensure the dough is not too sticky to handle.

Either beat the dough in the stand mixer on low speed for 5 to 7 minutes, or transfer the dough to a lightly floured surface and knead by hand for 5 to 7 minutes, incorporating more flour as needed so that the dough does not stick to the sides of the bowl or to your hands. The dough is ready when you gently press into it and it slowly bounces back. Coat a large bowl with 1½ teaspoons (7 ml) of olive oil oil. Form the dough into a ball and place in the bowl. Turn to lightly coat the ball with oil. Place a clean towel over the bowl. Let rest in a warm place until the dough has doubled in size, about 1 hour.

Meanwhile, pour the remaining ¼ cup (60 ml) of olive oil into a jelly-roll pan that is about 10 x 15 inches (25 x 38 cm) (see Sister Tip). Evenly spread so that it covers the bottom of the pan. Once the dough has doubled, place it on the pan and press the dough to fill the pan. Cover with plastic wrap or a clean towel (so that it sits directly on top of the dough) and let sit another hour, until it has doubled again.

During the last 10 minutes of the second rise, preheat the oven to 425°F (220°C).

(continued)

Garlic and Herb Focaccia (Continued)

FOR TOPPING

2 tbsp (30 ml) olive oil

2 tsp (2 g) dried rosemary

1 tsp dried basil

1 tsp dried parsley

4 cloves garlic, peeled and minced

1½ tsp (6 g) flaky sea salt

Once the dough has doubled, spread the 2 tablespoons (30 ml) of olive oil on top. Use your fingers to press dimples all over the dough. Sprinkle the top of the dough with the rosemary, basil, parsley, garlic and flaky sea salt.

Bake the focaccia: Bake for 22 to 26 minutes, until golden brown and crisp to your liking. Eat warm or allow to cool before slicing.

Sister Tip

A jelly-roll pan is a smaller version of a normal baking sheet. We recommend using this size pan for the best results with this recipe. If you choose to use a different-sized pan, you may need to adjust the cook time to account for a thinner or thicker focaccia.

Garlic Cheese Pull-Apart Bread

This pull-apart bread is absolute heaven. It's full of garlic, vegan butter and vegan cheese, and is a great dish to please a crowd. Serve it at any get-together, paired with marinara sauce or vegan Ranch Dressing (page 345).

PREP TIME:	COOK TIME:	YIELD:
35 minutes	*30 to 35 minutes*	*40 pull-apart bites*

DOUGH

1¼ cups (300 ml) warm water (heated to 100 to 110°F [37° to 43°C])

1 tbsp (12 g) granulated sugar

2¼ tsp (1 [7-g] packet) active dry yeast

3½ to 4 cups (437 to 500 g) all-purpose flour (spooned and leveled or weighed [see page 359 for How to Measure Flour]), plus more for kneading if needed

1 tsp garlic powder

1 tsp salt

¼ cup (56 g) vegan butter, cut into 4 pieces, at room temperature, plus more for pan (nut-free and/or soy-free if needed)

1½ cups (170 g) vegan Cheddar shreds (page 341) or store-bought (nut-free and/or soy-free if needed)

FOR RISING

1½ tsp (7 ml) canola oil

Make the dough: In a small bowl, whisk together the warm water and sugar. Sprinkle the yeast on top and whisk until it is mostly dissolved. Set aside for 5 to 10 minutes, until the mixture has foamed.

In the bowl of a stand mixer fitted with the hook attachment, or in a large bowl, stir together 3½ cups (437 g) of the flour, the garlic powder and the salt. Add the butter and beat until crumbly and well incorporated into the flour. Alternatively, you can mix it with a rubber scraper or large wooden spoon—the butter should break up slightly into the flour, but it's okay if large pieces remain. Once the yeast mixture is foamy, add it to the flour mixture. Beat the mixture on low speed or stir with the rubber scraper or wooden spoon, scraping the sides as necessary, until you have a soft but manageable dough. Add more flour, up to ½ cup (62 g), as needed, to ensure the dough is not too sticky to handle.

Either beat the dough in the stand mixer on low speed for 5 to 7 minutes, or transfer the dough to a lightly floured surface and knead by hand for 5 to 7 minutes, incorporating more flour as needed so that the dough does not stick to the sides of the bowl or to your hands. The dough is ready when you gently press into it and it slowly bounces back. Knead in the Cheddar shreds until they are well incorporated. Coat a large bowl with the canola oil. Form the dough into a ball and place into the bowl. Turn to lightly coat the ball in oil. Place a clean towel over the bowl. Let rest in a warm place until the dough has doubled in size, approximately 1 hour.

Meanwhile, butter a 12-cup (2.8-L) Bundt pan and set aside.

(continued)

Garlic Cheese Pull-Apart Bread (Continued)

BUTTER MIXTURE

½ cup (113 g) vegan butter, melted
(nut-free and/or soy-free if needed)

2 tsp (1 g) dried parsley

1 tsp garlic powder

1 tsp onion powder

1 tsp salt

Make the butter mixture: In a small bowl, stir together all the butter mixture ingredients.

Once the dough has doubled in size, punch into the dough to release any air bubbles. Divide the dough into 40 equal-sized balls. Dip each piece into the butter mixture, then place in the Bundt pan. You should have two or three layers of pieces. Cover with a clean towel or plastic wrap and set in a warm place to rise until the pieces double in size, 30 minutes to 1 hour.

Bake the bread: Once the pieces have almost doubled in size, preheat the oven to 400°F (200°C). Bake for 30 to 35 minutes, until golden brown.

SWEET TREATS

If you know us (well, especially if you know Mary-Kate), you know our cookbook would not be complete without a dessert section. For as long as we can remember, Mary-Kate has been the baker of the family. We can attribute just about every recipe in this chapter to her immeasurable talent when it comes to not only baking, but vegan baking. This chapter has 26 decadent sweet treat recipes, including Thick Chocolate Chip Cookie Bars (page 281), Funfetti Cake (page 324) and Cookie Dough Dip (page 291). Every single recipe will have you saying, "This can't be vegan!" (But it is!)

Thick Chocolate Chip Cookie Bars

Inspired by one of our most popular recipes, our Classic Chewy Chocolate Chip Cookies (page 297), these cookie bars are thick, chewy and loaded with chocolate. The best part? You only need ten ingredients to make these doughy, melt-in-your-mouth bars. We love keeping a stash in the fridge for when we're craving something sweet—they are great served warm or cold!

PREP TIME: 25 minutes

COOK TIME: 30 minutes

YIELD: 16 bars

3 cups (375 g) all-purpose flour (spooned and leveled or weighed [see page 359 for How to Measure Flour])

1½ tsp (7 g) baking soda

2 tsp (5 g) cornstarch

1 tsp salt

1 cup (2 sticks [227 g]) vegan butter (see Sister Tips) (nut-free and/or soy-free if needed)

1 cup (220 g) packed light brown sugar

½ cup (100 g) granulated sugar

¼ cup (60 ml) nondairy milk (nut-free and/or soy-free if needed)

1½ tsp (7 ml) pure vanilla extract

1¾ cups (294 g) vegan semisweet chocolate chips (soy-free if needed)

Preheat the oven to 350°F (180°C). Line an 8-inch (20-cm) square cake pan with parchment paper (see Sister Tips). In a medium-sized bowl, whisk together the flour, baking soda, cornstarch and salt. Set aside.

Using the microwave or the stovetop over low heat, partially melt the butter so that it's about halfway melted. Pour into a large bowl and whisk until it has a thick liquid consistency. Whisk in the brown sugar and granulated sugar, then the milk and vanilla. Add the flour mixture and mix again until incorporated. Fold in the chocolate chips.

Press the dough evenly into the prepared pan. Bake for 28 to 32 minutes, until a toothpick inserted into the center comes out clean or with just crumbs. Remove from the oven, allow to cool, then slice into 16 bars.

Sister Tips

For this recipe, we recommend using vegan buttery sticks, rather than from the tub.

If you'd like to make thinner bars in a 9 x 13–inch (23 x 32–cm) cake pan, change the bake time to 18 to 22 minutes.

Carmelitas

Carmelitas are dreamy bars layered with oatmeal cookie, chocolate chips and caramel. For this recipe, we use a homemade salted caramel that takes this dessert to the next level. It's the perfect combination of salty and sweet.

PREP TIME:
30 minutes

COOK TIME:
36 to 38 minutes

YIELD:
16 bars

CARAMEL

½ cup (100 g) granulated sugar

¼ cup (½ stick [56 g]) vegan butter, at room temperature (see Sister Tips) (nut-free and/or soy-free if needed)

2 tbsp (30 ml) nondairy creamer or soy milk, at room temperature (nut-free and/or soy-free if needed)

1 tsp pure vanilla extract

¼ tsp salt

COOKIES

1 cup (125 g) all-purpose flour (spooned and leveled or weighed [see page 359 for How to Measure Flour])

1 cup (90 g) old-fashioned rolled oats

1 tsp baking soda

½ tsp salt

¾ cup (1½ sticks [170 g]) vegan butter (see Sister Tips) (nut-free and/or soy-free if needed)

¾ cup (165 g) packed light brown sugar

1½ tsp (7 ml) pure vanilla extract

1 cup (168 g) vegan semisweet chocolate chips (soy-free if needed)

Make the caramel: In a heavy-bottomed saucepan, heat the granulated sugar over medium-low heat, stirring often, until it begins to clump and melt. Stir constantly until the sugar melts completely. Remove from the heat and add the butter. Stir until combined. Add the creamer and stir until combined. Place over medium heat and stir constantly until the mixture begins to boil. Cook, stirring, for another minute. Remove from the heat and whisk in the vanilla and salt. Strain the caramel into a heat-safe bowl. Set aside for later.

Make the cookie dough: Preheat the oven to 350°F (180°C). Line an 8-inch (20-cm) square pan with parchment paper. In a medium-sized bowl, whisk together the flour, oats, baking soda and salt. Set aside.

Using the microwave or the stovetop over low heat, partially melt the butter until it's about halfway melted. Pour into a large bowl and whisk until it has a thick liquid consistency. Add the brown sugar and vanilla and mix until combined. Add the flour mixture and mix until just combined. Press half of the dough into the prepared pan. Bake for 10 minutes.

Finish the bars: Meanwhile, check the consistency of the caramel by stirring it. If it seems too thick to pour, heat for 15 to 30 seconds in a microwave or on the stovetop until pourable. Remove the pan of parbaked dough from the oven and sprinkle the chocolate chips evenly over the dough. Evenly pour the warm caramel over the chocolate chips. Take pieces of the remaining dough, flatten them and place evenly on top of the caramel, covering as much of the surface as possible. Bake for another 16 to 18 minutes, until the top is golden brown. Remove from the oven and allow the bars to cool and set completely before slicing, about 4 hours. Slice into 16 bars.

Sister Tips

For this recipe, we recommend using vegan buttery sticks, rather than from the tub.

If your caramel seizes while adding in the butter and creamer, place it over low heat and whisk until the mixture comes back together.

Three-Ingredient Peanut Butter Cookie Dough Break-Apart Fudge

If you have just three simple ingredients on hand, you can make this easy peanut butter fudge. Not only is it vegan, but it's gluten- and soy-free. Enjoy it plain or with the addition of mini chocolate chips.

PREP TIME:
15 minutes

COOK TIME:
3 minutes

CHILL TIME:
3 hours

YIELD:
18 pieces

1 cup (90 g) gluten-free oat flour (spooned and leveled or weighed [see page 359 for How to Measure Flour])

½ cup (120 ml) pure maple syrup

½ cup (129 g) creamy peanut butter (soy-free if needed)

¼ cup (43 g) vegan semisweet mini chocolate chips (optional) (soy-free if needed)

Line an 8 x 4-inch (20 x 10-cm) loaf pan with parchment paper (see Sister Tip). Set aside.

Place the oat flour in a medium-sized bowl. Set aside. In a small saucepan, heat the maple syrup over medium-high heat until it begins to boil (showing large, bursting bubbles), then remove from the heat. Whisk the peanut butter into the maple syrup. Pour the mixture into the bowl of oat flour. Stir until combined. Leave at room temperature or place in the fridge until the dough cools completely.

If adding mini chocolate chips, fold them into the cooled dough. To form the fudge, press the chilled dough into the prepared pan. Carefully remove the parchment paper and flip the dough onto a cutting board so that the rounded corners face up. Using a knife, cut slits into the dough that almost reach the bottom, creating 18 pieces that are connected on the bottom. Place in an airtight container. Freeze until solid, at least 3 hours.

Once frozen, break off a piece every time you want a treat.

Sister Tip

You can use any size loaf pan you prefer—larger for thinner fudge or smaller for thicker fudge.

Texas Sheet Cake

This cake is not for the faint of heart. It's deliciously rich and sweet, pairing a moist and fudgy cake with chocolate icing. It's perfect for serving a crowd, as you can easily slice it into 24 or more pieces.

PREP TIME:
30 minutes

COOK TIME:
18 to 22 minutes

YIELD:
24 slices

CAKE
Nonstick spray, for pan

½ cup (120 ml) soy milk, at room temperature

1½ tsp (7 ml) lemon juice, white vinegar or apple cider vinegar

1 cup (2 sticks [227 g]) vegan butter (see Sister Tips) (nut-free if needed)

1 cup (240 ml) water

⅓ cup (35 g) unsweetened natural cocoa powder (spooned and leveled or weighed [see page 359 for tutorial])

2 cups (250 g) all-purpose flour (spooned and leveled or weighed [see page 359 for How to Measure Flour])

2 cups (400 g) granulated sugar

1 tsp baking soda

1 tsp salt

1 cup (240 g) vegan sour cream, plain nondairy yogurt or Cashew Cream (page 343), at room temperature (nut-free if needed)

2 tsp (10 ml) pure vanilla extract

Make the cake: Preheat the oven to 350°F (180°C). Spray a 13 x 18-inch (33 x 46-cm) baking pan with nonstick spray and set aside (see Sister Tips). In a small bowl, whisk together the soy milk and lemon juice. Set aside for 10 to 15 minutes, until curdled.

In a small saucepan over medium-low heat, heat the butter until melted. Add the water and cocoa powder. Whisk to combine. Increase the heat to medium-high and bring to a boil, whisking occasionally. Once it reaches a boil, remove the mixture from the heat and set aside to cool slightly.

In a large bowl or the bowl of a stand mixer fitted with the paddle attachment, whisk together the flour, granulated sugar, baking soda and salt. Pour the slightly cooled butter mixture into the flour mixture. Beat with a hand mixer or the stand mixer until just combined. Add the sour cream, vanilla and milk mixture and beat until just combined, scraping the sides as needed. Pour the batter into the prepared pan. Bake for 18 to 22 minutes, until a toothpick inserted into the center comes out clean or with just crumbs, no raw batter.

(continued)

Texas Sheet Cake (Continued)

ICING

½ cup (1 stick [113 g]) vegan butter (see Sister Tips) (nut-free if needed)

⅓ cup (80 ml) soy milk or nondairy milk of choice (nut-free if needed)

¼ cup (25 g) unsweetened natural cocoa powder (spooned and leveled or weighed [see page 359 for tutorial])

3 cups (375 g) powdered sugar

2 tsp (10 ml) pure vanilla extract

When the cake has about 10 minutes left in the oven, prepare the icing: In a medium-sized saucepan over medium-low heat, combine the butter, milk and cocoa powder. Whisk constantly until the butter is melted and the mixture is smooth and creamy. Lower the heat to low and add the powdered sugar. Whisk until the mixture is smooth. Remove from the heat and add the vanilla. Whisk until completely mixed and smooth.

Remove the cake from the oven, allow it to cool for 3 to 5 minutes, then pour the warm icing on top and spread it evenly over the cake. Allow the cake to cool completely, 1 to 2 hours, then slice into 24 pieces and serve.

Sister Tips

For this recipe, we recommend using vegan buttery sticks, rather than from the tub.

You can bake a half batch of this cake in a 9 x 13–inch (23 x 33–cm) baking pan, keeping the baking time the same.

No-Bake Chocolate Peanut Butter Bars

These no-bake, gluten-free bars are not only easy to make but also absolutely delicious. The peanut butter base is creamy and flavorful. It's topped with a delectable peanut butter chocolate ganache that'll have you craving a second slice.

PREP TIME: — *15 minutes* **COOK TIME:** — *none* **CHILL TIME:** — *1 to 2 hours* **YIELD:** — *8 slices*

PEANUT BUTTER LAYER

¾ cup (194 g) creamy no-stir peanut butter (soy-free if needed)

3 tbsp (45 ml) pure maple syrup

2 tbsp (30 ml) nondairy milk (soy-free if needed)

1 tsp pure vanilla extract

¾ cup (67 g) gluten-free oat flour (spooned and leveled or weighed [see page 359 for How to Measure Flour])

CHOCOLATE PEANUT BUTTER GANACHE

⅓ cup (56 g) vegan semisweet chocolate chips (soy-free if needed)

¼ cup (65 g) creamy no-stir peanut butter (soy-free if needed)

Make the peanut butter layer: Line a 9 x 5–inch (23 x 13–cm) loaf pan with parchment paper. In a large bowl or the bowl of a stand mixer fitted with the paddle attachment, combine the peanut butter, maple syrup, nondairy milk and vanilla. Beat with a hand mixer or the stand mixer until well mixed. Add the oat flour and mix to incorporate. Press evenly into the prepared loaf pan.

Make the ganache: In a small, microwave-safe bowl, combine the chocolate chips and peanut butter. Microwave in 15-second intervals, stirring in between each, until the mixture is smooth and creamy. Pour over the peanut butter layer.

Refrigerate or freeze until set, 1 to 2 hours, then remove from the pan and slice into eight bars. Store in an airtight container in the fridge or freezer.

Thin and Crispy Chocolate
Chip Cookies (page 292)

Cookie Dough Dip

This may just be the easiest dessert we have in this cookbook. This cookie dough dip requires no baking, one bowl, 5 minutes and just six ingredients. What could be better? It's sweet, creamy and the perfect dessert to serve at gatherings and parties. Serve it with vegan graham crackers, Thin and Crispy Chocolate Chip Cookies (page 292), vegan pretzels or whatever you'd like—the possibilities are endless.

PREP TIME:
5 minutes

COOK TIME:
none

YIELD:
8 servings

1 cup (226 g) vegan Cream Cheese (page 344) or store-bought, at room temperature (nut-free and/or soy-free if needed)

½ cup (1 stick [113 g]) vegan butter, at room temperature (nut-free and/or soy-free if needed)

½ cup (110 g) packed light brown sugar

1 tbsp (15 ml) pure vanilla extract

2 cups (250 g) powdered sugar

1 cup (173 g) vegan mini chocolate chips (soy-free if needed)

SERVING IDEAS
Vegan graham crackers

Vegan cookies

Pretzels

In a medium-sized bowl or the bowl of a stand mixer fitted with the paddle attachment, combine the vegan cream cheese, butter, brown sugar and vanilla. Beat with a hand mixer or the stand mixer until light and fluffy. Add the powdered sugar and beat until creamy. Mix in the chocolate chips.

Serve immediately, or place in the fridge until you are ready to serve. Serve with graham crackers, cookies, pretzels or your favorite sweet treat.

Thin and Crispy Chocolate Chip Cookies

If you love crispy, crunchy cookies, this recipe is for you. The addition of maple syrup helps these cookies spread and adds a perfect crunch. Be sure to leave lots of room on the pan for spreading, as these cookies will become almost the size of your hand. Serve them with Cookie Dough Dip (page 291) for an out-of-this-world combination.

PREP TIME: 20 minutes

COOK TIME: 18 minutes

YIELD: about 10 cookies

1⅓ cups (166 g) all-purpose flour (spooned and leveled or weighed [see page 359 for How to Measure Flour])

½ tsp baking soda

½ tsp salt

½ cup (1 stick [113 g]) vegan butter (see Sister Tips) (nut-free and/or soy-free if needed)

½ cup (100 g) granulated sugar

¼ cup (55 g) packed light brown sugar

2 tbsp (30 ml) pure maple syrup

2 tbsp (30 ml) nondairy milk (nut-free and/or soy-free if needed)

1½ tsp (7 ml) pure vanilla extract

1 cup (168 g) vegan semisweet chocolate chips (soy-free if needed)

Preheat the oven to 325°F (162°C). Line three baking sheets with parchment paper. In a medium-sized bowl, whisk together the flour, baking soda and salt. Set aside.

In a microwave-safe bowl, using a microwave, or in a saucepan over low heat, partially melt the butter until it's about halfway melted. Pour into a large bowl and whisk until it has a thick liquid consistency. Whisk in the granulated sugar and brown sugar, then whisk in the maple syrup, milk and vanilla until well combined. Add the flour mixture to the butter mixture and mix until just combined. Fold in the chocolate chips.

Roll 3-tablespoon (56-g) pieces of dough into balls and place well apart on the prepared baking sheets. These will spread a lot while baking, so we recommend placing only four on each baking sheet in a zigzag. Bake for 16 to 18 minutes (see Sister Tips). The cookies may look slightly underdone, but will firm up as they set. Remove from the oven and allow to cool on the baking sheets before serving.

*See in Cookie Dough Dip image on page 290.

Sister Tips

For this recipe, we recommend using vegan buttery sticks, rather than from the tub.

We recommend baking only one or two sheets at a time. If doing two sheets, swap the pans halfway through.

Oatmeal Chocolate Chip Cookies

These cookies are loaded with oats and chocolate chips, and spiced with a little bit of cinnamon. Are you "Team Oatmeal Raisin"? Feel free to swap out the chocolate chips for 1¼ cups (200 g) of raisins—they're delicious both ways.

PREP TIME:
20 minutes

COOK TIME:
9 to 11 minutes

YIELD:
3 to 3½ dozen

2 cups (250 g) all-purpose flour (spooned and leveled or weighed [see page 359 for How to Measure Flour])

1 tsp baking soda

1 tsp salt

1 tsp ground cinnamon

¾ cup (1½ sticks [170 g]) vegan butter, at room temperature (see Sister Tips) (nut-free and/or soy-free if needed)

½ cup (100 g) granulated sugar

¾ cup (165 g) packed light brown sugar

⅓ cup (80 ml) nondairy milk (nut-free and/or soy-free if needed)

2 tsp (10 ml) pure vanilla extract

2 cups (180 g) old-fashioned rolled oats

1½ cups (252 g) vegan semisweet chocolate chips (soy-free if needed)

Preheat the oven to 350°F (180°C). Line three to four baking sheets with parchment paper and set aside.

In a medium-sized bowl, whisk together the flour, baking soda, salt and cinnamon. In a large bowl or the bowl of a stand mixer fitted with the paddle attachment, combine the butter, granulated sugar and brown sugar. Beat with a hand mixer or the stand mixer until light and fluffy, about 2 minutes, scraping the sides as needed. Add the milk and vanilla and beat until smooth, about 30 seconds. Add the flour mixture to the butter mixture and mix until just combined. Fold in the oats and chocolate chips.

Place balls of about 1½ tablespoons (28 g) of dough on the baking sheets, leaving about 2 inches (5 cm) in between each for spreading. Bake for 9 to 11 minutes, until lightly golden brown (see Sister Tips). Enjoy warm or allow to cool before digging in.

*See in Peanut Butter Cookies image on page 295.

Sister Tips

For this recipe, we recommend using vegan buttery sticks, rather than from the tub. Let the butter sit out for 30 minutes to an hour before using.

We recommend baking only one or two sheets at a time. If doing two sheets, swap the pans halfway through.

Peanut Butter Cookies

These classic cookies are soft, chewy and loaded with peanut butter. Be prepared to make a second batch, as these cookies are always quick to be eaten. If you can't get enough of the raw cookie dough, be sure to check out our recipe for Edible Peanut Butter Cookie Dough (page 309).

PREP TIME:
20 minutes

COOK TIME:
8 minutes

YIELD:
2½ to 3 dozen cookies

1¾ cups (218 g) all-purpose flour (spooned and leveled or weighed [see page 359 for How to Measure Flour])

1 tsp baking powder

½ tsp baking soda

½ tsp salt

½ cup (1 stick [113 g]) vegan butter, at room temperature (see Sister Tips) (soy-free if needed)

½ cup (100 g) granulated sugar

½ cup (110 g) packed light brown sugar

¾ cup (194 g) creamy no-stir peanut butter (soy-free if needed)

¼ cup (60 ml) nondairy milk (soy-free if needed)

1 tbsp (15 ml) pure vanilla extract

Preheat the oven to 350°F (180°C). Line three baking sheets with parchment paper and set aside.

In a medium-sized bowl, whisk together the flour, baking powder, baking soda and salt. Set aside. In a large bowl or the bowl of a stand mixer fitted with the paddle attachment, combine the butter, granulated sugar and brown sugar. Beat with a hand mixer or the stand mixer until light and fluffy, about 2 minutes, scraping the sides as needed. Add the peanut butter, milk and vanilla. Beat again until combined, about 30 seconds. Add the flour mixture to the butter mixture and mix until just combined.

Roll about 1½ tablespoons (25 g) of dough into balls. Place on the prepared baking sheets, leaving 2 inches (5 cm) in between the balls of dough. Using a fork, make crisscross marks across each cookie, flattening them slightly in the process.

Bake for 7 to 9 minutes (see Sister Tips). The cookies may look a little under-done, but they will firm up as they cool—you don't want to overbake them. Remove from the oven and allow to cool on the baking sheets before serving.

*In the photo on the opposite page, these are shown in the middle-right column.

Sister Tips

For this recipe, we recommend using vegan buttery sticks, rather than from the tub. Let the butter sit out for 30 minutes to an hour before using.

We recommend baking only one or two sheets at a time. If doing two sheets, swap the pans halfway through.

**Classic Chewy Chocolate Chip
Cookies (page 297)**

**Peanut Butter Cookies
(opposite page)**

Snickerdoodles (page 296)

**Oatmeal Chocolate Chip
Cookies (page 293)**

Snickerdoodles

The perfect snickerdoodle has a soft and chewy center with a slightly crunchy cinnamon-sugar exterior, and these have just that. The addition of cream of tartar gives these cookies that classic snickerdoodle texture and flavor, so don't omit it—you can typically find it at the grocery store in the baking or spices section, or order it online.

PREP TIME:
25 minutes

COOK TIME:
7 to 9 minutes

YIELD:
about 1½ dozen

1½ cups (187 g) all-purpose flour (spooned and leveled or weighed [see page 359 for How to Measure Flour])

1 tsp cream of tartar

1 tsp cinnamon

½ tsp baking soda

¼ tsp salt

½ cup (1 stick [113 g]) vegan butter, at room temperature (see Sister Tips) (nut-free and/or soy-free if needed)

¾ cup (150 g) granulated sugar

2 tbsp (30 ml) nondairy milk (nut-free and/or soy-free if needed)

1 tsp pure vanilla extract

FOR ROLLING
2 tbsp (25 g) granulated sugar

1 tsp ground cinnamon

Preheat the oven to 375°F (190°C). Line two baking sheets with parchment paper.

In a medium-sized bowl, whisk together the flour, cream of tartar, cinnamon, baking soda and salt. Set aside. In a large bowl or the bowl of a stand mixer fitted with the paddle attachment, add the butter and sugar. Beat with a hand mixer or the stand mixer until light and fluffy, about 2 minutes, scraping the sides as needed. Add the milk and vanilla. Beat again until smooth, about 30 seconds. Add the flour mixture to the butter mixture and mix until just combined. Set aside.

In a small bowl, whisk the sugar and cinnamon together for rolling. Roll 1½-tablespoon (25-g) balls of dough and coat with the cinnamon sugar topping. Place on the prepared baking sheets, leaving 2 inches (5 cm) between the balls of dough. Bake for 7 to 9 minutes, until golden brown around the edges (see Sister Tips). Remove from the oven and allow to cool on the baking sheets before serving.

*See the image on the previous page (middle-left column).

Sister Tips

For this recipe, we recommend using vegan buttery sticks, rather than from the tub. Let the butter sit out for 30 minutes to an hour before using.

We recommend baking only one or two sheets at a time. If doing two sheets, swap the pans halfway through.

Classic Chewy Chocolate Chip Cookies

This recipe has been one of the most popular on our blog for years, and once you make it, you'll see why. It's our go-to cookie recipe for serving to friends and family or when we're craving a batch of warm, chewy chocolate chip cookies—the addition of cornstarch gives them an extra-chewy texture. If you find yourself sneaking cookie dough straight from the bowl, check out our Edible Chocolate Chip Cookie Dough recipe (page 310).

PREP TIME:	COOK TIME:	YIELD:
20 minutes	*9 to 11 minutes*	*3 to 3½ dozen*

2¼ cups (280 g) all-purpose flour (spooned and leveled or weighed [see page 359 for How to Measure Flour])

1 tsp salt

1 tsp baking soda

2 tsp (5 g) cornstarch

¾ cup (1½ sticks [169 g]) vegan butter, at room temperature (nut-free and/or soy-free if needed) (see Sister Tips)

1 cup (220 g) packed brown sugar

¼ cup (50 g) granulated sugar

¼ cup (60 ml) nondairy milk (nut-free and/or soy-free if needed)

2 tsp (10 ml) pure vanilla extract

1½ cups (252 g) vegan semisweet chocolate chips or 1¼ cups (216 g) vegan mini semisweet chocolate chips (nut-free and/or soy-free if needed)

Preheat the oven to 350°F (180°C). Line three or four baking sheets with parchment paper.

In a medium-sized bowl, whisk together the flour, salt, baking soda and cornstarch. In a separate large bowl or the bowl of a stand mixer fitted with the paddle attachment, combine the butter, brown sugar and granulated sugar. Beat with a hand mixer or the stand mixer until light and fluffy, about 2 minutes, scraping the sides as needed. Add the milk and vanilla and beat again until creamy, another 30 seconds.

Add about half of the flour mixture to the butter mixture and use a rubber scraper to mix until combined. Add the rest of the flour mixture and mix until just combined. Fold in the chocolate chips.

(continued)

Classic Chewy Chocolate Chip Cookies (Continued)

Using a cookie scooper, create 1½-tablespoon (28-g) balls of dough and place them on the prepared baking sheets, leaving about 2 inches (5 cm) between the balls of dough for spreading. Bake for 9 to 11 minutes (see Sister Tips), until they are slightly golden brown—they may look slightly underbaked, but will firm up as they set. Remove from the oven and allow to cool on the baking sheets before serving.

*See in Peanut Butter Cookies image on page 295.

Sister Tips

You can use either vegan buttery sticks or buttery spread from the tub for this recipe. You want the butter to be soft so that it incorporates well with the other ingredients. Typically, you should let the butter sit out for 30 minutes to an hour before using, but if you use buttery spread that is soft straight from the fridge, you can skip the softening step.

We recommend baking only one or two sheets at a time. If doing two sheets, swap the pans halfway through.

Cookie Dough Cupcakes

If you've never paired vanilla cake with chocolate chip cookie dough, you're missing out. This recipe stuffs (and tops!) frosted vanilla cupcakes with edible cookie dough. You'll only need a half batch of Edible Chocolate Chip Cookie Dough (page 310), but we recommend making an entire batch and saving the extra for eating on its own. That being said, if you'd prefer classic vanilla cupcakes, you can omit the cookie dough altogether.

PREP TIME:
40 minutes, plus prep time for cookie dough

COOK TIME:
16 to 20 minutes

YIELD:
about 14 cupcakes

CUPCAKES

1 cup (240 ml) soy milk, at room temperature

1 tbsp (15 ml) apple cider vinegar, white vinegar or lemon juice

1⅔ cups (190 g) cake flour (spooned and leveled or weighed [see page 359 for How to Measure Flour])

1 cup (200 g) granulated sugar

½ tsp baking soda

½ tsp baking powder

½ tsp salt

⅓ cup (80 ml) canola oil

1½ tsp (7 ml) pure vanilla extract

Make the cupcakes: Preheat the oven to 350°F (180°C) and line two cupcake pans with 14 cupcake liners. In a medium-sized bowl, whisk together the milk and vinegar, then set aside for 10 to 15 minutes, until curdled.

Sift the cake flour into a large bowl. Add the sugar, baking soda, baking powder and salt to the flour and whisk to combine. Add the canola oil and vanilla to the milk mixture and mix. Pour the milk mixture into the flour mixture and mix until just combined. Pour about 3 tablespoons (45 ml) of batter into each cupcake liner (add or remove cupcake liners depending on quantity of batter). Bake for 16 to 20 minutes, until a toothpick inserted into the center of a cupcake comes out clean or with only crumbs. Remove from the oven and set aside to cool completely.

(continued)

Cookie Dough Cupcakes (Continued)

FROSTING

½ cup (1 stick [113 g]) vegan butter, at room temperature (see Sister Tip) (nut-free if needed)

2 cups (250 g) powdered sugar

1½ tsp (7 ml) soy milk, or nondairy milk of choice, plus more as needed (nut-free if needed)

1 tsp pure vanilla extract

COOKIE DOUGH

½ batch Edible Chocolate Chip Cookie Dough (page 310)

Make the frosting: In a large bowl or the bowl of a stand mixer fitted with the paddle attachment, beat the butter with a hand mixer or the stand mixer until light and fluffy, scraping the sides as necessary. Add the powdered sugar, milk and vanilla, and beat until smooth and creamy. Stir in more milk, 1 teaspoon at a time, as needed, until a smooth but thick consistency is reached.

Assemble the cupcakes: Press a small hole into the center of each cupcake. Stuff each hole with a bit of cookie dough. Transfer the frosting into a piping bag fitted with a large drop flower tip or decorating tip of choice. Pipe a large swirl onto each cupcake. Divide the remaining cookie dough into 14 balls (or as many balls as there are cupcakes) and top each cupcake with a ball of cookie dough.

Sister Tip

For this recipe, we recommend using vegan buttery sticks, rather than from the tub. Let the butter sit out for 30 minutes to an hour before using.

Peanut Butter Cup Cookie Bars

If you love the combination of chocolate and peanut butter, you'll be head over heels for these bars. They combine a soft and chewy peanut butter cookie base with a chocolate peanut butter ganache and peanut butter cups. Obsessed with peanut butter? Make sure to try our Peanut Butter Cookies (page 294), No-Bake Chocolate Peanut Butter Bars (page 289) or Three-Ingredient Peanut Butter Cookie Dough Break-Apart Fudge (page 285).

PREP TIME:
25 minutes

COOK TIME:
14 to 16 minutes

YIELD:
24 bars

PEANUT BUTTER COOKIE LAYER

1¾ cups (218 g) all-purpose flour (spooned and leveled or weighed [see page 359 for How to Measure Flour])

1 tsp cornstarch

1 tsp baking powder

½ tsp baking soda

½ tsp salt

½ cup (1 stick [113 g]) vegan butter, at room temperature (see Sister Tip) (soy-free if needed)

½ cup (100 g) granulated sugar

½ cup (110 g) packed light brown sugar

¾ cup (194 g) creamy no-stir peanut butter (soy-free if needed)

¼ cup (60 ml) nondairy milk (soy-free if needed)

1 tbsp (15 ml) pure vanilla extract

CHOCOLATE PEANUT BUTTER GANACHE

1 cup (168 g) vegan semisweet chocolate chips (soy-free if needed)

½ cup (129 g) creamy no-stir peanut butter (soy-free if needed)

TOPPING

10 vegan mini peanut butter cups (soy-free if needed)

Make the cookie layer: Preheat the oven to 350°F (180°C) and line a 9 x 13-inch (23 x 33-cm) cake pan with parchment paper. In a medium-sized bowl, whisk together the flour, cornstarch, baking powder, baking soda and salt. Set aside. In a large bowl or the bowl of a stand mixer fitted with the paddle attachment, combine the butter, granulated sugar and brown sugar. Beat with a hand mixer or the stand mixer until light and fluffy. Add the peanut butter, milk and vanilla and beat again until creamy. Add the flour mixture to the butter mixture and stir until just combined. Press evenly into the prepared pan. Bake for 14 to 16 minutes, until a toothpick inserted into the center comes out clean or with only crumbs. Once baked, remove from the oven and set aside to cool completely.

Make the ganache: In a microwave-safe bowl, combine the chocolate chips and peanut butter. Microwave in 30-second intervals, whisking in between, until fully melted and creamy. Pour over the cooled cookie base and spread evenly.

Add the topping: Chop the peanut butter cups into halves or quarters. Sprinkle over the ganache. Let the bars sit at room temperature for 1 to 2 hours, or until the ganache sets, then slice into 24 bars.

Sister Tip

For this recipe, we recommend using vegan buttery sticks, rather than from the tub. Let the butter sit out for 30 minutes to an hour before using.

Fudgy Brownies

Nut-free option, Soy-free option

Years ago, we set out to create the perfect vegan brownie recipe, reminiscent of the nonvegan ones we grew up eating. After many trials and failures, it's safe to say we finally nailed the ultimate vegan fudgy brownies. They are rich, chocolaty and beyond delicious—everything you want in a brownie without the eggs or dairy.

PREP TIME:
25 minutes

COOK TIME:
34 minutes

YIELD:
24 brownies

3 tbsp (21 g) flaxseed meal

6 tbsp (90 ml) water

1⅔ cups (208 g) all-purpose flour (spooned and leveled or weighed [see page 359 for How to Measure Flour])

1¼ cups (125 g) unsweetened natural cocoa powder (spooned and leveled or weighed [see page 359 for tutorial])

1 tsp baking powder

¼ tsp baking soda

1 tsp salt

¾ cup (169 g) vegan butter (see Sister Tips) (nut-free and/or soy-free if needed)

1 (4-oz [113-g]) bar vegan semisweet chocolate (see Sister Tips) (soy-free if needed)

1¼ cups (250 g) granulated sugar

1 cup (220 g) packed light brown sugar

½ cup (120 ml) nondairy milk (nut-free and/or soy-free if needed)

1 tbsp (15 ml) pure vanilla extract

1½ cups (252 g) vegan semisweet chocolate chips (soy-free if needed)

Preheat the oven to 350°F (180°C). Line a 9 x 13–inch (23 x 33–cm) aluminum cake pan with parchment paper and set aside.

In a small bowl, whisk together the flaxseed meal and water. Set aside for 10 to 15 minutes, until gelled. In a medium-sized bowl, whisk together the flour, cocoa powder, baking powder, baking soda and salt. Set aside.

In a large, microwave-safe bowl, add the butter and chocolate. Microwave in 15-second intervals, stirring in between, until completely melted. Add the granulated sugar and brown sugar and whisk until combined. Add the milk, vanilla and flaxseed meal mixture. Mix until combined. Add the flour mixture to the chocolate mixture and mix until just combined. Fold in the chocolate chips.

Pour into the prepared pan and bake for 32 to 36 minutes. The top will look crackly and shiny, but the brownie may still be fudgy and seem underbaked—that's okay, it'll set as it cools. Remove from the oven and allow to cool completely in the pan, then carefully remove from the pan and slice into 24 bars.

Sister Tips

For this recipe, we recommend using vegan buttery sticks, rather than buttery spread from the tub.

Use a high-quality chocolate baking bar for the best outcome.

Sugar Cookie Bars

These bars are inspired by the store-bought frosted sugar cookies we grew up eating. The base is a soft sugar cookie that's topped with a creamy buttercream frosting and, of course, sprinkles. This recipe makes 24 bars, so it's great for serving a crowd.

PREP TIME:
30 minutes

COOK TIME:
14 to 16 minutes

YIELD:
24 bars

SUGAR COOKIE LAYER

2¾ cups (343 g) all-purpose flour (spooned and leveled or weighed [see page 359 for How to Measure Flour])

1 tsp baking powder

½ tsp baking soda

½ tsp salt

2 tsp (5 g) cornstarch

½ cup (1 stick [113 g]) vegan butter, at room temperature (see Sister Tip) (nut-free and/or soy-free if needed)

1 cup (200 g) granulated sugar

¼ cup (60 g) vegan sour cream, plain nondairy yogurt or Cashew Cream [page 343]) (nut-free and/or soy-free if needed)

3 tbsp (45 ml) nondairy milk (nut-free and/or soy-free if needed)

2 tsp (10 ml) pure vanilla extract

FROSTING

½ cup (1 stick [113 g]) vegan butter, at room temperature (see Sister Tip) (nut-free and/or soy-free if needed)

2 cups (250 g) powdered sugar

1½ tsp (7 ml) nondairy milk, plus more as needed (nut-free and/or soy-free if needed)

½ tsp pure vanilla extract

TOPPING

2 tbsp (17 g) vegan rainbow sprinkles (soy-free if needed)

Make the sugar cookie layer: Preheat the oven to 350°F (180°C). Line a 9 x 13-inch (23 x 33-cm) cake pan with parchment paper and set aside. In a medium sized bowl, whisk together the flour, baking powder, baking soda, salt and cornstarch. In a separate, large bowl or the bowl of a stand mixer fitted with the paddle attachment, combine the butter and granulated sugar and beat with a hand mixer or the stand mixer until well mixed. Add the sour cream, milk and vanilla. Beat again until smooth and creamy.

Pour about half of the flour mixture into the butter mixture and mix until just barely combined. Add the rest of the flour mixture and mix until just combined. Press the dough evenly into the prepared pan. Bake for 14 to 16 minutes, until golden. Remove from the oven and allow to cool completely in the pan while you prepare the frosting.

Make the frosting: In a large bowl or the bowl of a stand mixer fitted with the paddle attachment, beat the butter with a hand mixer or the stand mixer until light and fluffy, scraping the sides as necessary. Add the powdered sugar, milk and vanilla, and beat until smooth and creamy. Stir in more milk, 1 teaspoon at a time, as needed, until a smooth but thick consistency is reached.

Assemble the bars: Once the cookie layer is cool, evenly spread the frosting and immediately top with the sprinkles. Slice into 24 slices.

Sister Tip

For this recipe, we recommend using vegan buttery sticks, rather than buttery spread from the tub. Let the butter sit out for 30 minutes to an hour before using.

Edible Chocolate Chip
Cookie Dough (page 310)

Edible Peanut Butter Cookie Dough

It's almost impossible to make peanut butter cookies without grabbing a spoonful (or two) of the raw cookie dough, which is why we made this edible peanut butter cookie dough. With toasted flour and the lack of raw eggs, it is completely safe to eat. Craving a fresh peanut butter cookie now? Check out our Peanut Butter Cookies recipe (page 294).

PREP TIME:
10 minutes, plus inactive time to cool flour

COOK TIME:
5 minutes

YIELD:
6 servings

1 cup (125 g) all-purpose flour (spooned and leveled or weighed [see page 359 for How to Measure Flour])

¼ cup (56 g) vegan butter, at room temperature (see Sister Tip) (soy-free if needed)

¼ cup (65 g) creamy no-stir peanut butter (soy-free if needed)

⅓ cup (66 g) granulated sugar

⅓ cup (73 g) packed light brown sugar

1 tsp pure vanilla extract

3 tbsp (45 ml) nondairy milk (soy-free if needed)

¼ tsp salt

Preheat the oven to 350°F (180°C). Spread the flour on an ungreased baking sheet. Bake for 5 minutes. Remove from the oven and set aside to cool completely.

In a large bowl or the bowl of a stand mixer fitted with the paddle attachment, combine the butter, peanut butter, granulated sugar and brown sugar. Beat with a hand mixer or the stand mixer until light and fluffy. Add the vanilla and milk and beat until creamy. Add the cooled flour and salt and mix until combined. Eat right out of the bowl with a spoon or roll into bite-sized balls and place in an airtight container in the fridge or freezer to enjoy later.

Sister Tip

You can use either vegan buttery sticks or buttery spread from the tub for this recipe. You want the butter to be soft so that it incorporates well with the other ingredients. Typically, you should let the butter sit out for 30 minutes to an hour before using, but if you use buttery spread that is soft straight from the fridge, you can skip the softening step.

Edible Chocolate Chip Cookie Dough

If you're known for digging into the cookie dough before it goes into the oven, this recipe is for you. This dough is made with heat-treated flour and, of course, no raw eggs, making it perfectly safe to eat! It's not meant to be baked, so if you'd like fresh chocolate chip cookies, make our Classic Chewy Chocolate Chip Cookies (page 297).

PREP TIME:
10 minutes, plus inactive time to cool flour

COOK TIME:
5 minutes

YIELD:
6 servings

1 cup (125 g) all-purpose flour (spooned and leveled or weighed [see page 359 for How to Measure Flour])

½ cup (113 g) vegan butter, at room temperature (see Sister Tip) (nut-free and/or soy-free if needed)

¾ cup (165 g) packed light brown sugar

1 tsp pure vanilla extract

1 tbsp (15 ml) nondairy milk (nut-free and/or soy-free if needed)

½ tsp salt

½ cup (84 g) vegan mini semisweet chocolate chips (soy-free if needed)

Preheat the oven to 350°F (180°C). Spread the flour on an ungreased baking sheet. Bake for 5 minutes. Remove from the oven and set aside to cool completely.

In a large bowl or the bowl of a stand mixer fitted with the paddle attachment, combine the butter and brown sugar. Beat with a hand mixer or the stand mixer until light and fluffy. Add the vanilla and milk and beat until creamy. Add the cooled flour and salt and mix until combined. Fold in the mini chocolate chips. Eat right out of the bowl with a spoon or roll into bite-sized balls and place in an airtight container in the fridge or freezer to enjoy later.

*See in Edible Peanut Butter Cookie Dough image on page 308.

Sister Tip

You can use either vegan buttery sticks or buttery spread from the tub for this recipe. You want the butter to be soft so that it incorporates well with the other ingredients. Typically, you should let the butter sit out for 30 minutes to an hour before using, but if you use buttery spread that is soft straight from the fridge, you can skip the softening step.

Cookie Dough Bars

If there's one way to make our Edible Chocolate Chip Cookie Dough (page 310) taste any better, it's by adding more chocolate. In this recipe, we pair cookie dough with a two-ingredient chocolate ganache for a delicious treat that will please any dessert-lover. Obsessed with the combination of peanut butter and chocolate? Swap out the chocolate chip cookie dough for our Edible Peanut Butter Cookie Dough (page 309).

PREP TIME:
10 minutes, plus prep time for edible cookie dough

COOK TIME:
none

CHILL TIME:
1 to 2 hours

YIELD:
8 bars

1 batch Edible Chocolate Chip Cookie Dough (page 310) (nut-free and/or soy-free if needed)

1 cup (168 g) vegan semisweet chocolate chips (soy-free if needed)

1 tbsp (14 g) refined coconut oil

Line a 9 x 5-inch (23 x 13–cm) loaf pan with parchment paper (see Sister Tip). Press the prepared cookie dough evenly into the bottom of the pan. Set aside while you make the ganache.

In a microwave-safe bowl, combine the chocolate chips and coconut oil. Microwave in 15-second intervals, stirring in between, until the mixture is smooth and creamy. Pour the ganache over the cookie dough and spread so that it covers the dough evenly. Refrigerate until the chocolate hardens, 1 to 2 hours. Cut into eight bars.

Sister Tip

You can use an 8-inch (20-cm) square pan to yield 9 to 16 thinner bars.

Billionaire Bars

Our version of billionaire bars has four layers: shortbread, cookie dough, caramel and chocolate peanut butter ganache. These bars are rich, decadent and everything you could ask for in a dessert.

PREP TIME:
30 minutes, plus prep time for cookie dough

COOK TIME:
about 20 minutes

CHILL TIME:
1 to 2 hours

YIELD:
16 bars

SHORTBREAD BASE

¼ cup (½ stick [56 g]) vegan butter, at room temperature (see Sister Tips) (soy-free if needed)

¼ cup (31 g) powdered sugar

½ tsp pure vanilla extract

½ cup (62 g) all-purpose flour (spooned and leveled or weighed [see page 359 for How to Measure Flour])

COOKIE DOUGH

1 batch Edible Chocolate Chip Cookie Dough (page 310) (see Sister Tips) (soy-free if needed)

CARAMEL LAYER

½ cup (100 g) granulated sugar

¼ cup (½ stick [56 g]) vegan butter, at room temperature (see Sister Tips) (soy-free if needed)

2 tbsp (30 ml) nondairy creamer or soy milk, at room temperature (soy-free if needed)

1 tsp pure vanilla extract

¼ tsp salt

Make the shortbread: Preheat the oven to 350°F (180°F) and line an 8-inch (20-cm) square pan with parchment paper. In a large bowl or the bowl of a stand mixer fitted with the paddle attachment, beat the butter with a hand mixer or the stand mixer until creamy. Add the powdered sugar and vanilla and mix until combined. Add the flour and mix until just combined. Press evenly into the bottom of the prepared pan—the layer will be very thin. Use a fork to poke small holes all around the dough. Bake for 10 to 12 minutes, until golden. Remove from the oven and set aside to cool completely.

Once the shortbread has cooled, evenly press the prepared Edible Chocolate Chip Cookie Dough on top. Set aside.

Make the caramel: In a heavy-bottomed saucepan, heat the granulated sugar over medium-low heat, stirring often, until the sugar begins to clump and melt. Continue to stir until the sugar melts completely. The sugar will take 5 to 10 minutes total to melt. Remove from the heat and add the butter, whisking until combined. Add the creamer and whisk until combined (see Sister Tips). Place over medium heat, stirring constantly, until the mixture begins to boil. Cook, stirring, for another minute. Remove from the heat and stir in the vanilla and salt. Strain the caramel onto the cookie dough layer and spread evenly. Place in the fridge or freezer to set while you prepare the ganache.

(continued)

Billionaire Bars (Continued)

CHOCOLATE PEANUT BUTTER GANACHE

½ cup (84 g) vegan chocolate chips (soy-free if needed)

¼ cup (65 g) creamy no-stir peanut butter (soy-free if needed)

Make the ganache: In a microwave-safe bowl, combine the chocolate chips and peanut butter. Microwave in 15-second intervals, stirring in between, until completely smooth and creamy. Pour evenly over the caramel.

Place the bars in the fridge until the topping has set, 1 to 2 hours. Slice into 16 bars.

Sister Tips

For this recipe, we recommend using vegan buttery sticks, rather than from the tub. To soften, allow them to sit out for 30 minutes to an hour before using.

We recommend using freshly prepared cookie dough for this recipe. However, if using from the fridge, allow it to sit out for 30 minutes to 1 hour to soften before using.

If your caramel seizes while adding in the butter and creamer, place it over low heat and whisk until the mixture comes back together.

Triple-Layer Cookie Brownies

We grew up making these brownies—they are layered with a chocolate chip cookie base, a chocolate sandwich cookie center and a final layer of fudgy brownie. They are rich, chocolaty and a huge crowd-pleaser. Don't be discouraged by the amount of steps; these decadent brownies are absolutely worth the effort.

PREP TIME:
40 minutes

COOK TIME:
34 minutes

YIELD:
24 brownies

CHOCOLATE CHIP COOKIE LAYER

2¼ cups (280 g) all-purpose flour (spooned and leveled or weighed [see page 359 for How to Measure Flour])

1 tsp baking soda

1 tsp salt

2 tsp (5 g) cornstarch

¾ cup (1½ sticks [169 g]) vegan butter (see Sister Tips) (nut-free and/or soy-free if needed)

¾ cup (165 g) packed light brown sugar

½ cup (100 g) granulated sugar

3 tbsp (45 ml) nondairy milk (nut-free and/or soy-free if needed)

2 tsp (10 ml) pure vanilla extract

1¼ cups (210 g) vegan semisweet chocolate chips (soy-free if needed)

CHOCOLATE SANDWICH COOKIE LAYER

24 vegan chocolate sandwich cookies (soy-free if needed)

Preheat the oven to 350°F (180°C). Line a 9 x 13-inch (23 x 33-cm) aluminum cake pan with parchment paper and set aside.

Make the cookie dough: In a medium-sized bowl, whisk together the flour, baking soda, salt and cornstarch. Set aside.

Using the microwave or the stovetop over low heat, partially melt the butter so that it's about halfway melted. Pour into a large bowl and whisk until it has a thick liquid consistency. Whisk in the brown sugar and granulated sugar, then the milk and vanilla. Pour the flour mixture into the butter mixture and mix until just combined. Fold in the chocolate chips. Press into the prepared pan. Evenly line up the chocolate sandwich cookies on top of the cookie dough. Gently press the cookies into the dough. Set aside.

(continued)

Triple-Layer Cookie Brownies (Continued)

BROWNIE LAYER

1½ tbsp (8 g) flaxseed meal

3 tbsp (45 ml) water

1 cup (125 g) all-purpose flour (spooned and leveled or weighed [see page 359 for How to Measure Flour])

½ cup (50 g) unsweetened natural cocoa powder (spooned and leveled or weighed [see page 359 for tutorial])

½ tsp baking powder

⅛ tsp baking soda

½ tsp salt

6 tbsp (¾ stick [84 g]) vegan butter (see Sister Tips) (nut-free and/or soy-free if needed)

2 oz (56 g) vegan semisweet chocolate (see Sister Tips) (soy-free if needed)

⅔ cup (133 g) granulated sugar

½ cup (110 g) packed light brown sugar

¼ cup (60 ml) nondairy milk (nut-free and/or soy-free if needed)

1½ tsp (7 ml) pure vanilla extract

Make the brownie batter and bake: In a small bowl, whisk together the flaxseed meal and water. Set aside for 10 to 15 minutes, until gelled. In a medium-sized bowl, whisk together the flour, cocoa powder, baking powder, baking soda and salt. Set aside.

In a large, microwave-safe bowl, combine the butter and chocolate. Microwave in 15-second intervals, stirring in between, until completely melted. Add the granulated sugar and brown sugar and whisk until combined. Add the milk, vanilla and flaxseed meal mixture and mix until combined. Add the flour mixture to the chocolate mixture and mix until just combined.

Pour the batter over the cookie layer and evenly spread to cover. Bake for 32 to 36 minutes. The top will look crackly and shiny, but the brownie may still be fudgy and seem underbaked—that's okay. Remove from the oven, allow to cool completely, then remove from the pan and cut into 24 brownies.

Sister Tips

For this recipe, we recommend using vegan buttery sticks, rather than from the tub.

Use a high-quality chocolate baking bar for the best outcome. You will use half of a standard 4-ounce (113-g) bar.

Raspberry Crumble Bars

These bars come together with just seven ingredients that you most likely have sitting in your fridge and pantry. The sweet raspberry jam balances out the buttery oat crumble, making them a great dessert or the perfect complement to your morning cup of coffee or tea.

PREP TIME:
20 minutes

COOK TIME:
40 minutes

YIELD:
9 bars

1 cup (125 g) all-purpose flour (spooned and leveled or weighed [see page 359 for How to Measure Flour])

½ cup (110 g) packed light brown sugar

¼ tsp baking soda

¼ tsp salt

1 cup (90 g) old-fashioned rolled oats

½ cup (1 stick [113 g]) vegan butter, cold (see Sister Tip) (nut-free and/ or soy-free if needed)

¾ cup (240 g) raspberry jam

Preheat the oven to 350°F (180°C). Line an 8-inch (20-cm) square pan with parchment paper.

In a large bowl, stir together the flour, brown sugar, baking soda, salt and oats. Using a fork or a pastry cutter, incorporate the cold butter into the flour mixture by cutting it into smaller and smaller pieces, until you have a crumbly, sandlike texture.

Press about two-thirds of the crumble mixture into the prepared pan. Spread the jam on top, leaving a narrow bare margin around the sides. Top with the remaining crumble mixture and lightly press into the jam. Bake for 35 to 40 minutes, until lightly golden brown. Remove from the oven, allow to cool, then cut into nine bars.

Sister Tip

For this recipe, we recommend using vegan buttery sticks, rather than buttery spread from the tub.

Carrot Cake

This carrot cake has been a family favorite for years. Even our younger brothers, who would typically balk at a cake with vegetables in it, can't get enough. The addition of freshly shredded carrots results in a moist cake with the perfect texture. We pair it with a simple but delicious vegan cream cheese frosting that delightfully complements the gently spiced carrot cake layers.

PREP TIME:
45 minutes

COOK TIME:
36 to 40 minutes

YIELD:
10 slices

CAKE
Nonstick spray, for pan

1 cup (240 ml) soy milk, at room temperature

1 tbsp (15 ml) apple cider vinegar, lemon juice or white vinegar

2⅔ cups (333 g) all-purpose flour (spooned and leveled or weighed [see page 359 for How to Measure Flour])

1 tsp baking soda

1½ tsp (7 g) baking powder

1 tsp salt

2 tsp (5 g) ground cinnamon

¼ tsp ground nutmeg

1 cup (220 g) packed light brown sugar

1 cup (200 g) granulated sugar

½ cup (113 g) vegan sour cream, nondairy yogurt or Cashew Cream (page 343), at room temperature (nut-free if needed)

¾ cup (180 ml) canola oil

2 tsp (10 ml) pure vanilla extract

3 cups (330 g) freshly shredded carrots

Make the cake: Preheat the oven to 350°F (180°C). Spray two 8-inch (20-cm) round cake pans with nonstick spray and line the bottoms with parchment paper. In a small bowl, whisk together milk and vinegar, then set aside for 10 to 15 minutes, until curdled. In a medium-sized bowl, whisk together the flour, baking soda, baking powder, salt, cinnamon and nutmeg.

In a large bowl, mix together the brown sugar, granulated sugar, sour cream, oil, vanilla and the milk mixture until combined. Add the flour mixture and mix until just combined. Fold in the carrots. Divide the batter equally between the prepared pans. Bake for 36 to 40 minutes, until a toothpick inserted into the center of each cake comes out clean or with just crumbs, no raw batter. Remove from the oven and allow to cool completely in the pans.

(continued)

Carrot Cake (Continued)

CREAM CHEESE FROSTING

½ cup (1 stick [113 g]) vegan butter, at room temperature (see Sister Tip) (nut-free if needed)

½ cup (113 g) vegan Cream Cheese (page 344), or store-bought, at room temperature (nut-free if needed)

4 cups (500 g) powdered sugar

1 tsp nondairy milk, plus more as needed (nut-free if needed)

1 tsp pure vanilla extract

DECORATION

Crushed walnuts (optional; omit for nut-free)

Make the cream cheese frosting: In a large bowl or the bowl of a stand mixer fitted with the paddle attachment, combine the butter and cream cheese. Beat with a hand mixer or the stand mixer until light and fluffy, scraping the sides as necessary. Add the powdered sugar, milk and vanilla, and beat until smooth and creamy. Stir in more milk, 1 teaspoon at a time, as needed, until a smooth but thick consistency is reached.

Assemble the cake: Once the cake layers are cooled, remove from the pan and discard the parchment paper. Place one on a serving dish. Spread buttercream on top of the cake layer, then top with the second cake layer, upside down. Coat the entire cake with a thick layer of frosting. Decorate with the remaining frosting and crushed walnuts, if desired.

Sister Tip

For this recipe, we recommend using vegan buttery sticks, rather than from the tub. Let the butter sit out for 30 minutes to an hour before using.

Giant Chocolate Chip Oat Walnut Cookies

These cookies are loaded with oats, walnuts, chocolate chips and a touch of cinnamon. They are also giant—using ¼ cup (75 g) of dough per cookie—giving you lots (quite literally!) to love about them.

PREP TIME:
20 minutes

COOK TIME:
20 to 22 minutes

YIELD:
about 10 giant cookies

1¼ cups (156 g) all-purpose flour (spooned and leveled or weighed [see page 359 for How to Measure Flour])

½ tsp baking soda

½ tsp salt

¼ tsp ground cinnamon

½ cup (1 stick [113 g]) vegan butter, at room temperature (see Sister Tips) (soy-free if needed)

⅓ cup (66 g) granulated sugar

½ cup (110 g) packed light brown sugar

3 tbsp (45 ml) nondairy milk (soy-free if needed)

1 tsp pure vanilla extract

½ cup (46 g) old-fashioned rolled oats

1⅓ cups (223 g) vegan semisweet chocolate chips (soy-free if needed)

¾ cup (90 g) chopped walnuts

Flaky sea salt, optional

Preheat the oven to 300°F (150°C). Line two baking sheets with parchment paper and set aside.

In a medium-sized bowl, whisk together the flour, baking soda, salt and cinnamon. In a large bowl or the bowl of a stand mixer fitted with the paddle attachment, combine the butter, granulated sugar and brown sugar. Beat with a hand mixer or the stand mixer until light and fluffy, about 2 minutes, scraping the sides as needed. Add the milk and vanilla to the butter mixture, beating again until well combined, about 30 seconds. Add the flour mixture to the butter mixture and stir until just combined. Fold in the oats, chocolate chips and walnuts.

Scoop out ¼ cup (75 g) of dough for each cookie, roll into balls and place on the prepared baking sheets, leaving about 3 inches (7.5 cm) between the balls for spreading. Slightly press down each ball. If desired, top each with a sprinkle of flaky sea salt.

Bake for 20 to 22 minutes, until the edges are golden brown (see Sister Tips). They may look slightly underdone, but will set as they cool. Remove from the oven and allow to cool on the pans.

Sister Tips

For this recipe, we recommend using vegan buttery sticks, rather than from the tub. To soften, allow them to sit out for 30 minutes to an hour before using.

If your baking sheets are on different racks in the oven, swap the pans halfway through for the best results.

Funfetti Cake

Nothing says "let's celebrate" like a funfetti cake. This recipe is a tribute to the boxed funfetti cake we all grew up eating. It's perfect for birthday parties, anniversaries or holidays. Although it makes ten large slices, you can easily serve more by cutting this cake into smaller slices. Skip the store-bought and make this version instead.

PREP TIME:
45 minutes

COOK TIME:
20 to 24 minutes

YIELD:
10 large slices

FUNFETTI CAKE

Nonstick cooking spray, for pans

2 cups (480 ml) soy milk, at room temperature

2 tbsp (30 ml) apple cider vinegar, white vinegar or lemon juice

3 cups (375 g) all-purpose flour (spooned and leveled or weighed [see page 359 for How to Measure Flour])

2 cups (400 g) granulated sugar

1 tsp baking soda

1 tsp baking powder

1 tsp salt

⅔ cup (160 ml) canola oil

¼ cup (60 g) vegan sour cream, nondairy yogurt or Cashew Cream (page 343), at room temperature (nut-free if needed)

1 tbsp (15 ml) pure vanilla extract

½ tsp almond extract (optional; omit for nut-free)

½ cup (68 g) vegan rainbow sprinkles, plus more for decorating

VANILLA FROSTING

1½ cups (340 g) vegan butter, at room temperature (see Sister Tip) (nut-free if needed)

6 cups (750 g) powdered sugar

1 tbsp (15 ml) nondairy milk, plus more as needed (nut-free if needed)

1 tbsp (15 ml) pure vanilla extract

Make the cake: Preheat the oven to 350°F (180°C). Spray three 8-inch (20-cm) round cake pans with nonstick spray and line the bottoms with parchment paper. In a medium-sized bowl, whisk together the milk and vinegar, then set aside for 10 to 15 minutes, until curdled.

In a large bowl, whisk together the flour, granulated sugar, baking soda, baking powder and salt. To the milk mixture, add the oil, sour cream, vanilla and almond extract (if using), and mix. Pour the milk mixture into the flour mixture and mix until just combined. Gently fold in the sprinkles. Evenly distribute the batter among the three prepared pans. Bake for 20 to 24 minutes, until a toothpick inserted into the center of each cake comes out clean or with only crumbs, no raw batter. Remove from the oven and allow to cool in the pans completely.

Make the frosting: In a large bowl or the bowl of a stand mixer fitted with the paddle attachment, beat the butter with a hand mixer or the stand mixer until light and fluffy, scraping the sides as necessary. Add the powdered sugar, milk and vanilla, and beat until smooth and creamy. Stir in more milk, 1 teaspoon at a time, as needed, until a smooth but thick consistency is reached.

Assemble the cake: Remove the cooled cake layers from their pans. Place one cake layer on a cake stand or round cardboard cake board. Spread frosting on top. Place the second cake layer on top and spread more frosting on top. Place the final cake layer, upside down, on top. Spread a thick layer of frosting all around the cake. Decorate with the remaining frosting and extra sprinkles. We like using a piping bag fitted with a large drop flower tip to pipe extra frosting around the top of the cake. Slice and enjoy.

Sister Tip

For this recipe, we recommend using vegan buttery sticks, rather than from the tub. Allow them to sit out for 30 minutes to an hour before using.

Oatmeal Cream Pies

These nostalgic cookie sandwiches will bring you back to your childhood. This recipe combines soft oatmeal cookies with a sweet vanilla buttercream. They are the perfect dessert for impressing friends and family—nobody will guess that they're vegan!

PREP TIME:
30 minutes

COOK TIME:
9 to 11 minutes

YIELD:
12 to 14 pies

COOKIES

1½ cups (187 g) all-purpose flour (spooned and leveled or weighed [see page 359 for How to Measure Flour])

½ tsp baking soda

¼ tsp salt

½ tsp ground cinnamon

½ cup (1 stick [113 g]) vegan butter, at room temperature (see Sister Tips) (nut-free and/or soy-free if needed)

½ cup (100 g) granulated sugar

⅓ cup (73 g) packed light brown sugar

¼ cup (60 ml) nondairy milk (nut-free and/or soy-free if needed)

1 tsp pure vanilla extract

1½ cups (135 g) old-fashioned rolled oats

FILLING

¼ cup (½ stick [56 g]) vegan butter, at room temperature (see Sister Tips) (nut-free and/or soy-free if needed)

1 cup (125 g) powdered sugar

1½ tsp (7 ml) nondairy milk, plus more as needed (nut-free and/or soy-free if needed)

½ tsp pure vanilla extract

Make the cookies: Preheat the oven to 350°F (180°C) and line two or three baking sheets with parchment paper. In a medium-sized bowl, whisk together the flour, baking soda, salt and cinnamon. In a large bowl or the bowl of a stand mixer fitted with the paddle attachment, combine the butter, granulated sugar and brown sugar, and beat with a hand mixer or the stand mixer until light and fluffy, about 2 minutes, scraping the sides as needed. Add the milk and vanilla. Beat until combined, about 30 seconds. Fold in the flour mixture. Fold in the oats.

Roll the dough into 1½-tablespoon (25-g) balls and place on the prepared baking sheets, leaving 2 inches (5 cm) between the balls. Flatten each ball of dough slightly. Bake for 9 to 11 minutes (see Sister Tips), until golden brown. Remove from the oven and allow to cool completely.

Make the filling: In a large bowl or the bowl of a stand mixer fitted with the paddle attachment, beat the butter with a hand mixer or the stand mixer until light and fluffy, scraping the sides as necessary. Add the powdered sugar, milk and vanilla, and beat until smooth and creamy. Stir in more milk, 1 teaspoon at a time, as needed, until a smooth but thick consistency is reached.

Assemble the cookie sandwiches: Once the cookies are cooled, sandwich a heaping scoop of frosting between two cookies. Repeat with the rest of the cookies and frosting.

Sister Tips

For this recipe, we recommend using vegan buttery sticks, rather than from the tub. To soften, allow them to sit out for 30 minutes to an hour before using.

If your baking sheets are on different racks in the oven, swap the pans halfway through for the best results.

Hot Fudge Pudding Cake

This recipe may seem intimidating to make, but don't worry, it's surprisingly quick and easy. As it bakes, a layer of gooey hot fudge forms underneath the warm and fluffy chocolate cake. This cake is best served warm with a scoop of nondairy ice cream.

PREP TIME:
30 minutes

COOK TIME:
26 to 32 minutes

YIELD:
6 to 8 servings

Nonstick spray, for pan

LAYER 1
1 cup (125 g) all-purpose flour (spooned and leveled or weighed [see page 359 for How to Measure Flour])

½ cup (100 g) granulated sugar

¼ cup (25 g) unsweetened natural cocoa powder (spooned and leveled or weighed [see page 359 for tutorial])

2 tsp (9 g) baking powder

¼ tsp salt

¾ cup (180 ml) nondairy milk (nut-free and/or soy-free if needed)

¼ cup (60 ml) canola oil

1 tsp pure vanilla extract

LAYER 2
1 cup (220 g) packed light brown sugar

¼ cup (25 g) unsweetened natural cocoa powder (spooned and leveled or weighed [see page 359 for tutorial])

LAYER 3
1¼ cups (300 ml) boiling water

FOR SERVING
Nondairy ice cream (nut-free and/or soy-free if needed)

Preheat the oven to 350°F (180°C) and spray a 9-inch (23-cm) square cake pan with nonstick spray.

Prepare layer 1: In a medium-sized bowl, whisk together the flour, granulated sugar, cocoa powder, baking powder and salt. Add the milk, oil and vanilla, and mix until just combined. Pour into the prepared pan.

Prepare layer 2: In a small bowl, add the brown sugar and cocoa powder and mix until completely combined. Sprinkle over the first layer without mixing.

Add layer 3: Measure out the boiling water and pour on top of the first two layers without mixing. Let it sit on top.

Bake for 26 to 32 minutes, until the center has set; the bottom and sides will be puddinglike. Serve warm by scooping onto serving dishes and pairing with nondairy ice cream.

Tofu "Bacon" (page 335)

Steamed Seitan (page 332)

Parmesan-Crusted Tofu (page 334)

Simmered Seitan (page 333)

Crispy Seitan (page 336)

MEAT
SUBSTITUTES

In this chapter, you'll find seven of our favorite versatile meat substitutes—from various seitan and tofu recipes to a simple Easy Taco "Meat" (page 332). In addition to these meat substitutes, we love using jackfruit, textured vegetable protein and even avocado (hello, Fried Avocado Tacos [page 187]) in our recipes. You'll find many recipes that call for these substitutes throughout the book, such as Crispy "Chicken" Ranch Sandwich (page 179), Loaded Nachos (page 98) and Breakfast Sandwich (page 29).

Steamed Seitan

Seitan is one of our favorite meat substitutes—it's easy, flavorful and a great addition to many recipes. You can bread and fry it, use it as a pizza topping or enjoy it on sandwiches—the opportunities are endless. You'll find this Steamed Seitan in our Peanut Seitan Wrap (page 175), "Chicken Bacon" Caesar Salad Wrap (page 180) and our "Chicken Bacon" Ranch Pita (page 162), among other recipes.

PREP TIME:
5 minutes

COOK TIME:
10 to 14 minutes

YIELD:
14 oz (396 g)

1 cup (120 g) vital wheat gluten (spooned and leveled or weighed [see page 359 for tutorial])

¼ cup (20 g) nutritional yeast

1 tsp garlic powder

1 tsp onion powder

⅛ tsp ground turmeric

¾ cup (180 ml) vegetable broth

2 tbsp (30 ml) low-sodium soy sauce (or coconut aminos for soy-free)

In a large bowl or bowl of a stand mixer with a hook attachment, mix the vital wheat gluten, nutritional yeast, garlic powder, onion powder and turmeric. Add the broth and soy sauce, and mix well to form a dough. Knead by hand or with the stand mixer on low speed for 30 seconds to 1 minute.

Prepare a bamboo or metal steamer over boiling water. Slice the seitan into thirds, form the pieces into ½-inch (1.3-cm)-thick patties and place in the steamer, doing this in batches if necessary. Cover and steam for 14 minutes if using a bamboo steamer, and 10 minutes if using a metal steamer. Remove from the heat and allow to cool to the touch before using. Use as instructed in the recipe. This can also be sliced and used as a chicken substitute in your favorite dish.

Easy Taco "Meat"

As simple as this recipe is, it's the perfect recipe to have on hand for quick meals to have throughout the week, especially taco Tuesdays. Serve it in tacos, on Loaded Nachos (page 98) or in Loaded Burritos (page 185).

PREP TIME:
none

COOK TIME:
about 10 minutes

YIELD:
about 16 oz (453 g)

1 tbsp (15 ml) olive oil

16 oz (453 g) vegan ground "beef," defrosted if frozen (we like Impossible and Beyond beef) (gluten-free, nut-free and/or soy-free if needed)

¼ cup (36 g) Taco Seasoning (page 357) or store-bought

¼ cup (60 ml) water, plus more as needed

In a medium-sized skillet, heat the oil over medium-low heat. Add the vegan ground "beef." If your "beef" is in block form, break it up, using a spatula. Let cook for 3 to 5 minutes, or until lightly browned. Sprinkle the taco seasoning on top and stir until the vegan "beef" is coated. Add the water and stir to completely combine. Add more water, as needed, to fully mix in the spice blend and keep the "beef" from sticking. Sauté until the "beef" is completely cooked, 3 to 5 minutes. Serve this with your favorite toppings for tacos or in different recipes throughout our book.

*See in Loaded Nachos image on page 99.

Simmered Seitan

We often use simmered seitan as a beef substitute. You'll use this Simmered Seitan in our Philly Cheesesteak (page 165) and BBQ Seitan Sandwich (page 166). We also have a delicious variation of this seitan in our Seitan Gyro with Tzatziki Sauce (page 182). If you've never encountered seitan before, it's typically called "wheat meat," as it's made from vital wheat gluten, a flourlike substance that's high in gluten. When combined with liquid, it creates a stretchy, meatlike texture.

PREP TIME:	COOK TIME:	YIELD:
10 minutes	*1 hour, plus 30 minutes for cooling in broth*	*20 oz (567 g)*

SEITAN

1 cup (120 g) vital wheat gluten (spooned and leveled or weighed [see page 359 for tutorial])

¼ cup (20 g) nutritional yeast

1 tsp garlic powder

1 tsp onion powder

½ tsp dried sage

¾ cup (180 ml) vegetable broth

1 tbsp (15 ml) low-sodium soy sauce (or coconut aminos for soy-free)

BROTH MIXTURE

2 cups (480 ml) vegetable broth

2 cups (480 ml) water

1 tbsp (15 ml) soy sauce (or coconut aminos for soy-free)

1 tbsp (15 ml) maple syrup

Make the seitan: In a large bowl or the bowl of a stand mixer fitted with a hook attachment, whisk together the vital wheat gluten, nutritional yeast, garlic powder, onion powder and sage. Add the vegetable broth and soy sauce and mix until combined. Knead the mixture by hand or with the stand mixer on low speed for 5 to 7 minutes, or until it becomes firm and stretchy. Form into a round patty.

Prepare the broth mixture: In a medium-sized saucepan, whisk together the broth mixture ingredients and bring to a boil over high heat. Place the seitan patty in the broth mixture and lower the heat, bringing the mixture to a gentle simmer. Cover and allow to cook for about an hour, flipping halfway through. It will approximately double in size.

Once it is done, allow the seitan to cool in the broth for 30 minutes, then remove and place on a clean, absorbent towel to allow any excess liquid to drain off. Use as instructed in the recipe that calls for simmered seitan. This can also be sliced and used as a beef substitute in your favorite dishes.

Baked Tofu

This is an easy go-to recipe. We keep the flavor plain, which makes this tofu a versatile addition to many dishes for added protein. Serve it on top of Red Coconut Curry Noodles (page 137) or as a topping on salads—you'll come across it in the Roasted Veggie and Quinoa Salad (page 203).

PREP TIME:
5 minutes, plus inactive time for pressing tofu

COOK TIME:
20 to 30 minutes

YIELD:
40 to 50 pieces

1 (14- to 16-oz [396- to 453-g]) block extra-firm tofu

Canola or olive oil (or spray version), for pan

Drain the tofu and slice into four long, equal slices. Press the slices (see tutorial on page 358). Preheat the oven to 400°F (204°C). Prepare a baking sheet with parchment paper or by lightly oiling with canola or olive oil.

Chop the slices into ½- to 1-inch (1.3- to 2.5-cm) cubes. Place on the prepared baking sheet, making sure none are touching. Bake for 20 to 30 minutes, or until they are baked to your liking, flipping halfway through. Serve on top of your favorite pastas, rice dishes and salads.

*See in Roasted Veggie and Quinoa Salad image on page 202.

Sister Tip

Prior to placing on the baking sheet, you can toss the cubes of tofu in spices or coatings of choice, such as Garlic Salt (page 356), Italian seasoning and/or nutritional yeast. If doing so, we recommend first tossing in 1 tablespoon (15 ml) of canola or olive oil to aid in sticking.

Tofu "Bacon"

You won't miss bacon with this vegan recipe. It's deliciously sweet, smoky and baked to crispy perfection. Enjoy this "bacon" for breakfast, in our BLTA (page 169), or even on our Loaded Cheese Fries (page 118).

PREP TIME:
10 minutes

COOK TIME:
40 minutes

YIELD:
about 20 pieces

SAUCE
¼ cup (60 ml) pure maple syrup

¼ cup (60 ml) soy sauce (or tamari for gluten-free)

2 tbsp (30 ml) rice vinegar

1 tbsp (15 ml) liquid smoke

1½ tsp (3 g) smoked paprika

1 tsp garlic powder

TOFU
1 (14- to 16-oz [396- to 453-g]) block extra-firm or superfirm tofu (see Sister Tip)

Preheat the oven to 400°F (200°C). Line a large baking sheet with parchment paper.

Make the sauce: In a medium-sized bowl, whisk together all the sauce ingredients. Set aside.

Prepare the tofu: Slice the tofu into about 20 long, thin slices and pat dry with a towel. If the tofu seems soft and difficult to work with, follow our guide for pressing tofu (page 358) to remove any excess water.

Dip each slice of tofu into the sauce, covering it completely, then place on the prepared baking sheet. Reserve the remaining sauce. Bake for a total of 35 to 40 minutes, or until crispy, removing from the oven every 10 minutes and basting the tofu with the sauce, until no sauce remains. At the 20-minute mark, after basting, flip over the tofu slices and baste the other side. Allow to cool slightly before serving.

*See in Breakfast Sandwich image on page 28.

Sister Tip

If you can get your hands on superfirm tofu, that works very well in this recipe with no need for pressing.

Crispy Seitan

This recipe transforms our Steamed Seitan (page 332) recipe by breading and frying it to crispy perfection. You'll find it in our Crispy "Chicken" Ranch Sandwich (page 179) and Crispy "Chicken" Caesar Melt (page 176). It's also great sliced and topped on pasta dishes—including our Creamy Tomato Pasta (page 67), Creamy Roasted Garlic Pasta (page 85) or Creamy Garlic Orzo (page 115).

PREP TIME:	**COOK TIME:**	**YIELD:**
10 minutes	about 25 minutes	6 patties

SEITAN
1 cup (120 g) vital wheat gluten (spooned and leveled or weighed [see page 359 for tutorial])

¼ cup (20 g) nutritional yeast

1 tsp garlic powder

1 tsp onion powder

⅛ tsp ground turmeric

¾ cup (180 ml) vegetable broth

2 tbsp (30 ml) low-sodium soy sauce (or coconut aminos for soy-free)

BATTER
½ cup (62 g) all-purpose flour

½ cup (120 ml) water

BREADING
1 cup (60 g) vegan panko bread crumbs

½ tsp dried oregano

⅛ tsp dried thyme

¼ tsp dried rosemary

¼ tsp ground sage

¼ tsp dried basil

½ tsp garlic powder

½ tsp salt

FOR FRYING
Canola oil

Make the seitan: In a medium-sized bowl or the bowl of a stand mixer fitted with a hook attachment, mix together the vital wheat gluten, nutritional yeast, garlic powder, onion powder and turmeric. Add the broth and soy sauce, then mix well to form a dough. Knead by hand or with the stand mixer on low speed for just 30 seconds to 1 minute.

Prepare a bamboo or metal steamer over boiling water. Slice the seitan into thirds and form the pieces into patties about 4 inches (10 cm) long, 3 inches (7.5 cm) wide and ½ inch (1.3 cm) thick. Place in the steamer. Cover and steam for 14 minutes if using a bamboo steamer, and 10 minutes if using a metal steamer. Remove from the heat and allow to cool.

Prepare the batter and the breading: In a medium-sized bowl, whisk together the flour and water to make the batter. In a separate medium-sized bowl, mix the panko, oregano, thyme, rosemary, sage, basil, garlic powder and salt for the breading. Slice each piece of the steamed seitan in half horizontally (like a hamburger bun is sliced; do this carefully as you will have very thin slices), creating six thin patties.

Fry the seitan: Pour 1 to 2 inches (2.5 to 5 cm) of canola oil into a deep saucepan or pot over medium-low heat; alternatively, prepare a deep fryer according to the manufacturer's instructions. Bring the heat to about 350°F (175°C). Place a paper towel on a plate and set aside. Working with two or three patties at a time, dip each prepared seitan patty into the flour mixture, thoroughly coating, then dip into the breading, thoroughly coating. Using tongs, place the breaded seitan into the hot oil. Cook on each side for 2 to 3 minutes, until crispy and golden brown. Remove from the oil and place on the paper towel to absorb any excess oil. Repeat with the remaining patties. Serve as directed in the recipe you're following, or sliced on your favorite pasta dish.

*See in Creamy Tomato Pasta image on page 66.

Parmesan-Crusted Tofu

As kids (prior to going vegan), our dad would always make Parmesan-crusted chicken for us. This recipe emulates his method by first dipping the tofu in a vegan mayo mixture, followed by a Parmesan coating, then baking it to a perfect crisp. Serve this with Fettuccine Alfredo (page 71) or Creamy Garlic Orzo (page 115).

PREP TIME:
25 minutes

COOK TIME:
31 to 32 minutes

YIELD:
16 pieces

TOFU

1 (14- to 16-oz [397- to 453-g]) block extra-firm tofu

Canola or olive oil (or spray version), for pan

CASHEW PARMESAN COATING

¼ cup (38 g) raw unsalted whole cashews

⅓ cup (36 g) vegan traditional bread crumbs

3 tbsp (15 g) nutritional yeast

½ tsp onion powder

1 tsp garlic powder

½ tsp dried parsley

½ tsp salt

VEGAN MAYO MIXTURE

¼ cup (60 g) vegan Mayo (page 353) or store-bought

2 tbsp (30 ml) unsweetened plain rice milk

Prepare the tofu: Drain the tofu and slice lengthwise into four long, equal slices. Press the slices (see page 358 for tutorial). Use your hands to break each piece of tofu into four pieces, creating 16 roughly torn chunks.

Preheat the oven to 400°F (200°C) and oil a 9 x 13-inch (23 x 33–cm) baking dish with canola or olive oil.

Make the cashew Parmesan coating: In a high-speed blender, combine all the cashew Parmesan coating ingredients and blend to a powder. Transfer to a medium-sized bowl.

Make the vegan mayo mixture: In a separate, medium-sized bowl, mix together the vegan mayo and rice milk. Dip each piece of tofu into the mayo mixture, then coat well with the cashew Parmesan coating and place in the prepared dish.

Cover the dish with aluminum foil and bake for 25 minutes. Uncover and bake for another 5 minutes. Broil on high for 1 to 2 minutes to crisp, watching to make sure it doesn't burn.

*See in Creamy Garlic Orzo image on page 114.

Parmesan Cheese
(page 342)

Pesto
(page 352)

Mozzarella
(page 340)

Garlic Salt
(page 356)

Everything Seasoning
(page 357)

Cheddar
(page 341)

Ranch Dressing
(page 345)

Cream Cheese
(page 344)

Mayo
(page 353)

HOMEMADE
STAPLES AND
BASICS

This cookbook would not be complete without this chapter. We call for a lot of these staples and basics in a majority of recipes throughout this book, but don't fret; many of these can be replaced with store-bought options (as we always note in the recipe). From meltable cheeses and pizza dough to crunchy croutons, homemade spices and savory dressings, this chapter has a little bit of everything.

Mozzarella

Gluten-free, Soy-free

Making your own vegan cheese may sound intimidating, but with the right ingredients, it's actually much easier than you'd think. This cheese is capable of both shredding and melting, making it perfect for topping on pizza and melting into dips. You'll come across this cheese as part of the Crispy and Melty Mozzarella Sticks (page 236), Poutine (page 244) and Detroit-Style Cheese Pizza (page 77).

PREP TIME:	COOK TIME:	CHILL TIME:	YIELD:
5 minutes, plus inactive time to soak cashews	*5 to 10 minutes*	*4 hours*	*1 (27-oz [781-g]) block cheese (about 7 cups shreds)*

MOZZARELLA

1 cup (146 g) raw unsalted whole cashews, soaked (see page 358 for tips on soaking cashews)

⅓ cup (72 g) refined coconut oil

⅓ cup (40 g) tapioca flour (spooned and leveled or weighed [see page 359 for How to Measure Flour]) (see Sister Tip)

2 tbsp (12 g) kappa carrageenan (see Sister Tip)

1½ tsp (7 ml) lemon juice

1½ tsp (7 ml) apple cider vinegar

1 tsp granulated sugar

2 tsp (12 g) salt

2 cups (480 ml) water, at room temperature

FOR CHEESE SHREDS

Canola oil (1 tsp per 1 cup [113 g] of shreds)

Make the mozzarella: Have ready a 4-cup (960-ml) round or rectangular glass container with an airtight lid. In a high-speed blender, combine all the mozzarella ingredients and blend until smooth and creamy. Transfer the mixture to a large, nonstick saucepan over medium-low heat. Using a rubber scraper, constantly stir the cheese mixture, making sure to scrape the bottom and sides. As the mixture thickens, it will get chunky. Continue to stir until the chunks disappear and the mixture becomes smooth, stretchy and thick, but still pourable. This will take 5 to 10 minutes. Immediately pour into the container, cool at room temperature for 1 hour, then cover with the lid and chill in the refrigerator for at least 3 hours. Once it is a solid block, this can be stored in the fridge in its lidded container. We suggest using this within 5 to 7 days.

For cheese shreds: Shred the solidified mozzarella using a cheese grater (electric works great if you have one). Once shredded, toss each cup (113 g) of cheese shreds with 1 teaspoon of canola oil for the best melting capabilities. As shreds, these can be stored in a lidded airtight container or a resealable plastic storage bag, although we recommend shredding immediately prior to using.

*See on page 338 and in Poutine image on page 245.

Sister Tip

If you are unfamiliar with tapioca flour and/or kappa carrageenan, they are two ingredients that make this recipe successful. Tapioca flour helps the cheese get thick and stretchy, while kappa carrageenan helps it transition between a firm state and melted state. You can either find them at health food/specialty stores or order them online.

Cheddar

The first question we typically get asked when someone finds out that we are vegan is, "But, how do you live without cheese?" Our answer is always the same: We don't, we just eat cheese made from plants, not dairy. Not only is this vegan cheddar delicious when sliced and paired with crackers, but it can also be shredded and it even melts. Use for our Garlic Bread Grilled Cheese (page 163) or Garlic Cheese Bread (page 270).

PREP TIME:
5 minutes, plus inactive time to soak cashews

COOK TIME:
5 to 10 minutes

CHILL TIME:
4 hours

YIELD:
1 (29-oz [825-g]) block cheese (7 to 7½ cups shreds)

1 cup (146 g) raw unsalted whole cashews, soaked (see page 358 for tips about soaking cashews)

⅓ cup (72 g) refined coconut oil

⅓ cup (40 g) tapioca flour (spooned and leveled or weighed [see page 359 for How to Measure Flour]) (see Sister Tip)

2 tbsp (12 g) kappa carrageenan (see Sister Tip)

1½ tsp (7 ml) lemon juice

1½ tsp (7 ml) apple cider vinegar

1 tsp granulated sugar

2 tsp (12 g) salt

3 tbsp (15 g) nutritional yeast

1½ tsp (7 g) Dijon mustard

1½ tsp (9 g) white miso paste (gluten-free if needed)

⅛ tsp ground turmeric

1½ tsp (3 g) paprika

2 cups (480 ml) water, at room temperature

FOR CHEESE SHREDS
Canola oil (1 tsp per 1 cup [113 g] of shreds)

Have ready a 4-cup (960-ml) round or rectangular glass container with an airtight lid.

In a high-speed blender, combine all the ingredients (except the canola oil) and blend until smooth and creamy. Transfer to a large, nonstick saucepan over medium-low heat. Using a rubber scraper, constantly stir the cheese mixture, making sure to scrape the bottom and sides. As the mixture thickens, it will get chunky. Continue to stir until the chunks disappear and the mixture becomes smooth, stretchy and thick, but still pourable. This will take 5 to 10 minutes. Immediately pour into the container, cool at room temperature for 1 hour, then cover with the lid and chill for at least 3 hours. Once it is a solid block, this can be stored in the fridge directly in its lidded container. We suggest using this within 5 to 7 days.

For cheese shreds: Shred the solidified Cheddar, using a cheese grater (electric works great if you have one). Once shredded, toss each cup (113 g) of cheese shreds with 1 teaspoon of canola oil, for the best melting capabilities. As shreds, these can be stored in a lidded airtight container or a resealable plastic storage bag, although we recommend shredding prior to using.

*See on page 338 and in Twice Baked Potatoes image on page 100.

Sister Tip

If you are unfamiliar with tapioca flour and/or kappa carrageenan, they are two ingredients that make this recipe successful. Tapioca flour helps the cheese get thick and stretchy, while kappa carrageenan helps it transition between a firm state and melted state. You can either find them at health food/specialty stores or order them online.

Parmesan Cheese

This is one of the simplest recipes in our cookbook. Don't let its short ingredient list fool you—it's flavorful, cheesy and perfect on top of pasta, dips and salads. You'll use it in our Artichoke Parmesan Dip (page 229) and as a topping on Breadsticks (page 266), Fettuccine Alfredo (page 71) and Pesto Pasta (page 62).

PREP TIME:
5 minutes

COOK TIME:
none

YIELD:
about ¾ cup
(3.25 oz [85 g])

¼ cup (73 g) raw unsalted whole cashews

2 tbsp (10 g) nutritional yeast

½ tsp Garlic Salt (page 356) or store-bought

In a high-speed blender or food processor, combine the cashews, nutritional yeast and garlic salt and blend or process until a powder has formed. Store in an airtight container in the fridge.

*See on page 338 and in Pesto Pasta image on page 63.

Cashew Cream

This is a staple that should be in your fridge at all times. It's so easy to whip up and is extremely versatile. Not only do we use it in savory dishes, but it's also a great replacement for sour cream in baking. You'll use this Cashew Cream in Loaded Nachos (page 98), Baked Mac and Cheese (page 86) and Classic Stuffed Shells (page 89).

PREP TIME:
5 minutes, plus inactive time to soak cashews

COOK TIME:
none

YIELD:
1 heaping cup (about 270 g)

1 cup (146 g) raw unsalted whole cashews (see Sister Tip)

½ cup (120 ml) water, plus more for soaking

1 tsp lemon juice, apple cider vinegar or white vinegar

½ tsp salt

Place the cashews in a medium-sized bowl. Cover with room-temperature water. Soak for at least 2 hours, up to 12 hours (see page 358 for alternative options and tips). Drain and rinse the cashews.

In a high-speed blender, combine the soaked cashews, ½ cup (120 ml) of fresh water, lemon juice and salt, and blend until creamy, scraping the sides as needed. Transfer to an airtight container and refrigerate. Use within 3 to 5 days.

*See Jackfruit Taquitos image on page 234.

Sister Tip

For the best flavor, the cashews should be raw and unsalted, but in a pinch, you can use any you have on hand. If the cashews are salted, reduce the added salt down to ¼ teaspoon, then taste and add more if desired.

Cream Cheese

This recipe took years (yes, *years*) to perfect. Inspired by our absolute favorite tofu cream cheese that we get from authentic bagel shops in New York City, this vegan cream cheese is light, fluffy and perfect in both sweet and savory dishes; it's the best vegan cream cheese recipe you'll find. Transform this classic recipe by making our Bagels with Veggie Cream Cheese (page 21).

PREP TIME:
10 minutes, plus inactive time to soak cashews

COOK TIME:
none

CHILL TIME:
4 hours

YIELD:
about 2½ cups (565 g)

⅔ cup (97 g) raw unsalted whole cashews, soaked (see Sister Tips)

8 oz (226 g [about ½ of a standard package]) silken tofu, drained

⅓ cup (72 g) refined coconut oil

1 tsp lemon juice

1 tsp apple cider vinegar

3 tbsp (45 ml) plain, unsweetened rice milk

¼ cup (60 g) nondairy plain, unsweetened yogurt

1½ tsp (6 g) granulated sugar

1½ tsp (9 g) salt

½ tsp xanthan gum (see Sister Tips)

In a high-speed blender, combine the cashews, tofu, coconut oil, lemon juice, vinegar, rice milk, yogurt, sugar and salt, and blend until smooth and creamy. Add the xanthan gum and blend for another 15 seconds to 1 minute; the mixture will thicken. Pour into an airtight container and refrigerate for at least 4 hours before using. Use within 3 to 5 days.

*See in Bagels with Veggie Cream Cheese image on page 22.

Sister Tips

To soak cashews, place them in a bowl and cover completely with water. Let sit for at least 2 hours, then drain, rinse and pat dry (see page 358 for more options and tips).

Xanthan gum helps thicken the cream cheese and keeps it from separating in the fridge. It's imperative for this recipe and cannot be omitted. You can find it at most specialty/health food stores or online.

Ranch Dressing

Gluten-free, Nut-free option, Soy-free option

This is our mom's secret recipe that she is allowing us to share with you all. This recipe is seriously the *best*—we've never come across a better vegan ranch dressing. Once you make this, you will always be sure to have a batch in your fridge. You'll find it used in our Crispy "Chicken" Ranch Sandwich (page 179) and Hummus Ranch Wrap (page 181).

PREP TIME:
5 minutes

COOK TIME:
none

YIELD:
about 2⅓ cups (560 ml)

1 cup (226 g) vegan Mayo (page 353) or store-bought (soy-free if needed)

1 cup (226 g) vegan Cream Cheese (page 344) or store-bought (nut-free and/or soy-free if needed)

¼ cup (60 ml) plain, unsweetened rice milk, plus more as needed

1 tbsp (15 ml) apple cider vinegar

2 tsp (1 g) dried parsley

2 tsp (0.1 g) dried chives

1 tsp onion powder

1 tsp garlic powder

1 tsp dried dill

¼ tsp salt, plus more to taste

In a blender, add all the ingredients and blend until smooth. Thin out with extra rice milk, as needed, to get a smooth, semi-thick consistency. Taste and add more salt, if desired. Store in an airtight container in the refrigerator and use within 5 to 7 days.

*See in Crispy and Melty Mozzarella Sticks image on page 237.

Peanut Vinaigrette

Extra peanutty and flavorful, this vinaigrette will quickly become a staple in your house-hold. You'll find it served cold in our Crunchy Cabbage Peanut Salad (page 201) or warm in our Peanut Seitan Wrap (page 175).

PREP TIME:
5 minutes

COOK TIME:
5 to 7 minutes

YIELD:
1¼ cups (300 ml)

2 tsp (5 g) cornstarch

1 tbsp + ⅓ cup (95 ml) water, divided

1 tbsp (16 g) creamy peanut butter (soy-free if needed)

¼ cup (60 ml) unseasoned rice vinegar

¼ cup (60 ml) low-sodium soy sauce (or tamari for gluten-free, or coconut aminos for soy-free)

1½ tsp (7 ml) pure (untoasted) sesame oil

1 tbsp (12 g) granulated sugar

½ tsp garlic powder

¼ tsp onion powder

½ tsp chili powder

⅛ tsp ground ginger

1 tsp vegan sriracha

2 tbsp (30 ml) toasted peanut oil

In a small bowl, whisk together the cornstarch with 1 tablespoon (15 ml) of the water. Set aside. In a small saucepan, add the peanut butter, rice vinegar, soy sauce, sesame oil, remaining ⅓ cup (80 ml) of water, sugar, garlic powder, onion powder, chili powder, ginger and sriracha and whisk over medium-low heat.

Increase the heat to medium-high, bringing the mixture to a gentle boil while whisking constantly. Add the prepared cornstarch slurry and whisk. Lower the heat to low and allow to simmer, whisking often, until slightly thickened, 2 to 3 minutes. Remove from the heat and whisk in the peanut oil until well combined.

If not using immediately or if you prefer a chilled vinaigrette, place in the refrigerator for at least an hour, or until cooled. Store any extra in an airtight container in the refrigerator and use within 1 week.

Chipotle Ranch

This isn't your average ranch dressing. It's loaded with flavor—the added seasonings and chipotle pepper in adobo sauce take it up a notch. We use it in our Taco Salad (page 209) and Fried Avocado Tacos (page 187).

PREP TIME:	COOK TIME:	YIELD:
10 minutes	*none*	*about 2 cups (480 ml)*

½ cup (120 ml) plain, unsweetened soy milk, at room temperature

1½ tsp (7 ml) apple cider vinegar

1½ tsp (7 ml) fresh lime juice

1 tbsp (15 ml) maple syrup

1½ tsp (2 g) garlic powder

1 tsp onion powder

1 tsp ground cumin

½ tsp dried dill

½ tsp dried parsley

¼ tsp paprika

½ tsp crushed red pepper flakes

⅛ tsp cayenne powder

½ tsp hot sauce

½ tsp salt

¼ cup (60 g) Roasted Tomato Salsa (page 217) or salsa of choice

1 chipotle pepper + 1 tbsp (15 g) adobo sauce (see Sister Tips)

1 cup (240 ml) canola oil

In a high-speed blender (see Sister Tips), combine all the ingredients, except the oil, and blend until creamy. Reduce the blender speed to low. While the mixture is still blending, remove the lid and slowly add the canola oil.

Once all the oil is added, blend on high speed for about 30 seconds, or until a thick consistency is reached. Add a little water, as needed, to reach a smooth, slightly thick consistency. Store in an airtight container in the refrigerator and use within 5 to 7 days.

Sister Tips

Alternatively, you can use an immersion blender to blend all the ingredients until thick and creamy.

Chipotle peppers normally come in a small can with adobo sauce.

Creamy Caesar Dressing

As we mentioned in the introduction to our Caesar Salad recipe (page 206), Caesar salad was one of the things we missed when we went vegan. So (of course), we had to make our own Caesar dressing that rivals the nonvegan version—and this recipe hits the spot. You'll use this in our Crispy "Chicken" Caesar Melt (page 176) and "Chicken Bacon" Caesar Salad Wrap (page 180).

PREP TIME:
10 minutes

COOK TIME:
none

YIELD:
about 2 cups (480 ml)

⅓ cup (80 ml) plain, unsweetened soy milk, at room temperature

3 cloves garlic, peeled, or 1 tbsp (9 g) jarred minced garlic

1 tbsp (15 ml) maple syrup

2 tbsp (24 g) capers + 1 tbsp (15 ml) caper brine (see Sister Tips)

3 tbsp (45 ml) lemon juice

2 tbsp (10 g) nutritional yeast

1 tbsp (15 ml) vegan Worcestershire sauce (gluten-free if needed)

1 tsp garlic powder

1 tsp onion powder

1 tsp salt

½ tsp freshly ground black pepper

1 tbsp (15 g) Dijon mustard

1 cup (240 ml) avocado oil

In a high-speed blender (see Sister Tips), combine all the ingredients, except the avocado oil. Blend until smooth, then reduce the blender speed to low. While the mixture is still blending, remove the lid and slowly add the avocado oil. Once all the oil is added, blend on high speed for 15 to 30 seconds, or until a thick consistency is reached. Add water, as needed, to reach a smooth, slightly thick consistency.

Chill before serving, if desired. Store any extra in an airtight container in the refrigerator and use within 5 to 7 days.

Sister Tips

Caper brine is simply the liquid in the jar of capers.

Alternatively, you can use an immersion blender to blend all the ingredients until thick and creamy.

Homemade Croutons Three Ways

No need to buy store-bought croutons when homemade take just 15 minutes and are perfectly crispy. This recipe is super easy and a great way to use up stale bread and the end pieces. Enjoy these croutons on top of your favorite salad or even eat them on their own.

PREP TIME:
5 minutes

COOK TIME:
10 to 12 minutes

YIELD:
2 heaping cups (115 g)

ORIGINAL

¼ cup (60 ml) olive oil, plus more for pan

¼ tsp salt

¼ tsp garlic powder

¼ tsp dried parsley

3 cups (100 g) vegan bread of choice (about 6 slices), diced into 1″ (2.5-cm) cubes (gluten-free if needed)

CAESAR VARIATION

2 tbsp (14 g) vegan Parmesan Cheese (page 342) or store-bought (nut-free and/or soy-free if needed)

¼ tsp dried oregano

⅛ tsp ground thyme

1 tsp lemon juice

ROSEMARY VARIATION

2 tsp (3 g) fresh rosemary

Preheat the oven to 400°F (200°C) and oil a baking sheet.

In a large bowl, stir together all of the ingredients, except the cubed bread, until well combined. If making a variation, stir in the additional ingredients. Add the diced bread and stir to coat completely. Spread evenly on the prepared baking sheet. Bake for 10 to 12 minutes, or until crispy. Store any extras in an airtight container or resealable plastic bag and use within a week.

*See in Tomato Soup image on page 195.

Perfect White Rice

This simple white rice recipe comes out perfect every time. It's our go-to rice to pair with many of our dishes, including Sweet and Sour Tofu (page 128), Sticky Sesame Cauliflower (page 151), Sweet Fire Tofu (page 134) and Peanut Vegetables (page 249).

PREP TIME:
2 minutes

COOK TIME:
17 to 21 minutes,
plus 10 minutes
with no heat

YIELD:
3 cups (500 g)

1 cup (200 g) long-grain white rice

1½ cups (360 ml) water

½ tsp salt, plus more to taste

CILANTRO LIME RICE VARIATION
1 tbsp (15 ml) fresh lime juice

2 tbsp (2 g) chopped fresh cilantro leaves

Place the rice in a strainer and rinse under running cold water until the water runs clear. Shake around to remove any excess water. In a medium-sized saucepan over high heat, stir together the rice, water and salt. Cover and bring to a boil. Once boiling, stir well, then lower the heat to low, bringing the mixture to a simmer.

Simmer, covered, for 17 to 21 minutes (the time can depend greatly on your burner), or until all liquid has been absorbed. Turn off the heat and let sit, covered, for another 10 minutes. Add more salt, if desired, and fluff up with a fork. Serve warm.

For Cilantro Lime Rice, stir the lime juice and cilantro into the cooked rice.

*See in Balsamic Roasted Veggies and Tofu image on page 104.

Coconut Rice

This is arguably one of the best and most delicious ways to enjoy rice. Using coconut milk makes this rice richer than the classic version (page 350), but still light enough to pair with other dishes. It's amazing served with Peanut Vegetables (page 249) or Peanut Tofu and Broccoli (page 146).

PREP TIME:
2 minutes

COOK TIME:
20 to 25 minutes, plus 10 minutes with no heat

YIELD:
4 to 6 servings

1½ cups (300 g) long-grain white rice

1 (13.5-oz [382-ml]) can full-fat coconut milk

1 cup (240 ml) water

1 tsp salt, divided, plus more to taste

Place the rice in a strainer and rinse under running cold water until the water runs clear. Shake around to remove any excess water. In a medium-sized saucepan over high heat, stir together the rice, coconut milk, water and ½ teaspoon of salt.

Cover and bring to a boil. Once boiling, stir well, then lower the heat to low, bringing the mixture to a simmer. Simmer covered, for 20 to 25 minutes, or until all the liquid is absorbed. Turn off the heat and let sit, covered, for 10 minutes. Fluff with a fork and stir in the remaining ½ teaspoon of salt. Taste and add more salt, if desired.

*See in Peanut Vegetables image on page 248.

Pesto

Gluten-free, Soy-free

We've been making this homemade pesto for years—especially in the summertime when we can use the fresh basil from our mom's garden. It's quick and easy, coming together in just five minutes. You'll use it in our Pesto Pasta (page 62), Pesto Mozzarella Melt (page 160) and Pesto Seitan Pizza (page 82).

PREP TIME:
5 minutes

COOK TIME:
none

YIELD:
1½ cups (390 g)

2½ cups (70 g) lightly packed fresh basil

1 cup (117 g) walnuts

1 tbsp (15 ml) lemon juice

3 cloves garlic, peeled, or 1 tbsp (9 g) jarred minced garlic

¼ tsp salt, plus more to taste

¾ cup (180 ml) olive oil

In a food processor, add all of the ingredients except the olive oil. Process until finely minced. With the food processor running, slowly pour in the oil. Once all of the oil has been added, continue to process until smooth and creamy. Taste and add more salt, if desired. This is best if used immediately, but will keep in the fridge for 3 to 5 days.

*See in Pesto Pasta image on page 63.

Mayo

There's no need for store-bought vegan mayo when you can easily make your own at home. Our homemade recipe uses easy-to-find ingredients and takes five minutes to whip up. We always have a batch on hand to spread on sandwiches and use in many of our recipes including Kale Artichoke Dip (page 231), Tofu Banh Mi (page 170) and Parmesan-Crusted Tofu (page 337).

PREP TIME:
5 minutes

COOK TIME:
none

YIELD:
about 1⅔ cups (380 g)

½ cup (120 ml) plain, unsweetened soy milk, at room temperature

1½ tsp (7 ml) apple cider vinegar

1½ tsp (7 ml) lemon juice

1 tsp salt

1 tsp granulated sugar

1 cup (240 ml) avocado oil

In a high-speed blender (see Sister Tip), add the soy milk, vinegar, lemon juice, salt and sugar. Begin blending on a low speed. While the mixture is still blending, remove the lid and slowly add the avocado oil. Once all of the oil is added, blend on high speed until a thick consistency is reached, 15 to 30 seconds. Store in an airtight container in the refrigerator and use within 5 to 7 days.

Sister Tip

Alternatively, you can use an immersion blender to blend all the ingredients until thick and creamy.

Garlic Aioli

This homemade aioli combines vegan Mayo (page 353) with garlic, lemon juice and spices. It's great smothered on sandwiches, used as a dip for Fries (Baked or Fried) (page 259), or drizzled on pizza (hello, "Bacon" and Caramelized Onion Detroit-Style Pizza [page 78] with Garlic Aioli). We love keeping a batch in our fridge for when we're craving creamy, garlicky deliciousness.

PREP TIME:
5 minutes

COOK TIME:
none

YIELD:
1 heaping cup
(about 260 g)

1 cup (226 g) vegan Mayo (page 353) or store-bought (soy-free if needed)

4 cloves garlic, peeled and minced, or 4 tsp (12 g) jarred minced garlic

1 tbsp (15 ml) lemon juice

½ tsp garlic powder

1 tsp salt

½ tsp freshly ground black pepper

In a small bowl, whisk together all the ingredients. Use immediately or refrigerate. Store in an airtight container in the refrigerator and use within 5 to 7 days.

*See in "Bacon" and Caramelized Onion Detroit-Style Pizza image on page 79.

Pizza Dough

Nut-free, Soy-free

Want the secret to making your own pizza that tastes like (if not better than) takeout? Homemade dough! This pizza dough is extremely versatile—not only do we use it for our two Detroit-Style Pizza recipes (pages 77 and 78) and two hand-tossed pizza recipes (pages 81 and 82), but also for Garlic Cheese Bread (page 270). This recipe makes enough for two hand-tossed pizzas or one Detroit-style.

PREP TIME:
15 minutes, plus inactive time for rising

COOK TIME:
none

YIELD:
enough dough for two 12" (30-cm) round pizzas or one 9 x 13" (23 x 33-cm) rectangular pizza

1 cup (240 ml) warm water (heated to 100 to 110°F [37 to 43°C])

1 tbsp (12 g) granulated sugar

2¼ tsp (1 [7-g] packet) active dry yeast

2¾ to 3¼ cups (343 to 406 g) all-purpose flour (spooned and leveled or weighed [see page 359 for How to Measure Flour]), plus more for kneading if needed

1 tsp salt

2½ tbsp (37 ml) olive oil, divided

Sister Tip

To freeze: Either cut in half to freeze separately if using for hand-tossed pizzas or keep whole if using for Detroit-style pizza or garlic cheese bread. Coat the outside of dough ball(s) with olive oil or nonstick spray and place in a large plastic bag, then freeze. Prior to using, place in the fridge for about 8 hours, until defrosted. Remove from the fridge and let sit at room temperature for 30 minutes to 1 hour before using. Use as directed in the recipe.

In a small bowl, whisk together the warm water and sugar. Sprinkle the yeast on top and whisk until it is mostly dissolved. Set aside for 5 to 10 minutes, until the mixture has foamed.

Meanwhile, in the bowl of a stand mixer fitted with the hook attachment, or in a large bowl, stir together 2¾ cups (343 g) of the flour and the salt. Once the yeast mixture has foamed, add it and 2 tablespoons (30 ml) of the olive oil to the flour mixture. Beat on low speed or stir with a rubber scraper or wooden spoon, scraping the sides as necessary, until you have a soft but manageable dough. Add more flour, as needed, up to ½ cup (62 g), to ensure the dough is not too sticky to handle.

Either beat the dough in the stand mixer on low speed for 5 to 7 minutes, or transfer the dough to a lightly floured surface and knead by hand for 5 to 7 minutes, incorporating more flour as needed so that the dough does not stick to the sides of the bowl or to your hands. The dough is ready when you gently press into it and it slowly bounces back. Coat a large bowl with the remaining 1½ teaspoons (7 ml) of olive oil. Form the dough into a ball and place in the bowl. Turn to lightly coat the ball in oil. Place a clean towel over the bowl. Let rest in a warm place until the dough has doubled in size, about 1 hour. Use as directed in the recipe or freeze for later (see Sister Tip).

*See in Pesto Seitan Pizza image on page 80.

Homemade Seasonings

Garlic Salt

No need to buy garlic salt when you can make your own. With just four ingredients, this recipe comes together in two minutes and is a key ingredient for Garlic Bread Grilled Cheese (page 163), Parmesan Cheese (page 342) and Garlic Cheese Bread (page 270).

PREP TIME:
2 minutes

COOK TIME:
none

YIELD:
about 5 tbsp (56 g)

2 tbsp (36 g) salt

2 tbsp (12 g) garlic powder

1 tbsp (1 g) dried parsley

2 tsp (5 g) cornstarch

In a small bowl, mix together all the ingredients. Store in an airtight container.

Everything Seasoning

You know that Everything but the Bagel seasoning that everyone is obsessed with? Well, this is like that. But better. It's homemade, simple to make and ready in less than five minutes. Take homemade bagels (page 21) or avocado toast to the next level by topping with this seasoning.

PREP TIME:
2 minutes

COOK TIME:
none

YIELD:
about ½ cup (2.5 oz [72 g])

1½ tbsp (13 g) poppy seeds

2 tbsp (18 g) white sesame seeds

1½ tbsp (16 g) dried minced garlic

1 tbsp (8 g) dried minced onion

1½ tbsp (18 g) flaky sea salt

In a small bowl, mix together all the ingredients. Store in an airtight container.

Taco Seasoning

Skip the packets and make your own taco seasoning—it's simple to make and great to keep in your pantry. You'll use this seasoning in our Easy Taco "Meat" (page 332) and Jackfruit Quesadillas (page 97).

PREP TIME:
2 minutes

COOK TIME:
none

YIELD:
about ½ cup (2.5 oz [72 g])

3 tbsp (25 g) chili powder

2 tbsp (17 g) ground cumin

1½ tbsp (10 g) paprika

2 tsp (4 g) garlic powder

1 tsp onion powder

2 tsp (3 g) dried oregano

2 tsp (12 g) salt

½ tsp freshly ground black pepper

½ tsp crushed red pepper flakes

In a small bowl, mix together all the ingredients. Store in an airtight container.

Handy How-Tos

As you may know, we've been bloggers and recipe creators for more than five years now (but cooking and baking for much longer than that!) and we've picked up some handy tricks along the way! The following are tips and how-tos that we encourage you to follow whenever possible to ensure you have the best success with every recipe.

HOW TO SOAK CASHEWS

Place the required amount of cashews in a large bowl, mason jar or desired container. Cover completely with water and soak for at least 2 hours at room temperature, or up to 12 hours in the refrigerator.

If you're in a time crunch, pour boiling water over the cashews and soak for 20 minutes, or up to 1 hour.

Prior to using in your recipe, drain the cashews and rinse. Lightly dry by shaking around in the strainer or by placing on a large, clean, absorbent towel and patting them dry. Use the soaked cashews immediately in the recipe you're following.

HOW TO PRESS TOFU

To press tofu, you can either do so by using a tofu press, which can be found at some home goods stores or online, or by using common items found in a kitchen. If using a tofu press, follow the manufacturer's instructions. Here are instructions for how to press tofu using common kitchen items.

Drain the water from the tofu package. Slice into desired sizes or leave as a whole (this works best if you're crumbling the tofu rather than chopping). Lay flat on a thick, clean, absorbent towel. Place another thick, clean, absorbent towel on top of the tofu. Find a heavy cutting board, skillet or something similar and lay it on top of the towel-covered tofu (you can even stack multiple heavy items on top to aid in pressing).

Let sit for at least 30 minutes, up to 1 hour. The longer it sits, the better. Remove the tofu from the towels and pat with a fresh, clean towel to remove any excess water that remains. Prepare your tofu as directed in your recipe.

HOW TO FREEZE TOFU

Freezing tofu creates a chewier, meatier texture. As tofu freezes, the water molecules expand, creating small holes in the tofu and giving it a spongelike consistency. This not only changes the texture, but also allows it to absorb more flavors. You can repeat the freezing and defrosting method once for an even chewier texture. We recommend this method in our Crispy Buffalo Tofu Sliders recipe (page 173), but you can use it any time you'd like your tofu to have a meatier texture.

Freeze. The day before you plan on using tofu (or 2 days before, if you plan on repeating this process), drain the tofu and place in a resealable plastic bag or a container with a lid. Seal. Freeze overnight.

Defrost. Let sit out for at least 6 hours, or until completely defrosted. If in a time crunch, place in a pot of boiling water and boil for 15 to 20 minutes, or until completely defrosted, or microwave for 8 to 10 minutes, turning over halfway through, until completely defrosted. For an even chewier texture, repeat the freezing and defrosting process once more.

Slice and press the tofu as directed in your recipe.

HOW TO MEASURE FLOUR (AND OTHER FLOURLIKE SUBSTANCES)

Measuring flour correctly is extremely important to ensure the success of a recipe, especially in baked goods. You can do so either by using a kitchen scale to weigh your flour or by using dry measuring cups, following the instructions below. It is also important to measure other flourlike substances, such as cocoa powder and vital wheat gluten, this way.

Stir the flour around in its container to fluff it. Using a spoon, gently scoop the flour into your dry measuring cup until the cup is overfilled. Using the back of a knife, scrape the excess flour off the measuring cup. Use as directed in the recipe.

HOW TO CUT BUTTER

Cutting butter is when you incorporate cold butter into a flour mixture by chopping the butter into smaller and smaller pieces, until you have a crumbly, sandlike texture.

Begin with cold vegan butter in stick form. Chop it into small chunks, then add the chunks to your flour mixture. Using a pastry cutter or fork, cut the butter into smaller and smaller pieces until you end up with a crumbly texture (see Sister Tip).

Another way to easily and quickly incorporate cold butter is by beginning with extremely cold vegan butter in stick form, then using a cheese grater to grate the butter into the flour mixture. Stir to incorporate the small chunks of butter into the flour mixture. You will come across this method in Buttermilk Biscuits (page 265).

Sister Tip

Pastry cutters are made specifically for cutting butter and can be found at some home goods stores or online.

Acknowledgments

To our mom, Kate, our biggest inspiration and the mastermind behind many recipes throughout this book. Thank you for never complaining when you walk into a messy kitchen. We truly could not have done this without you.

To our dad, John, our greatest fan since the beginning. Thank you for always seeing what this platform could become and for always pushing us to think bigger.

To our brothers, John, Jack and Lance, thank you for being the best nonvegan taste testers we could ask for and for never complaining when we force you to try three versions of the same dish.

To the special men in our lives (you know who you are), thank you for your constant support and for always being there to finish our leftovers.

To our grandparents, Sharon and Larry, thank you for being the inspiration (and taste testers) for many recipes in this book.

To all of our friends and extended family who have taste tested, recipe tested and supported us from the very beginning. We love and appreciate you.

To the publishing company that made this all happen, Page Street Publishing, thank you for trusting us and bringing our vision to life. A special thank-you to Sarah Monroe, our amazing editor, and Meghan Baskis and Julia Tyler, the creative visionaries behind the design of this cookbook.

To our rockstar photographer, Hayden Stinebaugh, thank you for your creative eye and for putting up with the chaos that went behind each photo.

To every follower and subscriber, thank you. We would not be where we are today without every single one of you.

In memory of our late grandparents, Leila and Ray. We miss you every day, but know you're looking down on us and smiling with pride.

About the Authors

Molly Davis, Emily Letchford, and Carrie, Mary-Kate, Hannah and Shannon Lynch are the founders, content creators and recipe developers behind the successful food blog Six Vegan Sisters and social media platform @sixvegansisters. Reaching millions of people each year, the Six Vegan Sisters have turned their passion for vegan cooking and baking into a thriving business. Some of their features include *VegNews*, *Thrive Magazine*, *Legends of Change*, *Plant-Based by Nafsika* on FYI by A&E and *The Dr. Oz Show*. When the sisters aren't cooking, baking or working on their blog, you can typically find them spending time with family, staying active, watching Detroit sports or traveling. Their blog can be found at www.sixvegansisters.com.

Index